BREADWINNING DAUGHTERS:
YOUNG WORKING WOMEN IN A DEPRESSION-ERA CITY, 1929–1939

One of the most trying periods of the twentieth century, the Great Depression left few Canadians untouched. Based on research that included more than eighty interviews with women who lived and worked in Toronto in the 1930s, *Breadwinning Daughters* examines the consequences of these years for women in their homes and workplaces, and in the city's court rooms and dance halls.

In this insightful account, Katrina Srigley argues that young women were central to the labour market and family economies of Depression-era Toronto. The oral histories give voice to women from a range of cultural and economic backgrounds, and challenge readers to consider how factors such as race, gender, class, and marital status shaped women's lives and influenced their job options, family arrangements, and leisure activities. *Breadwinning Daughters* brings to light previously forgotten and unstudied experiences and illustrates how women found various ways to negotiate the burdens and joys of the 1930s.

(Studies in Gender and History)

KATRINA SRIGLEY is an assistant professor in the Department of History at Nipissing University.

STUDIES IN GENDER AND HISTORY

General Editors: Franca Iacovetta and Karen Dubinsky

Breadwinning Daughters

Young Working Women
in a Depression-Era City,
1929–1939

KATRINA SRIGLEY

UNIVERSITY OF TORONTO PRESS
Toronto   Buffalo   London

ISBN 978-1-4426-4029-0 (cloth)
ISBN 978-1-4426-1003-3 (paper.)

∞

Printed on acid-free, 100% post-consumer recycled paper with vegetable-based inks.

Library and Archives Canada Cataloguing in Publication

Srigley, Katrina, 1973–
    Breadwinning daughters: young working women in a depression-era city,
    1929–1939 / Katrina Srigley.

    (Studies in gender & history)
    Includes bibliographical references and index.
    ISBN 978-1-4426-4029-0 (bound)   ISBN 978-1-4426-1003-3 (pbk.)

    1. Young women – Employment – Ontario – Toronto – History – 20th century.
    2. Women employees – Ontario – Toronto – History – 20th century.   3. Women
    employees – Ontario – Toronto – Social conditions – 20th century.   4. Women
    employees – Ontario – Toronto – Economic conditions – 20th century.
    5. Toronto (Ont.) – History – 20th century.   6. Depressions – 1929 –
    Ontario – Toronto.   I. Title.   II. Series: Studies in gender and history

    HD6100.T6S75 2010   305.242'20971354109043   C2009-904055-7

University of Toronto Press acknowledges the financial assistance to
its publishing program of the Canada Council for the Arts and the
Ontario Arts Council.

 Canada Council   **Conseil des Arts**
    for the Arts   **du Canada**

 ONTARIO ARTS COUNCIL
    CONSEIL DES ARTS DE L'ONTARIO

University of Toronto Press acknowledges the financial support for
its publishing activities of the Government of Canada through the
Book Publishing Industry Development Program (BPIDP).

This book has been published with the help of a grant from the Canadian
Federation for the Humanities and Social Sciences, through the Aid
to Scholarly Publications Program, using funds provided by the
Social Sciences and Humanities Research Council of Canada.

For my parents

'It was the best of times, it was the worst of times ...'
Charles Dickens, *A Tale of Two Cities*, 1859

Contents

Acknowledgments

Breadwinning Daughters is about young working women who lived through one of the most challenging decades of the twentieth century, the Great Depression. It began as a doctoral thesis at the University of Toronto and was inspired by my desire to learn more about my grandmother, a young woman who left high school in the 1930s to look after her ill and unemployed father. It became a book because more than eighty women and men welcomed me into their homes and shared their memories. It is their generosity of spirit that made this study possible. For this, I thank them first and foremost.

As I worked on my thesis and later my manuscript, I received help from many people. The skilled archivists and reference librarians at the Archives of Ontario, City of Toronto Archives, Thomas Fisher Rare Book Library, and the Government Document collection, Robarts Library, helped me tackle the documentary record. This study is much richer because of the impressive and valuable collections at the Multicultural History Society of Ontario. Curator Pasang Thackchooe offered important assistance in my efforts to sort through hundreds of interviews. Enrico Cumbo generously shared recordings from his own research, which broadened my source base in important ways. June Elliott and Ian Hamilton carefully read and edited the manuscript. Dick Duffin spent hours perfecting the images for the book. At the University of Toronto Press, I would like to thank my editor Len Husband for his support for this project, along with Frances Mundy, who helped me through the very last stages of editing and indexing. My anonymous reviewers provided thoughtful and inspiring critiques. You have all helped make this a better book.

In graduate school and as an assistant professor, I have benefited from the support of many friends and mentors. Despite her busy schedule, Franca Iacovetta has always offered her advice and support. She taught me how to navigate academia. For this and much more, I am very thankful. My thesis supervisor, Carolyn Strange, provided calm, consistent, and honest critiques. She taught me how to be a better academic, writer, and teacher. Far more than he realizes, Michael Wayne's unfailing support has been integral to my success. Thank you to the members of the Toronto Labour Studies Group for reading the thesis at various stages and for challenging me to think and write more clearly. The Centre for Criminology, University of Toronto, provided me with an exciting intellectual community and space to write (!) in the last years of my PhD. As I transitioned from graduate student to professor, and this project moved from thesis to book, I benefited from the encouragement and enthusiasm of my colleagues and students at Nipissing University, particularly those in the history department. Thank you.

For their friendship and support, I thank: Kimberly Berry, Heidi Bohaker, Bettina Bradbury, Jenny Carson, Anne Clendinning, Heather DeHaan, Hilary Earl, Jennifer Evans, Nancy Fan, Andrea Gilbert-Clark, Dave Goutor, Valerie Hébert, Craig Heron, Maxine Iversen, Linley Jesson, Kyra Knapp, Kate Macnamara, Kyle Marsh, Claude Morin, Gordon Morrell, James Murton, Catherine Murton-Stoehr, Derek Neal (who looked over my shoulder at a Senate meeting and changed my book title), Françoise Noël, Ruth Percy, Ian Radforth, Barb Smith, Nathan Smith, Robert Teigrob, and Lisa Todd.

My family has been essential to the completion of this book. Henning Helms has dealt with suitcases filled with books, lost computer files, and frantic telephone calls. He patiently understands long work hours and longer parenting hours, and is always supportive of my academic life, even if it makes him shake his head sometimes. In the early months of her life, my daughter Klarissa Srigley shared her time with this project as she slept, fussed, ate, and played. My brother Chris Srigley inspires me with his adventurous spirit. He never fails to make me laugh. My parents, Sam and Penny Srigley, are my greatest champions, and my first and most important teachers. They are the reason I have had the privilege to pursue a career that I love and to write this book. For these reasons and many more, *Breadwinning Daughters* is dedicated to them.

BREADWINNING DAUGHTERS:
YOUNG WORKING WOMEN IN A DEPRESSION-ERA CITY, 1929–1939

Introduction

It was 1932, one of the worst years of the Great Depression, when fifteen-year-old Norma Vineham pushed open the front door of her Toronto home, stepped onto the porch, and paused. It was a beautiful spring morning, yet the normally buoyant young woman was weighted down with anxiety and regret. For the first time since she started school, she would not walk to her nearby high school but take a streetcar across the city to her new job at Dominion Silk Mills, a textile factory in downtown Toronto. The preceding year had been exceedingly difficult for Norma and her family: her mother lost her battle with pneumonia, and her father's company, Golden Awl Metal Weatherstripping, went bankrupt. Aside from the emotional impact of these events on the family of five, Norma, her older sister Grace, and soon after her younger sister Isabelle, found themselves earning wages to support their father and two brothers.[1]

In the Depression context, the Vineham girls were not alone. Young daughters from across Toronto had similar responsibilities. Rose Edelist and her sister, who immigrated from Poland in the late twenties, supported their family by working as seamstresses in the garment district. Margaret Gairns's salary from her job as a high school teacher secured her parents' retirement and their home in the middle-class neighbourhoods of north Toronto. Claire Clarke's work at a hat factory alleviated financial pressure on her parents who were relying on rent from boarders drawn from Toronto's small West-Indian community.[2] In many ways these stories are not remarkable: despite the gender expectations that surrounded employment, women had long worked for money and, by the interwar years, were working in greater numbers than ever before. In fact, wage earning had become an expected stage in women's lives between schooling and marriage. What is noteworthy about the 1930s is the sheer number of families who were coping with the vulnerabilities of the decade through the employment of young daughters.[3] When 'men's' jobs in primary industry were disappearing, leaving fathers and sons from a wide social and economic faction of the city with few places to turn and few ways to support their families, young women continued to have viable wage-earning options in the secondary and tertiary sectors of the economy, including textile manufacturing, office work, domestic service, teaching, and nursing.[4] This meant that gendered divisions of labour, which relegated women to lower-wage and -status jobs than men, also offered them greater opportunity and stability, something Alice Kessler-Harris has noted few people celebrated but many found essential to survival.[5] For young women, wage earning placed them in breadwinning positions that could be rewarding and burdensome. Many felt fulfilled supporting their families and realized a degree of social and economic independence they had not experienced before. Others sacrificed schooling opportunities and personal freedom, entering the labour market with the obligations of breadwinners rather than supplementary wage earners.

In spite of their important place in the Depression-era economy, we know almost nothing about these young women, where they lived and worked, how they felt, or what they thought. What roles did these workers play in the labour market? What did wage earning mean to their lives? How did it affect their families? Did it expose them to danger? Did it limit or expand their independence? *Breadwinning Daughters* answers these questions by examining the experiences of young wage-earning women in Toronto's economy, homes, and places of leisure in the 1930s. It does so by drawing upon more than one hundred interviews with women and men, collected between 1997 and 2005. These interviews give us access to personal and unique perspectives and remind us of the subjective nature of experience and memory and of the many and varied ways that lives are different, shaped in turn by context, social and economic status, culture, and individual identity.[6] In addition to interviews, I have used contemporary newspapers – the *Toronto Daily Star* and *Evening Telegram* – census data from 1931 and 1941, along with various government reports and documents, police records, photographs, and magazines to provide a sense of the social and cultural world of the city. Together these sources give different dimensions to our understanding of the Depression and its impact on the lives of Canadians.

Breadwinning Daughters focuses on the individual and the local because, as historians Kerry Abel, Kathleen Canning, Mrinalina Sinha, and others have argued, examining specific 'historical conjunctures' allows us to uncover and understand the complex results of systems of social power, such as citizenship or patriarchy, for historical actors without erasing agency or individuality.[7] To do so is not to ignore the nation or issues of national importance, but instead to recognize the fundamental material and ideological links that scholars of transnationalism have urged us to recognize between individuals, their particular context, and the much larger world that surrounds them. This book develops themes of work and identity, privilege and disadvantage, that speak to the place of young women in Toronto, and to their place in urban labour markets and families and their connection to cultural systems that were important to many people in North America and Western Europe in these tumultuous years.

Scholars interested in the everyday lives of women, particularly those from working-class and immigrant communities, have always been challenged by a documentary record that tends to be written for, by, and about white, wealthy, and powerful men. This has encouraged historians interested in women's lives to seek out, talk to, and record individual stories, the results of which are evident in Karen Hagemann's book on wage-earning women in Germany's Weimar Republic, Franca Iacovetta's work on Toronto's postwar Italian community, or Selina Todd's scholarship on young working-class women in mid-twentieth-century London, England, to name only a few in a considerable field of scholarship.[8] These and other feminist studies of working-class, immigrant, and racialized women have used taped interview techniques to gather and reconstruct women's lives and subjectivities, to analyse historical actors' recollections, and to understand women's experiences.

As one of the most difficult decades in a troubled century, the 1930s has generated considerable study through the tools of oral history. In Canada, it is one of the few historical periods to have been recorded in this way for more than thirty years.[9] With the notable exception of Denyse Baillargeon's scholarship on the living conditions, life cycle, and strategies used by francophone housewives in 1930s Montreal, and a few recent articles on women in the Great Depression, this interest has not encouraged a significant number of studies that focus on women or their experiences.[10] Until quite recently, the history of the Great Depression in Canada and elsewhere has focused on the unemployed male and the economic and political shifts that were the harbinger and backdrop to his world. The questions of economic and political historians have driven most of this scholarship, leaving the 1930s curiously understudied by scholars interested in the questions of social historians.[11] Recent and older work on the history of the welfare state, labour, and women and gender does not ignore the Depression, but this scholarship tends to consider the 1930s through an analysis of the interwar years or to trace a larger theme of which the Depression context is only a small part.[12] This does not shed much light on or explain how the decade shaped the lives of young women.

It is notable that the Great Depression had a significant and distinct impact on the lives and memories of the women in this study. Like many scholars, historians Veronica Strong-Boag in *New Day Recalled*, Susan Porter-Benson in her posthumously published *Household Accounts*, and Tamara Myers in *Caught*, conceptualize the 1930s as an 'interwar' decade. They argue for and show noteworthy continuity in the expected life stages of women, the conditions of the working class, and the regulation of juvenile delinquents; but this periodization does not capture women's understanding of and experiences during the Depression.[13] They never used the term 'interwar' nor discussed feelings of continuity. For them the 1930s was about rupture. If *ideas* about the appropriate life stages of women and the inequalities wrought by gender and class had great permanence, women's *experiences* of these social structures shifted after the onset of the lengthiest economic downturn since industrialization. The degree of poverty that working-class women lived with may only have shifted, but the unemployment that shook these young wage earners' households had a significant impact, for better and for worse, on the choices they made about schooling, work, and marriage.

Aside from generating source material that provides access to individual experiences and memories, oral histories have another important role: they allow scholars, as Paul Thompson notes in his classic *The Voice of the Past*, to 'change the focus of history itself.'[14] Memories can be used with political purpose to tell the stories of those whose pasts have been ignored and to challenge dominant narratives that silence those histories.[15] In this vein, *Breadwinning Daughters* is a feminist project. It argues that women are central to our understanding of the history of 1930s. As obvious and logical as this might seem, existing historical scholarship does not make this clear. And, furthermore, the political imperatives of writing a history that recognizes the importance of women are still important to give us a broader sense of the past and to, through attrition if nothing else, change the way people understand the place of women in Canadian society. As Franca Iacovetta points out in a recent issue of the *Journal of Women's History*, 'Tokenism ... is still widespread' in the field of history, and moving away from this mentality will require more than the occasional article or course on women and gender to 'fix' the problem.[16]

Breadwinning Daughters also joins an ever-expanding field of scholarship in women's and gender history that is committed to challenging dominant national narratives that privilege the stories of the white British majority and do so without considering the complicated and thorny issues that characterize life in a (post-)colonial society. Much like other major cities in North America, Britain, Australia, and New Zealand, Toronto was largely an Anglo-Protestant city in the 1930s, but it had growing immigrant and racialized communities, especially Jews, Italians, and East Europeans, as well as Irish Catholics, African Canadians, and francophones.[17] As such, Toronto's young workers were not a homogeneous group. While they shared the same sex (and even this is contested) their gender could have altogether different meanings depending on time and place and other sources of identity, including class differences, gender ideals, and heterosexuality, along with racial and ethnic identities. To use Patricia Hill Collins's well-known phrase, 'interlocking systems of oppression' and, I would add, privilege shaped these women's experiences.[18] This meant that in certain contexts some of them enjoyed more economic and cultural power than other women, and other men for that matter.

Classic books such as Jennifer Brown's *Strangers in Blood* and Sylvia Van Kirk's *Many Tender Ties* indicate how early historiography on Canadian women dealt with questions of difference and the power relations they created.[19] Socialist feminists have made equally important contributions to our understanding of working-class women, their wage-earning capabilities, union representation, and protests,[20] as have historians who more recently have asked questions about how ethnicity and sexuality (along with gender and class) shaped employed women's lives and experiences.[21] The significant historiographical shifts that encouraged this and other scholarship have offered new perspectives on women's wage earning and activism that are particularly sensitive to, for example, immigrant women's different cultural understandings and expressions of femininity, waged work, resistance, and dissent.[22] They have also shown us that women's notions of their respectability and the ways in which they forged and articulated their identities as women, workers, foreigners, wives, and mothers differed significantly from both middle- and working-class Anglo-Protestant models of ideal womanhood and female respectability. Studies of supposedly unruly ethnic 'female mobs,' of Italian and other 'Latin' women's direct action on the streets, and of neighbourhood and community-based mobilizations led by mothers and daughters remind us of the need to pay closer attention to homeland strategies that women imported to North America, including some important cultural tools such as women's stories of resistance that were told and retold at the kitchen table and in children's plays performed at the socialist hall.

Even with these significant challenges to our ways of understanding differences among women, race suffers a particular neglect in Canadian women's and gender history, particularly as it relates to questions of power and privilege. With some notable exceptions, Canadian historians have not examined how the 'invention of race,' which was fundamental to the objectives of the British Empire in Canada as elsewhere, has shaped the experiences of historical actors.[23] Race, by which I mean whiteness and blackness, was a 'foundational colonial sorting technique' that was used as a tool for social mobility and exclusion during and well beyond the disintegration of the British Empire; the power that racial markers generated has not been fully explored in Canadian history.[24] Though political ties with Britain were weakening in the 1930s, particularly with the passage of the Statute of Westminster in 1932, the cultural elements of Britishness, including religious, racial, and class identities, still held great power and social cachet in Canadian society. Canadians turned out by the thousands to show their adoration for King George VI and Queen Elizabeth on their tour in 1939 (figure 1), and, more importantly, in their everyday lives they mobilized 'Britishness' to assert privilege. This was particularly important in a context where power, economic and otherwise, was slipping through so many people's hands. For some young women this translated into advantages that gave economic security and social acceptance, making it easier for them to navigate the challenges of the Great Depression. For others it had disastrous consequences, relegating them to the margins of Canadian society.

Along with their value for examining the impact of systems of privilege and disadvantage on women's lives, the relevance of oral histories has expanded in the last twenty years because scholars are using memory sources to understand connections between the past and the present. Recent feminist scholarship dealing with refugee women, wartime rape victims, and Holocaust survivors, as well as feminist anthropologists who collect the stories and narratives of Aboriginal women and South American peasant women, have developed sophisticated understandings of the form, content, and silences of women's narratives and have also introduced us to female subjects who set the criteria and pace for telling their stories. They remind us that the subjective and spatial contexts of remembering, including collective ideals, identities, and silences, are essential analytical tools for understanding recollections.[25] Narratives of human rights, which became entrenched in the vocabulary of Western

1   Geraldine Windeatt pulling up her stockings before joining the crowd waiting to see King George VI and Queen Elizabeth in Toronto on their Royal Tour of Canada on 22 May 1939. Photo courtesy of Penny Srigley.

nations after the Second World War, heavily influenced the memories of the women in *Breadwinning Daughters*. In Canada this has been expressed most clearly through multiculturalism, a core element of national identity despite significant evidence of ongoing state-based and societal racism, and through the 1982 Charter of Rights and Freedoms. Such narratives produced a tension in women's memories between contemporary and historical understandings of inequality based on difference. Shifting ideas about class status and material wealth had an equally powerful influence on women's memories. Though many of the women in this study lived through incredibly difficult times in the 1930s, their more stable economic positions at the end of the twentieth century and the ongoing importance of class to privilege encouraged them to emphasize that their families 'made it through' and to downplay the economic difficulties of these times. As scholars of memory have shown us, it is important to recognize this interplay of past and present when examining the reminiscences of historical actors.

While informed by societal patterns and collective ideals of the present, memories are also influenced by interview context, including when, how, and who participated in the interview.[26] A photograph taken after my last visit with Norma Vineham in 2005 (figure 2) helps illustrate some of the issues that shape the recollection process, including age, generation, gender, and racial and ethnic background. Vineham, like the rest of the women in this study, is elderly and during our meetings was engaged in a process that oral historians call life review. In some cases this encouraged her to emphasize the positive rather than the negative experiences of her life. When looking across seventy years, it is common (though certainly not universal) for people to focus on good events and positive experiences, a phenomenon understood colloquially as a rose-coloured view of the past. While this has typically been cited as a source limitation, oral historians recognize that life review produces memories in which experiences, whether positive or challenging, are placed more clearly within their historical context. As Fred Allison points out in his interesting article on one veteran's memories of the Vietnam War, recollections of events recorded many years later can sometimes be more useful because interviewees have a better sense of themselves and the world around them.[27]

Memories generated for this study were also shaped indelibly by generational issues. As a woman in my late twenties, I was more akin to a granddaughter who needed help with her school project than a researcher armed with a tape recorder. This encouraged Vineham and many of my interviewees to adopt a didactic tone typical of elder–youth relationships in mainstream Canadian culture. In interviews with the elderly, memories are often 'imparted to the young as part of one's role as an older person in society.'[28] Recollections often included, therefore, persistent criticism of younger generations, who were described as spoiled and oblivious to 'how good they have it' because they had not endured the likes of the Great Depression. This narrative would, interviewees hoped, heighten my and others' appreciation of Canada and the type of life Canadians lead. Such generational differences also influenced what topics were and were not covered in interviews: while work and wage earning, leisure and family were topics dealt with easily, and political shifts inspired by the feminist movement made stories of gender inequality more transparent, issues of sexuality were far trickier to get at. Indicators of normative heterosexuality, including courtship and marriage, were discussed quite freely, but

2 Katrina Srigley with Norma Vineham, 15 April 2005. Photo courtesy of Katrina Srigley.

questions about sexual expression, violence, or non-normative sexual preferences were very difficult to address. In these interview contexts, the generational divide shaped memories and could act as a silencer.

In addition, my 'Britishness' gave and denied me access to certain people. I speak English without a foreign accent; I am aware of the cultural protocols that shape interaction with elders, which were familiar to the majority of the participants in this study; my fair complexion eased my entry into some people's homes and encouraged others to view me with scepticism. I had great difficultly, for instance, securing interviews with people in Toronto's Italian communities. I am not Italian, and many people were not interested in sharing their stories, particularly those from the era of fascism and Mussolini. For these memories I turned to interviews conducted by Enrico Cumbo for his study of the Italian community in Toronto and existing collections of oral histories found at the Multicultural History Society of Ontario.[29]

Though they were in their eighties and nineties, Toronto's elderly recalled the 1930s clearly. The Depression years were impressed on their minds for good reason. From the emblematic stock market crash to the onset of the Second World War, the 1930s was one of the most difficult decades in the twentieth century and Canada was among the hardest hit of Western nations. There had been other economic depressions, two as recent as 1913–14 and 1921, but the troubles of the 1930s were marked by greater and more long-lasting unemployment, economic vulnerability, and environmental disaster. By 1933, conservative estimates placed unemployment at nearly 30 per cent with close to 2 million Canadians relying on relief. Though marginally better than in the prairie provinces or single-industry towns such as nearby 'blue-collar' Hamilton, the situation in Toronto was still dire.[30] For the majority of families who belonged to the working or lower middle class and whose earnings (if they were lucky enough to have them) just covered expenses, Toronto was not a place of opportunity. More typical were situations of unemployment that forced thousands of the city's fathers and sons to take to the streets in search of work, line up for food, and ride the rails, hoping for better options.[31] The collapse of the male-dominated construction industry was one of the first indicators of the severity of the situation. The market was so slow that the number of houses in the city barely altered over the entire decade.[32] Ethel Bird's father experienced this first-hand when his construction company went belly up and he and Bird's mother had to rely on their daughter's modest wages from a factory job at Canada Wire and Cable. Fred Marks's earnings from his job as a salesman were based on commission. When things started slowing down he widened his base, travelling as far as Montreal, his backseat piled high with various and sundry products, mostly magazines, in search of customers. As the Depression lengthened it became clear that this strategy was not helping. Marks may not have been jobless but the Depression had left him without money. By 1932, he and his family were relying on food relief and the wages his daughter Agnes earned at her factory job.[33]

The plight of the unemployed was virtually ignored by Canada's federal government. The country's wealthy leaders, Richard Bedford Bennett and William Lyon MacKenzie King, were well versed in laissez-faire economics and highly suspicious of the philosophies of economists such as John Maynard Keynes and the New Deal politics being practised south of the border. They had great trouble extricating themselves from atavistic notions of entitlement and spent far more time worrying about balanced budgets and how to avoid a state-based relief program than assisting Canadian citizens. They hoped that private charity would be sufficient for those in need. Many organizations and the city's families did their best to help the destitute. Hobos, as homeless people were called then, could regularly be found eating meals on the back porch of the MacMillan household in Toronto's east end. As Audrey MacMillan, who worked as an office girl at Bell Telephone, explained, 'Mother always kept special cutlery, special plates in a little back shed we had off the kitchen. These people would sit on the back stoop and eat what we had.' She added: '[My mother] was not a benevolent person, but she did do that.'[34] These measures, while helpful, were hardly sufficient. As the Depression dragged on, more and more provinces and those directly responsible for the unemployed, municipalities, were crying out for help from the federal government.

When relief came, as it did in fits and starts, it was given out grudgingly, in keeping with the belief that Canada should never 'become committed to a dole system' and that Canadians be given 'work not charity.' In 1930, the City of Toronto established a Civic Unemployment Relief Committee to oversee the development of relief jobs.[35] This ill-conceived public works project was an attempt to keep men working, an approach government officials hoped would not promote laziness or erode work ethic. In the first year of the program, Toronto's municipal government 'spent three times as much on outdoor work as on the dole' with no measurable change in economic conditions or benefit to the city's unemployed.[36] Until 1933, the House of Industry, which was publicly funded but privately administered, was the main source of food relief in the city. Agnes Marks often travelled to the Elm Street location with her mother. 'You'd get bags of stuff,' she recalled. 'I remember syrup, always getting syrup and flour and baking powder and sugar and those dry ingredients, rolled oats and things like that.' After waiting in line for a large or small allotment (families with children received more food), Marks remembered that 'people would come out, sit on ... the curb and exchange stuff.' Each week families received the same bland staples, variety was expensive, and fruit and vegetables were rare. Aside from economic expediency, the government used all means possible to discourage people from relying on aid, failing to recognize that most people would much rather work than accept relief, a demoralizing and very public indication of family crisis. Not long after they started going to the House of Industry, the relief official asked Marks's mother, 'Where is your husband? You got a husband?!' She wanted to make sure the family was not 'double dipping' by collecting relief and the wages of a male breadwinner. In order to make certain they received support in the following weeks Marks's father started collecting their food, but he found it difficult, yelling 'That's out! That's it ... I am not going to go through that stuff!' and refusing to go after his first visit.[37] At this point, Agnes's factory job became exceptionally important. In 1933, a voucher system replaced the House of Industry as the main source for food relief in Toronto. Those on assistance redeemed coupons for food (for a set price rather than a set amount) at various pre-approved locations in the city, which left people vulnerable to price increases.[38] When MacKenzie King returned to office in 1935, he reduced aid to the provinces by 25 per cent. He did not listen to Canada's unemployed and, ultimately, like Bennett before him, he failed to provide sufficient relief. Torontonians had to come up with alternative or at least supplementary ways to pay the bills. Though it was hardly ideal to place daughters in the position of breadwinner, their workforce participation was less demoralizing and typically more profitable than relief.

Women were an integral part of the economic and cultural fabric of Toronto in the 1930s. They pounded the pavement in search of work, toiled among pots and pans, listening to popular radio serials like *Fibber McGee and Molly*, sweated on the line, danced the night away at the Palais Royal, turned tricks on street corners, and strolled along the boardwalk with their boyfriends or husbands or girlfriends. Organized thematically, *Breadwinning Daughters* takes us into this world. Chapter 1 places these women within the social, cultural, and economic milieu of Depression-era Toronto. While young women met the economic challenges of the 1930s by finding jobs in a rather favourable economic market, they also had to negotiate the social and cultural world around them. This included expectations about their behaviour and the disappointments that the 1930s generated for them. Though women of their age and marital status had worked before, they had not typically been forced to make similar sacrifices or commit themselves to wage earning for such a significant amount of time. For some women, this was easy and exciting, offering opportunities for adventures away from home. For others it proved burdensome, shattering their dreams and expectations about schooling and marriage.

Many of the greatest challenges of the Depression were felt most acutely within households. Stories of struggling families fill historical accounts of the thirties. Chapter 2 offers a glimpse into the private worlds of Toronto's working daughters. Here young women were positioned more centrally than ever before as wage earners and as caregivers, shifting economic and social relations in reality if not in thought. In their families, young women dealt with alcoholism, depression, and desertion, but also felt great joy and support. The employment that young women had access to in Toronto's labour market was central to these changes. Through an analysis of women's paid work in domestic service, clerical work, manufacturing, and teaching, chapter 3 enters the female world of work. By exploring the contours of privilege and disadvantage, it shows that some women enjoyed access to a greater number of more lucrative jobs than others in Toronto.

As young females in a society with particular perceptions of ideal feminine behaviour and structured around patriarchal relations of power, it is no surprise that women faced specific dangers in their homes, workplaces, and in the spaces in between. Chapter 4 considers the threats women workers faced in the city. The shocking 1935 murder of Ruth Taylor indicates that the city could be a perilous place for women. While such murders acted as powerful cautionary tales for working girls, they also diverted attention from the far more typical dangers women faced in their workplaces and homes. Domestic complaints (desertion, wife abuse, and assault) dominated the city's courts in these years; and, as interviews reveal, young women were vulnerable to psychological and physical abuse at the hands of destitute parents. As breadwinners whose wages were essential to family survival, they suffered, usually in silence, through sexual harassment in their workplaces in order to ensure they received their pay cheques.

Though public space was a source of real and perceived danger for women, the fifth and final chapter demonstrates that young employed women also managed to 'kick up their heels' and have fun in the Depression. The financial insecurities of the decade meant that many working girls had to spend their free time economically, but they still negotiated the time, space, and funds to embrace commercial amusements found at the city's dance halls and movie houses. As in previous decades, such 'public' pastimes raised the spectre of compromised respectability, but, as this chapter demonstrates, young women adopted and resisted such precepts depending on the context, their self-identities, and desires.

As the stories of young working women such as Vineham, Gairns, and Marks unfold in the following chapters, a unique window into the Depression also opens. These young working women did not ride boxcars, become members of Parliament, or live in hobo camps, but their stories are equally important to our understanding of the social change, economic downturn, and political upheaval that was the 1930s.

As workers in Canada's second-largest urban centre they earned wages in factories and classrooms, the houses of the wealthy, and the offices of Toronto businesses in order to feed, clothe, and house their families in a period when unemployment had made male breadwinning particularly precarious. In the process they dealt with discrimination, negotiated insecurity, and carved out space for happiness and amusement in one of the most difficult periods of the twentieth century.

Chapter 1

Young Working Women
in a Depression-Era World

As the streetcar rumbled across the city to Dominion Silk Mills, Norma Vineham bravely faced her first day of work. When her father's small business faltered in the early thirties he put 'every bit of insurance money' that the family had into it, but this strategy proved futile in the face of the Great Depression. By 1932, savings were depleted, including money set aside for schooling. As the labour market offered few options for Vineham's father, she and her sisters became the sole wage earners in the household. Someone had to put food on the table, and the family's best options rested with their young daughters. This economic reality had a profound impact on the lives of young women like Vineham: it placed them in positions typically occupied by their fathers in the family economy and altered life stages they had been taught were a 'natural' part of life between childhood and adulthood, including schooling, wage earning, and marriage. Norma Vineham was not anxious and unhappy because of her new factory job. She expected to earn wages before she married. She just did not imagine giving up school to do so.

This chapter examines what this negotiation of societal expectations, economic realities, and individual dreams meant to Toronto's young working women. As such, it examines the place of young women workers within Depression-era discussions of employment and unemployment. For a young woman to be accepted as a worker, it was essential for her to adopt the behaviour and appearance of a dutiful daughter, including working in women's jobs and not transgressing dominant notions of feminine respectability. The economic realities of the decade forced women to negotiate these expectations carefully and to make sacrifices they did not anticipate, forgoing schooling and delaying or abandoning plans for marriage, life stages they had been taught were appropriate for women their age.

That Vineham and other young women like her were workers places them at the heart of a long-standing debate in women's history about the place and power of employed women within societies that associate the workplace, and more broadly the public sphere, with men and masculinity. We now have extensive scholarship questioning the utility of the public/private divide for understanding women's lives and experiences in a variety of contexts. Scholars have asked how and when the waged work of women disrupted these gendered associations; they have considered how women as workers, mothers, and protesters have negotiated and challenged such ideals.[1] In examining these issues, scholars have given a significant amount of attention to young working women. This is hardly surprising, as they occupied the majority of positions in industrialized workplaces, were the victims of some of its darkest tragedies, and were involved in far greater numbers than older, married workers in unions and political organizations. They also inspired the greatest angst among the middle-class observers of their time, who initially saw them as vulnerable to the evils of the city but by the 1920s were rather convinced they were symptomatic of a 'girl problem' that was threatening the moral fabric of North American society. Young workers who flocked to city centres in search of work were realizing a greater degree of financial and social independence than their mothers or grandmothers. This, along with their love of clothing and makeup and their penchant for urban amusements, symbolized a 'new day' for young women that fit uncomfortably with dominant notions of domestic femininity and threatened to push holes in one of the most important foundations of Canadian society, the heterosexual nuclear family.[2] Thus working girls faced censure from the state, legal system, and their communities (gossip was one of the most powerful forms of social control) for violating or appearing to challenge societal expectations about their position and role.

What was the place of the young Depression-era worker in such discussions? She certainly continued to have a place in the consciousness and agenda of reform-minded individuals and organizations. As existing historiography on interwar women workers makes clear, women lived in a world structured by male privilege and power: their behaviour, particularly their sexuality, was regulated by their family and people in their community, the state, and middle-class organizations such as the Young Women's Christian Association (YWCA). Their right to protection from sexual exploitation was shaped by perceptions of their respectability that were based on their ability to assert Britishness; they also dealt with tenacious inequalities rooted in gender and class that consigned them to lower-paying jobs and positions as temporary workers in North American labour markets and households.³ This is, however, only part of the story. The individual experiences and memories of working women add a new dimension to this tale of regulation and inequality, highlighting the impact the Great Depression had on young women's lives and the degree to which broader social norms can obscure our view of historical actors and contexts that do not fit neatly into such ideals and perceptions.

By the 1930s, Toronto was becoming more a city of working women than it had ever been before. Between 1931 and 1941 the number of women between the ages of fifteen and thirty-five who found jobs in Toronto steadily increased, which meant that more and more wage earners like Norma Vineham were criss-crossing the city each day by streetcar or on foot. More young women were also living in the city, which was a result of their ongoing movement from Canada's rural to urban areas. Observing a 'trend towards smaller families' in the countryside in these years, census analysts attributed it to 'the increasing drift from the farms to the cities on the part of young people, especially girls.'⁴ Marion Forsythe, who shared her memories with me in her small room at one of Toronto's retirement homes in 2002, moved from the then-rural township of Scarborough to the city of Toronto in the mid-thirties to find employment. Forsythe had just finished high school. She knew she was expected to find work to help reduce costs for her parents, but she saw few employment prospects on her family's dairy farm or in the surrounding rural community. Ontario's largest city held more promise for a young woman with commercial training, and with little trouble she landed a job in the Toronto law offices of Wadsworth, Wadsworth and Wadsworth. She was then able to pay her own way; when she returned home, she 'always brought gifts,' 'a new blouse' for her mother, which helped out in important ways. When Luella Luno left Barrie, Ontario, in the mid-1930s she, like Forsythe, was looking for work. Unlike her older brother whose labour was needed on the farm, Luno was a financial burden to her family, whose small beef-cattle operation had seen better times. She thus headed to Toronto and found a domestic position in Rosedale, one of Toronto's wealthiest neighbourhoods. Luno remembered these years with a great deal of fondness. She met her husband at this time, whom she noted 'drove a motorcycle,' and though her workday was long she did not live in, which meant that when she finished work she did as she pleased. This was a freedom she would not have enjoyed on the farm.⁵

Unlike their predecessors who embodied the spectre of a 'girl problem' in the city, these young women were typically cast as dutiful daughters: young women who worked to support their families rather than thrill-seeking adventurers who were likely to undermine the stability of the nation with their work and independence. When young workers came into the focus of social commentators, who had long monitored their behaviour, it was more often in relation to the perceived crisis in the family, brought about by unprecedented levels of male unemployment rather than as a result of their wage earning. The creation of Toronto's Family Court in 1929 and the veneration of non-lawyer experts who would deal with 'all matters concerning the family' point to the emphasis placed on the need to solve the problems of domestic space in these years.[6] Targeting families as the 'social incubator' of instability did little to help them deal with the problems of the Depression years, but for young women it did mean that their wage earning was perceived as necessary and rather normal. The unemployed male who was out riding the rails or languishing at home was a far more pressing concern in this regard.

To be understood as a dutiful and normal working daughter it was necessary for young women to avoid contravening other expectations about proper feminine behaviour. In this sense, gender ideals had not loosened their hold on the societal acceptance or rejection of young women. It was important, for instance, for young women who lived away from home to board with a family rather than to live independently. Though she often went home in the summer months, for most of the year Marion Forsythe boarded in the east end of Toronto, where she had her own room, took meals with the family, and was rather certain her rent 'included laundry.'[7] This arrangement cost less money than living alone and reduced the responsibilities of shopping and cooking. In addition to such costs, city planners characterized apartment living as morally dubious. In his study of residential zoning in Toronto, historical geographer Richard Dennis notes that apartment houses were 'a deviation from the North American ideal of single-family, owner-occupied homes' and therefore were thought to undermine the city 'morally and economically.' Critics declared that apartments 'could never be homes' and, in fact, felt that 'they promoted race suicide' by making 'life too easy for women' or by removing them from the controls of a conventional family.[8]

While living in a family situation it was also important for young women to recognize their place as temporary workers; lifelong employment was still understood as a male prerogative. As in decades before and after the 1930s, the road to matrimony and offspring was 'routinely presented to girls in all walks of life as the fulfillment of every true woman's ambitions,' while education and employment were presented as transitory.[9] Women were not expected to become wage earners for life. The fear that work might take women away from the home found expression in the right-to-work debate, one of the most consistent editorial themes of the Great Depression. As Margaret Hobbs has uncovered for the Canadian context, and Alice Kessler-Harris and Lois Scharf highlight for the United States, concerns about overturned gender roles inspired women and men across the continent to pick up their pens to write to local and national newspapers to argue that female employment was threatening the family and the male breadwinner.[10] Rising numbers of well-dressed salesgirls behind department store counters or the working women who crowded the garment district after their shift ended certainly provided a stark contrast to the ever-increasing number of downtrodden and unemployed men in relief lines. 'It is a striking fact,' one man wrote in the *Evening Telegram,* one of Toronto's dailies, 'that from 1901 to 1931, the number of women in business has more than tripled, and proportionately, the number of men out of work has shown a constant increase.' Speaking to 'the average young business women,' this writer contended that they were 'being fooled and allowed to believe that there [was] a position for every girl.' Such behaviour was drawing women away 'from the natural course of home-making,' the result of which would be for women 'a lonely old age and the prospect of spending one's last days in some institution or in the frigid atmosphere of relatives who really don't want one.'[11] Such chilling threats were accompanied by anti-feminist rhetoric which characterized women workers as 'a flock of clucking biddies [who] blandly usurp men's position as breadwinner.' They seemed to be everywhere, this writer continued with exaggeration, 'women in street cars, women in crowded places, women in general bulldoze their way to the goal in view, unmindful of all facts but one, their sex will get them by if their brain cannot.'[12] In the monthly women's magazine *Chatelaine,* one commentator insisted that it would be 'a fantastic idea' if the House of Commons decided that 'every woman employed in a gainful occupation shall remain at home and permit her nearest male relative who is out of work to take over the said position.' Because, continued critic Merderic Martin, 'a full dinner pail for thousands and thousands of women has made the Depression worse for all of us – men, women and children.'[13]

Workers and leaders within both the mainstream and radical sections of the Canadian labour movement also opposed the employment of women by heralding their 'natural' domesticity. Joe Salsberg, a Communist activist during the 1930s, recounted: '*You heard it in every union!* It was an open cry: Send them back to the kitchen!'[14] Edward Mann, a member of the Cooperative Commonwealth Federation during the Depression explained:

'It was a male-dominated, left-wing group ... women weren't looked on as being politically significant or politically interested.'[15] Leaders of the Quebec-based Canadian Catholic Confederation of Labour, including those who represented the women textile workers in their union, went so far as to petition the Quebec government to bar all women from waged work except in special cases of acute necessity.[16] Women on the left were well aware of the contradictions implicit in a reform agenda that argued for class equality while promoting gender inequality. As poet and left-activist Dorothy Livesay said: 'Such were the dichotomies I found in male-female relationships in the thirties. In theory, we were free and equal as comrades on the left. In practice, our right hand was tied to the kitchen sink!'[17] Canadians from across the social and political spectrum accepted the dominant gender and family ideology of the day. It assumed that a stable society, built on families with employed fathers who earned a family wage and homemakers who served and nurtured husbands and children, was the surest cure for abnormal economic conditions.

Proclamations of domesticity evident in such discussions did not impact all women equally, however. Within the Depression-era economy, single working daughters had much greater latitude and space to be workers than their married counterparts. This was due, in part, to the greater sense of normalcy that surrounded the presence of young working women in the city, but also because they were not a long-lasting threat to the gender order as long as they held jobs in women's occupations and planned to abandon the workplace for marriage and motherhood.[18] Married women in non-domestic positions did present such a threat. In a letter to Ontario Premier Mitchell Hepburn, Miss Evelyn Bast demanded that any woman with a husband should not work. Miss Asselin of Renfrew had similar concerns: writing to the Ontario minister of labour in 1936, she asserted that 'a man that's getting big wages should be able to help his wife at home and other women that are married can well afford to stay out of there and give a young girl a chance to make a clean living without going astray.'[19] One self-named 'Canadian daughter' insisted that 'in most every case ... these positions in offices, factories etc. could be filled by boys and girls who ha[d] unemployed fathers, or [were] entirely dependent on themselves for a living.'[20] Interviewees unanimously affirmed that married women were not allowed to work in the 1930s, and this despite the fact that many had mothers who earned wages as domestics or seamstresses or who themselves continued to earn wages after marriage. The Tapp sisters' mother worked cleaning offices during the Great Depression. She did so to supplement relief payments and later the wages of her daughters, which were insufficient to feed a family of nine. She was not, however, a worker. As her daughter Joyce Cahill explained, she was not schooled, and as a married woman she could not have gotten employment anyhow. Another daughter, Marg McLean, affirmed this reality: 'My goodness no!' In our interview, Wilfred Wood recalled that many women worked 'but not married women. That was the difference. It didn't seem to be a custom then. Once a girl got married she stayed home. And it was a sort of a stigma attached to a husband that couldn't afford his wife without her working.'[21] 'You see,' asserted Anne Hinsta who was a married domestic worker in the Depression, 'you did not want to go around with the fellas because they had no money and you feared, how could they look after you? You'd be looking after a man.'[22] Helen Campbell, who worked as a secretary before and after she married in 1938 (figure 3), also affirmed that 'no job, [meant] no marriage,' for Toronto's young men and no husbands for the city's young women.[23] Despite obvious contradictions between married women's wage earning and ideals, it was clear at the time and in women's memories that married women were not legitimate workers.[24]

That none of the working women in this study recalled any animosity to their employment highlights the degree to which young, single wage earners skirted such enmity and were instead accepted workers. With regards to her sisters who were working throughout the Depression, Audrey Macmillan remarked, 'I don't remember anything about that as far as my sisters were concerned. I don't remember my father feeling like that about his daughters. He was in a male profession.'[25] Ivy Phillips thought women were underpaid, but she has no recollection of resistance to young women working. 'No I don't remember that.'[26] As to why there would be any concern about women working, Phillips was not sure. After all, she continued, women were not trained at school to be the breadwinners, a fact that made the work of single women in women's jobs acceptable. Similarly, Mary Macnamara thought her 'wages were ridiculous'; as for the right-to-work debate, she said, 'I don't remember this about women. I guess I was too busy living to worry about that sort of thing, you know, going about my business, getting there and coming back and sleeping at night and having some fun in between.'[27] Macnamara was not the only woman who claimed work demands got in the way of awareness of such disputes. Thelma Plunkett hardly had time to read the newspaper at the end of the day. When asked about the backlash against women who worked in the Depression years Plunkett replied: 'No, I can't really [remember]. I guess I didn't read as much as some people might have because I didn't have the time because by the time I got home so late and [had] my supper and you know. I just didn't really [have time] and we

3   From left to right, Darryl and Helen Campbell on their wedding day, 28 May 1938, with matron of honour Geraldine Windeatt. Photo courtesy of Penny Srigley.

had to go into work on Saturday morning. We were supposed to go in Saturday morning till noon and we never got out of there until three.'[28]

The vast majority of women, both married and single, worked because they had to or were expected to, not because of selfish indulgence. As long as they did not present a significant threat to domesticity, they did not attract much attention anyway. This allowed young single women who were temporary workers and dutiful daughters to avoid societal derision. It also allowed women who were married to work in certain female jobs. These women's memories remind us of the gender divisions of labour, which made the idea of competition between men and women for employment rather moot. Young single women who earned wages in 'women's' jobs, were rarely competitors for 'men's' jobs, and as long as they planned to marry, they were hardly threatening to societal ideals.

This does not mean that young single workers did not have to protect their identity as workers by behaving appropriately for Canadian women. In the 1930s as before, a young woman's respectability crystallized in her appearance and behaviour and determined societal acceptance or rejection. Avoiding poverty or at least the appearance of poverty was of crucial importance for young women in these years. Relying on government relief was seen as an indication of moral and individual failure. Young women, therefore, went to great lengths to hide their destitution. If relief was necessary, they hoped no one would notice the government truck that stopped outside their home or the mass-produced relief clothing they wore. Tapp sisters Marg McLean and Joyce Cahill were horribly embarrassed by their relief shoes, which routinely fell apart and made horrible flapping and squeaking noises as they walked. They did what they could to modify their shoes, stuffing cardboard in the soles and urging their father to repair them with his tools in the basement. Art Ballantine stuffed his relief sweater in the family mailbox, preferring the cold air to arriving at school dressed in that manner. Young people knew that how they looked mattered and, as a consequence, did their best to modify their appearance to ensure acceptance.

Clothing styles provide an interesting window into the ways in which working women could and did use their appearance to secure approval in the face of difficult economic times. Fashion communicates visually the values and sensibilities of a particular time and place. It also exposes 'subtle links' between individuals and the world around them.[29] Such standards exerted considerable influence over young working women who strove to emulate these images and were well aware that appearing as a respectable Canadian woman was key to desirability. In our interview, Norma Vineham was keen to assure me that irrespective of the economic challenges of the Great Depression she and her family always had clean clothes; they could always present themselves in public.[30] Vineham shared images with me she had collected for our visit that revealed this desired image and the meaning that she invested in her clothing (figure 4). In this image, her outfit is simple, neat, and feminine. Importantly she is also wearing a hat, which was an adornment that symbolized femininity and an economic status that was, at the very least, above destitution. In the second image (figure 5), working girls Geraldine Windeatt and Nora Windeatt cut fine figures in their fur-trimmed coats and hats, conveying a respectability that belied their difficult economic situations. In the thirties far more than in previous decades, the ability of young working women to maintain a respectable and desirable image was circumscribed by their economic responsibilities; however, women like Vineham and the Windeatt sisters-in-law could perform 'ladyhood' by dressing appropriately and not, publicly at least, transgressing societal boundaries in a manner that would weaken their social acceptance. This helped them mitigate the challenges of economic destitution.

4   Norma Vineham, nineteen years old, 1936. Photo courtesy of Norma Vineham.

5   Fashionable working women Nora and Geraldine Windeatt. Photo courtesy of Penny Srigley.

As widely syndicated advice columnist Dorothy Dix reported, clothing influenced heterosexual desire, a key element of acceptability. The Depression years witnessed a clear shift in popular feminine attire from the fashions of the 'new day,' which were boyish and androgynous, to those that emphasized the female form, waists, hips, and breasts. Short hemlines fell to calf level, and 'traditional corsets and girdles, all designed to mould and flatten various female figures into perpendicular lines' were abandoned for more curvaceous styles that celebrated motherhood.[31] In a column titled 'Modern Girl Out! Feminine in Style,' Dix reported that men no longer desired the independent flapper of the 1920s. Rather, a survey conducted on university campuses indicated 'fluffy ruffles won out by long odds' and 'eighty per cent of the men questioned declared that girls who smoke and drink and swear and overdo the use of rouge and lipstick ma[d]e no hit with them.' Men, Dix argued, wanted their women 'sweet and feminine.'[32] In 1936, she went so far as to claim that 'long skirts and clinging gowns [were] responsible for increasing [numbers of] marriages.'[33] A short story titled 'Femininity' published in Toronto's *Evening Telegram* provided a similar message. In the story, two women, Clodene and Pamela, vie for the attention of athletic and handsome Perry Norton while on a ski vacation. 'Clodene was distinctly the athletic type.' Pamela, for her part, 'hated cold and snow and rugged physical exercise.' Ultimately, Pamela's femininity wins her Perry, who points out to her: 'You're a woman, not like these other male imitators. And that's what I, what all men want in a female, femininity.'[34] In such stories, it was clear that a woman's greatest asset was her feminine appearance. By abandoning flapper styles for more traditional images, young women signalled their conformity to such ideals.

Few working women had 'pin money' to spend on a marcel wave or make-up, let alone a fur coat or new wardrobe. This forced them to be imaginative about how they achieved their desired appearance. Sewing skills became incredibly important to help women, as the Women's Institute of Toronto advertised, make 'prettier clothing than ever before' at half the price. As one graduate of courses offered by the Institute told a reporter, 'It is really smart these days to be thrifty, and with thousands of women turning to the needle, it has become positively fashionable to make your own clothes.'[35] Ivy Phillips, who worked as a domestic and sales girl during the thirties, was so talented with needle and thread that her five sisters often called on her to make clothes for them. She happily complied and was even able to make them clothes out of fabric previously used for curtains. Her sisters were very proud of Phillips's abilities and agreed that her skills meant that they had 'new' and fashionable dresses in the 1930s. Creating inexpensive but respectable clothing did not work for all women.

Claire Clarke employed her mother's Singer sewing machine, brought all the way from Barbados, to produce clothing that helped her deal with the racial discrimination she faced in Toronto. Retail establishments such as Simpsons and Eaton's, insurance offices, and many other companies would not, in Clarke's words, 'hire blacks in the door.' They were welcome to work for the company from home in the cottage industry, but they were not welcome to be the face of Toronto's businesses. In defiance, Clarke learned how to sew and began to produce clothing and do alterations for middle-class women. These skills also meant that Clarke 'never lacked clothing' of good quality. In one interview, she recalled that when most women were buying stockings for fifteen cents, her earnings allowed her to buy the high-grade ones for sixty-five cents.[36] Clarke was certainly not going to appear unemployed. By donning more expensive and classy clothing, Clarke rejected those who cast her as an unsuitable office worker and presented an alternative, respectable image.

Window shopping and mail-order catalogues also gave working women the opportunity to learn about the latest styles in inexpensive ways. It was popular during the Depression for working-class women to make weekend trips to the shops just to browse. There they evaluated the 'eye-catching outfits' worn by mannequins, compared prices, planned how to make similar apparel, and dreamed about themselves in those clothes. Audrey Macmillan's mother was talented enough to replicate clothing from display windows. This was particularly fruitful for her daughters. 'We were four girls,' Macmillan explained. 'As we got older, my older sisters would go downtown to Simpsons and the French Room and check out their expensive clothes and run home and my mother could cut it free hand.'[37] On Saturdays, Mabel Duncan regularly walked the eight kilometres from her home to a nearby shopping area just to look at the nice 'millinery stores and the dress stores.'[38] Duncan rarely purchased anything, but she, along with her friends, enjoyed the fashion and the shops. Catalogues, on the other hand, brought the latest styles to the doorsteps of women's homes. Young women waited with excitement for new publications and spent hours pouring over them perched on the edge of their beds or nestled in living-room chairs. Sometimes images were clipped out and stuck on bedroom mirrors or in scrapbooks as reminders of the perfect hat or dress. Browsing, window shopping, and flipping through catalogues were forms of 'mental consumption' that allowed women to imagine themselves dressed in clothes they could not afford but could sometimes replicate with sewing skills.[39] The Depression was a perfect time to employ these skills of production to achieve your desired image. The act of replicating clothes displayed in windows or catalogues allowed women

to fulfil their desires for fashionable clothes when their economic situation prevented them from buying these items. Though their families may
have been down and out, young women like Claire Clarke and the Tapp
sisters used their clothing to reject the identities and experiences the
1930s had thrust upon them; they did this to ensure that they would not
be denied access to workplaces or to the dances that young women loved
to attend. As they remembered these times many years later, it also allowed them to reflect on clothes that were not worn and tattered and re-
affirm their respectability in the face of the Great Depression.

While the thirties had a significant impact on the ability of young women
to maintain a respectable appearance, young working women also recalled
with great sadness how the 1930s truncated their educations. By the 1920s,
unlike in nineteenth-century Toronto, schooling was widely acknowledged
as useful for girls of all classes, at least until sixteen; therefore, many more
young women were attending school to this age and beyond.[40] Reduced or
eliminated school fees, the emergence of more 'female' subjects like
household science, and the economic benefits of white-collar employment all helped smooth the way for their increased enrolment.[41] Schooling
nonetheless 'remained tied to the rhythms of the family economy,' and
recently won educational gains did not come to fruition for daughters
who provided essential economic support for their families.[42]

Like their mother, who was a nurse, Vineham, then seventeen, and her
sister Grace both had career aspirations. They wanted to attend university. 'Mother hoped that Grace would go to university. She wanted her to
be a librarian.' With her thirst for learning still evident, Vineham observed: 'Grace and I, we *so* wanted to go to school. I wanted to be a teacher.
Well I guess our parents had ambitions for us.'[43] For Ivy Phillips 'the hardest thing' about the Depression 'was when [she] quit school, having to
quit school and having to work.' Phillips hoped to be a nurse 'more than
anything in the world'; however, like many other young women of her
generation, her need for a job forced her to give up her educational
dreams. When she turned sixteen her mother told her matter-of-factly,
'"You're finished." I didn't go to school that day,' Phillips said wistfully.
She had already been going 'from school to people's houses' to earn
wages, but after her birthday she began housework full-time. 'I'm not
sure whether I missed things' as a consequence of the Depression, she
mused, but 'the hardest thing was having to quit school.'[44]

Like the Vineham sisters and Phillips, Helen Wilks had to alter her educational aspirations when her father lost his business. 'He was a printer,'
Wilks told me as we sat at the dining room table of her Toronto home. 'He
had a small shop and two of his big accounts went bankrupt. So he didn't

get paid. So that was the end of that.'[45] Shortly thereafter, things changed for Wilks. Suppressing her unhappiness with difficulty, Wilks acknowledged the tough choices that the thirties thrust upon her: 'My education [ended] because of the Depression and I was a top student at school,' said Wilks, tears slipping discreetly from her eyes. 'There was no possibility even to go to high school.' Unlike Vineham, Wilks did not leave school immediately. Instead of going to an academically focused collegiate, Wilks went to a commercial high school. At a collegiate, her mother noted, she would 'go for five years' and still be unable to 'do anything about making money.' At a commercial school 'they taught shorthand, typing, bookkeeping; we took some English and a bit of French,' Wilks explained. These technical skills could be turned into wages more easily. Though she 'fought like mad' to stay at an academic institution, Wilks felt that her position as third child gave her little leverage. She had to follow the path set for her by her older brothers and sisters. Unlike many young women, Wilks's family had the economic stability to ensure that she did not 'work in a factory,' though their position was not sufficient for her to spend time learning skills that would not earn her money afterward.

Now justifiably proud of the Bachelor of Arts degree she earned at the University of Toronto in 1984, Claire Clarke recalled the 1930s as a particularly difficult time when it came to schooling. She characterized those years between 1929 and 1939 as a 'time of shattered dreams.'[46] Clarke graduated from Central High School of Commerce in 1932. Though she had worked hard to earn the marks to be eligible for a collegiate, she was, like Wilks, strongly encouraged to choose the more practical route at a commercial high school. Job availability influenced Clarke too, but her memories emphasized different issues. Clarke's teachers told her to leave the academic stream because they saw few employment prospects for a young black girl. As Clarke recalled, they assumed that when she finished she 'would be cleaning pots just like the rest of them.'

It was not simply the white teachers who advocated more practical academic aspirations; people within Clarke's West-Indian community felt that even a commercial education was extravagant. They assumed that by allowing their daughter to pursue higher education, the Clarkes were acting beyond their station. Particularly in the lean thirties, no one understood why the family was not benefiting from their daughter's breadwinning, however nominal her wages might have been in the domestic service occupations open to her. Despite such pressure, Clarke's parents, her mother in particular, insisted that her daughter get an education. 'The time would come,' Clarke recalled her mother saying, 'when opportunities would present themselves,' and then she would be ready.

In the 1930s, expanded schooling for young women did not always translate into opportunity. In fact, one of the most difficult consequences of the Depression for women of this age group was their inability to continue with their schooling. Working girls' earnings were invaluable to their families in a time of economic crisis. These responsibilities limited the aspirations of many young women. For others, racial discrimination in schools and workplaces meant that they could not contribute as much money as they hoped to the family wage until the Second World War arrived. Whatever the case, the 1930s forced women to adapt their lives to different economic and social demands, which caused upset then and remained a particularly acute sign of disadvantage at the end of the twentieth century when the importance of schooling for stable careers was even greater.

Along with educational limitations, young working women also found that their wage-earning responsibilities prevented them from getting married as early as they might have liked. Marriage rates plummeted during the Depression more drastically than during any other decade in the twentieth century, as young workers found themselves forced to choose between employment and marriage.[47] This put young women in difficult situations. Ethel Bird still felt guilty in 2002 about her decision to marry seventy years earlier at the age of twenty-four. Before her marriage, Bird worked at Canada Wire and Cable. She recounted: 'I worked in a little tiny office with another chap measuring the contents of the batteries for the cars and small batteries and radios and measuring on a slide-scale ruler.' She only made thirteen cents an hour but it was enough for her to pay board to her parents. She also looked after her ill mother. When her family's construction company went bankrupt her father 'couldn't find a job. They weren't hiring. People were doing with what they had. There wasn't jobs to be had. We went on welfare. My Dad went to the town and they gave him work collecting garbage, thirteen dollars a week.' Bird's decision to marry coincided with these events, which meant that she left her job and moved out of her family home. Her feelings of shame about this decision come through clearly in her recollections: 'They couldn't keep the house. I always feel very guilty that I shouldn't have got married. I might have been able, you know, thirteen cents an hour, I could have helped out there.[48]

Faced with these situations, some working daughters did not marry. Alice Chrysler shared the story of Ethel Charlton with me. Charlton was a school teacher and a family friend. As Chrysler recalled, Charlton wanted to marry her beau William; however, William was not a 'go getter, shall we say.' He had not been able to land employment sufficient to support a wife and her family. 'The truth of it was the woman was supporting her invalid parents.' If she married she would lose her job. This story was a rather sad one, Chrysler felt, but she explained that women accepted the situation 'because that was the way it was ... you didn't think to complain. There weren't these movements of women's rights.'[49]

In certain banks and insurance companies, men risked dismissal if they married before they had reached a salary level considered sufficient to support a family.[50] When Bill Pearson proposed to his wife Margie in 1936, the couple had to postpone their nuptials until he earned enough money. He shared his recollections with me by reading a letter he had written to his grandchildren: 'Gran and Gramp got engaged one night when they were attending a dance on Gram's twenty-fourth birthday. This was just before Gramp had to move to Montreal. His company sent him to Montreal in 1936, but for the next two years he and Gram wrote to each other regularly ... and as soon as he was earning 125 dollars a month, they got married.'[51] Mutual Life, a Toronto insurance company, did not allow their male employees to marry until they had reached an income of $1500 a year.

For women the legal sanctions on employment after marriage were more far-reaching. In many fields, but particularly in teaching, nursing, and clerical work, a woman lost her job if she married. Canada's provincial and federal governments were especially notorious for 'rigorously pursu[ing] a policy of discrimination' based on marital status.[52] Margie Pearson worked at Eaton's as a comparison shopper. After her engagement, she wore her ring on her necklace rather than on her hand. It was important not to disclose that she would soon be married because she might lose her job. Similarly, if a nurse married she was automatically fired. Distress over the social relationships that nurses established preceded and lasted long past the Depression; however, during these years reprisals for transgressing rules sometimes had dire consequences.[53] When she finished her nursing education at Toronto General Hospital, Elizabeth Gammon 'was offered a job as Assistant Head nurse on Ward A.' She was excited about her new job and the young man who had been courting her for several months. 'That was when I got into difficulties,' Gammon recalled. At Christmas that year, her beau, who 'had been sent to Winnipeg' for work, came home 'for a bit of a holiday.' He asked Gammon to marry him. When the head nurse got word that Gammon was engaged, she informed her, 'We won't need your services anymore.' With amazement Gammon recalled how she was fired, 'just like that because I was *getting* married!'[54]

Some women had to choose between their family and matrimony. Others lost partners in the First World War or found no 'suitable male contacts.'[55] Irrespective of what shaped decisions about marriage, women who remained single were known derisively as career women or, still more derogatorily, as spinsters. In describing the career woman, one working girl claimed that she had 'been told by her mother and all the relations on both sides of the family, from Great Aunt Hodge down to [her] kid brother that [she was] improving [her] chances every day of being pushed in behind the pickle jars on the shelf and bringing lasting disgrace on the family.' As for spinsters, she continued; they were pitifully described as 'faithful old sort[s], very competent' though rather 'set in [their] ways and ... old fashioned.'[56] Connie Lancaster, who was 94 at the time of our 2002 interview, shared her feelings about her single status. When asked whether she had chosen not to marry, Lancaster replied with great emotion, 'My choice? I guess nobody wanted me really.' Pausing to contain herself, she continued: 'Okay, okay, I am not worried. I was busy, still am.'[57] Marion Forsythe never planned to marry. 'I played the field, but no I guess I was just never interested in marrying. I just didn't want to have to be committed to wash, iron, and make meals. I saw the drudgery.' In later years, Forsythe met and lived with a female colleague from Imperial Oil. 'Our desks were next to one another,' Forsythe recalled. They lived together for thirty-seven years. 'What great love we shared,' she explained; 'what a blow not to have her at home.'[58] For Forsythe, marriage meant labour; it had very little to do with a loving, satisfying, supportive relationship. Young women, like Forsythe, would also have been aware, from observing their parents and relationships in other homes, that marriage could also mean unhappiness, even violence and desertion. She was happiest forming a partnership with another woman. This was a choice that other women made as well, though they, like Forsythe, would have been ostracized had they publicly affirmed such desires in the 1930s.

For most women at the time, the expectation that they leave work for marriage was considered 'normal' rather than as a limitation based on gender difference. Rather than expressing concern about the fact that she lost her job when she married, Nora Windeatt remarked: 'In those days that was the thing. You had a job at home taking care of the family, and the man ... would feel terrible if he thought his wife had to go to work. He was the provider. You thought that was great and fine and had no problem with that.' She proudly shared her wedding photograph with me, urging me to take it for my project (figure 6).[59]

6   James and Nora Windeatt on their wedding day, 2 September 1938. Photo courtesy of Nora Windeatt.

When asked whether she was particularly upset that her employer, General Electric, forced office workers to quit when they married, Norma Hall commented that she was 'quite happy not to work.' In those days that was the thing, she continued, 'married women did not work then. [They] just stayed home and wore little housedresses.'[60] In 1998, Hall's recollections convey a critical appraisal of past ideals. However, during the Depression she understood that this was simply the way things were. In 1938, a survey of 167 young women who were graduating from Quebec and Ontario universities showed that just under 90 per cent desired marriage over a career.[61] That they were expected to leave work for marriage did not upset most young women. For most of them it was a 'natural' transition in their lives that the Depression had disrupted. Some working women preferred careers instead of marriage; some had no desire to form heterosexual unions; others would have wed, but the social and economic context of the 1930s worked against them. Had they been permitted to combine employment and matrimony, they might have made different choices and many certainly would have enjoyed greater economic security.

More young women than ever before were living and working in Toronto during the Depression. In the city, they found employment, which was particularly important to the economic well-being of their families. As we will see in chapter 5, they also, like Luella Luno, found freedom and excitement in these spaces. Their presence in the city did not, however, draw nearly the attention it had in earlier decades. Instead, concerns about how the Depression was affecting the 'ideal' family took centre stage. Upheaval at all levels of Canadian society in these years found expression in images of and discourses about women who challenged traditional divisions between home and work. But young single women did not undermine traditional gender divisions with their work, and therefore they emerged from the decade relatively unscathed by hyperbolic rhetoric or widespread moralistic interference characteristic of earlier periods. As long as they worked in women's jobs, behaved and appeared respectable, they were not a source of discontent. They were, instead, dutiful daughters who intended to follow the path to matrimony and offspring. This does not mean that the decade did not have a significant impact on their lives. The decade altered the life stages of Canada's young working women. It changed educational trajectories, forcing them to abandon or reduce their schooling aspirations. It led to delayed or cancelled marriages. These consequences were felt acutely by these women and remain clear indicators of what the Depression meant to their lives.

Chapter 2

Breadwinning Girls and Substitute Mothers: Negotiating Family Responsibilities

When Norma Vineham and her sisters headed out to work each morning, they left behind their unemployed father, an ailing mother, and three brothers who were still in school. The sisters became the primary breadwinners while their father took over daily domestic tasks, upsetting the traditional arrangement of their household. 'When Grace and I and Isabelle started to work,' recalled Vineham, 'Dad would have the dinner ready ... It was much the same most of the time, soup and stew, plain food, but again as I say we didn't go hungry.'[1] The Vinehams' situation was not at all unusual in the 1930s. The extent and nature of male unemployment during the Great Depression shifted roles within many families. It is interesting to consider what this meant to daughters. Did such adjustments upset the dominant cultural order that prioritized male breadwinning and female domesticity?

This chapter examines the place of young women within their households, highlighting the Depression-era conditions that brought breadwinning daughters to centre stage. Though social commentators responded to these changes in various ways, respectable working daughters remained an acceptable and desirable alternative to welfare and poverty. For their part, women workers remember that such shifts in the family economy brought greater responsibility and vulnerability to their lives.

For the majority of Torontonians, 80 per cent according to the 1931 census and 85 per cent in the 1941 census, families were based upon economic and social relationships formed between a husband, wife, and children who lived in the same home.[2] In such households, husbands were supposed to be the primary breadwinners, while wives worked in domestic space and, as childrearing literature from the period indicates, were the primary caregivers for children.[3] Despite the image of normalcy

upheld by such numbers, the vast majority of families had more complicated arrangements. Historians of the family and the working class have
established that women have always earned wages inside and outside the
home to supplement the family economy, but the place of young daughters within these arrangements has not been the focus of significant
study. As census analysts explained it in 1936, during the Great Depression
offspring bore 'a considerable share of the burden of supporting their
families,' shouldering nearly 86 per cent of the secondary sources of income in households where fathers continued to work and 90 per cent
where fathers were unemployed.[4] As in other periods, roles within family
economies were elastic to meet needs and daughters played particularly
crucial breadwinning roles in efforts to deal with such vulnerabilities.

Such shifts did not go unnoticed by family experts, including social
workers, psychologists, the police, and others who worked in Toronto's
legal system. Court records for the newly minted Family Court reflect an
increasing fear that domestic violence, desertion, and mental illness were
threatening the conventional family. There were also alarming statistics,
including falling birth and marriage rates, which suggested the 1930s
were 'provok[ing] a series of changes' in the family.[5] The Social Service
Council of Canada and others attributed 'modern unrest' in Canadian
homes to wide-ranging sources including new leisure activities and the
First World War, but the 'changing economic order' and high male unemployment were at the heart of such concerns.[6] Toronto's chief of police, Dennis Draper, saw joblessness as a harbinger of increasing rates of
delinquency. In his annual reports, Draper focused overwhelmingly on
the condition of Toronto's families and their ability to draw young citizens away from crime by inculcating them with appropriate morals and
a sound respectability. This, Draper believed, was a preventive measure
that would help vanquish problems generated by groups of downtrodden men. In 1935, Draper expounded on the steps necessary to establish
and maintain security: 'First and of primary importance is to re-establish
the home' because home training would 'serve as a bulwark of defense
against temptation to deviate from the path of clean and honest living in
later years.'[7] Young working daughters benefited from a strong home
because it prevented them from turning to immoral paths such as prostitution to stave off destitution.[8] *Hush*, a scandal sheet published weekly
in Toronto, reported in 1930 that the city was 'seething under a wave of
semi-professional and amateur prostitution, the direct result of starva-
tion wages' and the practice of hiring married women by companies like
Eaton's department store.[9] This coverage was undeniably sensational,

but it was reflective of broader perceptions espoused by people like Draper who did not want male unemployment to interfere with the transition of working girls into married women who were healthy and respectable. In keeping with these beliefs, promiscuous or even potentially deviant women were 'transformed into an "allegorical threat" to family and nation' in the thirties.[10] As Jennifer Stephen reveals in her analysis of the policy objectives of Ruth Low, director of Social Services and International Affairs of the YWCA, independent women, particularly if they were 'without home ties,' threatened Canada's families and 'the reproductive identity of all women.'[11] High male unemployment certainly shook the idea of the family to its core.

The decision to send female children out to earn wages in a time of economic crisis was not novel in the thirties. The working class and poor had used such strategies in the past irrespective of aspirations for a lone male breadwinner.[12] Before and after industrialization daughters had taken up domestic service occupations to help increase family income. Families sent daughters to Toronto from as far away as Britain and continental Europe to find jobs and, hopefully, send remittances home; however, in times of economic need, it had been far more common for brothers, particularly the eldest, to be the first line of defence because they typically earned more and had access to a wider range of jobs. Daughters worked if there were 'no brothers of an age to earn' and were rather more important for the domestic help they provided in the home.[13] During the Depression brothers continued to contribute to their families by scavenging (and in some cases stealing), selling papers, and using their bikes to deliver goods for local drug and grocery stores, but fewer of them were finding permanent paid employment.[14] As a consequence of such changes, Judge Helen Gregory MacGill noted in 1930: 'More daughters than sons [were] found giving all or a large proportion of their earnings to, and accepting responsibility for, the family.' This was due in part, she explained, to economic conditions and the gendered division of labour. 'In times of depression women and children because of their low standard of pay can often get work more easily than men.'[15] Young single women were no longer part of a 'hidden economy' of workers and, instead, enjoyed access to a range of employment in less vulnerable sectors of the economies of urban centres such as Toronto.

Breadwinning daughters were central the survival of the Tapp family. In the early years of the Depression, George Tapp was a prosperous and, as his daughters recalled, happy man. He left the house each day with his lunch pail in hand while his wife remained home caring for, and getting off to school, their seven children: Nell, Vivian, Ella, Ivy, Margaret, Joyce, and Bill. As daughter Ivy Phillips recollected: 'I remember going over and waiting for him to come off his shift at the corner of Gerrard and Main Street. He'd have his lunch box and whoever got there first got, well he'd always leave a cake or something in his lunch box for the first one that got there. I can remember that.'[16] As a motorman for the Toronto Transit Commission (TTC), Tapp would have earned an average yearly income of approximately $700.[17] This was a stable though barely adequate income for a family of nine. The average family in the city was earning between $900 and $1500 a year, and even this income did not provide for luxuries. To extend household earnings Tapp participated in the 'informal' economy. Daughter Joyce Cahill offered the details with great amusement: 'You know, here is a man who was supposed to be working on the TTC as a driver, but [he] had a great big car, a new Buick every year, [or] a Durant, and his two oldest daughters had fur coats! And, he's working for the TTC.' A car of this size cost between $800 and $1000 in the early thirties; this was not an expense that was manageable on Tapp's salary (figure 7). Cahill's sister Margaret McLean provided an explanation for the economic stability reflected in this photograph: 'Father was a bookie.'[18] Gambling outside of racetracks was illegal in Ontario, and, throughout the Depression, Toronto's chief constable, Dennis Draper, was focused overwhelmingly on 'organized professional gamblers' who were 'sinking [their] tentacles into the vitals' of a society struggling with economic deprivation.[19] There was significant fear that Toronto's citizens might fall victim to greedy bookies, risk their last dollar for an elusive fortune, and, in doing so, squander their family's much-needed livelihood. Irrespective of such concerns, Tapp's participation in criminal activity was not exceptional; a variety of crimes were used to help families deal with economic difficulties in the thirties. Children stole coal, lumber, and even ice from the railway yards.[20] There was tacit acceptance of such crimes among parents and sympathetic court officials.[21] In fact, for a time George Tapp had an arrangement with the police and ran a very lucrative business. As McLean recalled, 'he even more or less had the Number Ten police station in the palm of his hand.' Number Ten was conveniently located at the end of their street, and Tapp 'was most generous' with his alcohol and money.[22] The Tapp children all participated in covert operations. 'When we were kids,' McLean explained mischievously, 'we would have to go to various places to tell them, Bill the Barber and Happy at the Drugstore, don't phone in bets, don't phone in bets!' It was Ivy's job to pull the phone cords. 'If you

7   James Tapp and his daughters from right to left, Ivy, Margaret, Joyce, and Ella. Photo courtesy of Margaret McLean.

[went] down the cellar way on the wall of the cellar there was two things that affected the phone; the family had it organized and you pull the thing and the phone would go dead.'[23] This system worked flawlessly for a time: the police would 'raid' the house but leave without any incriminating evidence. When 'they changed every policeman in Number Ten' and staged a legitimate raid things began to fall apart.[24]

In McLean's words, 'Dad went down. So my very proud, darling mother went out and worked. She scrubbed floors.' Their mother's day began quite differently after their father's arrest. Early each morning, she headed to the offices of Labatt's Brewery. As her youngest daughter, Joyce Cahill, recalled, 'She couldn't do anything. Our mother was not schooled.' She did start to clean office. 'She would go, she'd leave about three o'clock in the morning … for two hours come back get us kids ready for school or whatever, then go again.' Along with her work outside the home, as McLean remembered it, their mother always had 'a pot of porridge' waiting on the wood stove. 'Remember that Joyce! We'd come downstairs and there was always a pot of oatmeal at the back of the old black stove in the kitchen.' After tending to childcare, their mother would return to work, sometimes with one of her daughters in tow. Even at a very young age, Cahill recalled, 'sometimes I would go along and she would give me a cloth to dust the chairs.' However, their mother's wages were insufficient to support the family. Soon thereafter daughters Nell, Ivy, and Ella found employment. They cleaned houses for a time but eventually found other work. Nell Moran and Ivy Phillips acquired work at Jenny Lind, a chocolate store, while their sister Ella worked at a Toronto-area factory.[25]

While Claire Clarke's father did not lose his job at the foundry where he worked as a wheelwright, his hours were reduced during the Depression. This was 'hard work,' Clarke observed. 'He used to say how he would be pounding these wheels, they were big train wheels,' but this was preferable to work as a railway porter, one of the few avenues of employment open to black men in these years. In an attempt to compensate for lost time, Clarke's father did odd jobs in his off hours. Through the winter he would 'get himself dressed, get the shovel, the snow shovel, and go out the door going to see if he could find a job with the city.' Her mother worked from home as a seamstress. The family also had boarders, drawing upon those in need of housing in the West-Indian community. Sometimes they had more than one family living with them; Clarke and her sister had to sleep in the dining room on cots. These strategies barely covered the costs of their home, newly purchased in June 1930.

Claire Clarke knew her family needed her wages to help make ends meet. They had already made sacrifices to ensure that she and her sister could finish high school. Clarke had clerical training, had even earned an award for her skills, but she had no luck finding work in this field. Here race denied her access to Toronto's offices. Refusing to take the domestic service jobs that were available for young black women, she learned how to sew and began using her mother's sewing machine to make alterations and clothing. She also found work at a hat factory in downtown Toronto. The Jewish proprietor, Mr Wise, hired her 'to sit and make hats.' During all of this Clarke continued 'lobbying, writing civil service exams' and keeping up her qualifications so that she might eventually find an office job. This would not happen until the Second World

War, when Clarke found a job in the offices of the Canadian Navy. After her first day of work she came home and told her parents with relief: 'No more boarders.'[26]

The Edelist family relied on the wages of their eldest daughter Rose for their immigration from Poland to Canada and for their economic stability through the early years of the Depression. In 1922, fourteen-year-old Rose Edelist left her academic studies in Poland to apprentice as a seamstress. Much like families from the British Isles and northern Europe who had sent their daughters to earn wages as domestics in the colonies during the nineteenth century, this decision was premised on a plan to get the family to Canada. Word had arrived that work was plentiful for Jewish women in Toronto's garment industry. Within four years, Edelist arrived at her aunt's door in the Kensington Market area of the city with the training and experience necessary to find work as a seamstress, which she did with little problem. Soon after, she began sending 'ten dollars a month every month' to Poland. Within the year, Rose's younger sister had arrived. The sisters worked to first bring their father to Toronto and by 1929 had managed to collect the money necessary for their mother and remaining siblings to arrive, just before Canada effectively closed its doors to immigrants.[27] It was not easy, Edelist explained. 'Well I will tell you I was worn out. I worked hard since I was very young and [it was] a lot of tension to bring over ... seven children and my parents.' Reuniting their family in Canada did not end the sisters' financial responsibilities. When the Depression set in no one else could find work. 'My sister and I had to carry the whole load ... to make enough money there should be food on the table and rent and clothing.' When she married in 1932, Edelist's husband moved into their already crowded house because her wages were so essential to the household and the young couple could also rely on the support of their extended family.[28]

Margaret Gairns's situation was slightly different, though her wages were equally important to her parents during the 1930s. I sat with Gairns, a spirited 92-year-old, on more than one occasion in her Toronto retirement home in the spring of 2002. Disappointment characterized Gairns's memories of the early Depression years because when she graduated from the Ontario College of Education (OCE) in 1932, there were no teaching positions available for her. Gairns found this unemployment particularly upsetting. However, in lieu of a job, her father, 'a *fine* jewellery engraver,' urged his daughter to complete her Master of Arts degree at Victoria College, University of Toronto. 'My father didn't want me to go way up to northern Ontario' for a teaching job, Gairns explained. 'I was an only child and I was living at home and he said "Look we are not that hard up. You always wanted to do graduate work. Why don't you just settle down?"' That is exactly what Margaret Gairns did.

Such options were a privilege that few of Toronto's daughters enjoyed. In explaining the social class of her family and friends, Gairns said: 'We were a middle-class group that managed to struggle through without sending the girls out to work.' Nevertheless, schooling was no small financial burden. Gairns's father rented rooms to tenants to bolster family income. 'Not boarders!' Gairns corrected me, but 'tenants.' She explained: 'Father had bought the house. It was a single-family house, but he altered it or had it altered. We lived on the ground floor and there were one, two, three apartments and I think they cost about thirty-five dollars a month.' These tenants lived in the house as long as the Gairns family lived there. The income was necessary 'because his income from his chosen work was not [pause] I never knew what it was,' explained Gairns, 'but there was no question about me going to college and there was no need for me to look for a bursary or anything.'[29] While Gairns's father may not have earned a substantial amount of money as a jewellery engraver, Gairns carefully established her family's middle-class status, something that was important to her sense of acceptance in and access to the halls of Victoria College in the early thirties and her retirement home more than seventy years later.

When Gairns found a permanent teaching job in 1937, her father was ill and had closed his business. They decided to move closer to Gairns's job in north Toronto. 'Father wanted to move for me, really ... He was retired. Mother had never worked after she was married; women didn't in those days.' They moved to a five-room bungalow, which her father called '"a wee box." He was a Scot you see, born in the north of Scotland.' They were 'cookie cutter houses,' but 'the little five-roomed house was plenty of room for us.' Gairns lived with her parents until they passed away. As for marriage, she said, 'I was never tempted. I was dedicated to the teaching. I just loved it. I wasn't interested in housekeeping and that kind of thing. I didn't want little children all around my feet.' As a former student explained in Gairns's obituary, 'Admirers? Many. Married? Never! Kids? Thousands.'[30]

Gairns was a devoted teacher who clearly adored her profession. As marriage would have forced her to abandon teaching, her limited choice came easily. She remembered her decision to remain single: 'I was lucky living at home. I paid something into the family [expenses], but I didn't have to pay high and I had security living at home.' She was unsure about the amount of her monthly payments, but she does remember that she 'paid a substantial contribution to the first Frigidaire' the family purchased. Gairns also appreciated her mother's domestic support, describing her as 'a wonderful manager. You see she did all this canning and making marmalade. All those things were made at home by Mom ... mind you, she worked very hard at times. When the things were ripe and ready and you couldn't say "Well I'll do that three weeks from now" because it wouldn't be available.' On the domestic side of things, Gairns recalled that she 'wasn't very much help.'[31] The demands of her teaching career meant that she had little time to be involved in the responsibilities of cooking or cleaning. As Gairns's memories suggest, daughters could benefit from remaining at home. An editorial cartoon published in the *Evening Telegram* in 1935 provides commentary on this situation. In it an anxious wife meets her work-weary husband at the door to explain that their daughter has married and brought home an unemployed fellow she barely knows. As the young daughter unabashedly serves food to her new husband in the background, her parents struggle with the burden of her foolhardy decision.[32]

An employed daughter could also provide significant economic security for her parents. The teaching profession, like nursing, was one of the most stable and lucrative areas of work for women in the interwar years. A female teacher in Toronto earned between $1300 and $1600 per year, compared with a female clerical worker, who earned (if she was given the minimum wage of $12.50 per week) $900, or a male carpenter, who made just under $900 in 1931.[33] When she started working at Lawrence Park Collegiate Institute in 1937, Gairns received a raise. Banging her hand on the table for emphasis, she said: 'I jumped to $1800 a year and I thought I was a millionaire!' she said with laughter.[34] In the winter months of 1930–1, the average family of five in Canadian urban centres spent between $18 and $20 a week on rent, staple foods, fuel, and lighting.[35] Gairns was earning almost $38 a week. Though she was hardly wealthy, this salary certainly offered her family stability in her father's retirement.

Given the economic security that such a salary could bring to an entire family, it is not surprising that, as one woman noted in *Chatelaine,* 'feminine social isolation [was] particularly common among teachers.'[36] Another *Chatelaine* writer felt that 'married woman [were] more needed in the teaching profession than in making doilies or playing afternoon bridge, or even making layer cake or those other peculiarly virtuous occupations, making jam and pickles.'[37] Until the 1950s, however, the Toronto Board of Education forced women to give up their teaching jobs once they were married.[38] Consequently, only two of the six teachers interviewed for this study married. Like Gairns, teacher Dora Wattie did not marry. When asked whether this was a problem for her she responded, 'No, no. A lot of people did not marry at that time because they had family responsibilities.'[39] Those who did marry often faced economic hardship as a consequence. For instance, Mary Chenhall, who taught math and physics at Markham District High School, lost her job when she married in 1935. 'I got fired because they didn't hire married women,' she explained.[40] Chenhall remembered this restriction with mixed feelings: '[I was] not too happy,' Chenhall began, but 'looking back I am happy that it happened that way. We had four boys in ten years and then I was home.' Losing her job 'was hard to take,' but, she explained, 'now I see my granddaughters with full-time jobs and I think we were lucky to stay home.' In the Depression years, Chenhall's unemployment meant that she and her husband struggled to make ends meet on his salary as a music instructor. In fact, the Chenhalls were 'living hand to mouth.' Martin Chenhall was not, like his wife, a formally trained teacher. During the 1930s it was very difficult for him to compete for employment in an already restricted labour market.

As the adjustments of the Vineham family make clear, a household did not run on wages alone. Sometimes it was necessary for fathers to complete domestic tasks when their daughters and wives took up breadwinning responsibilities. This upset the traditional power structure of households along gender and generational lines and in some families contributed to difficulties like depression, alcoholism, and violence; however, as Joy Parr demonstrates in her analysis of Paris, Ontario, seldom did such shifts transgress gender division of labour entirely.[41] Fathers and brothers did certain jobs and helped out at home, but in most cases the organizing and running of domestic space were still left to women, both mothers and daughters. As Parr explains, 'being a dutiful daughter implie[d] both unpaid labour and cash contributions to kin.'[42] The memories of Toronto's working daughters point to their roles as substitute mothers who cleaned, cooked, and cared for younger siblings, particularly in cases where mothers were earning wages or were absent through death or desertion.

Grace Michaels, who was born in Leicester, England, in 1910, came to Canada in 1924 with her younger brother. Their father, who had come to Toronto two years earlier in search of work, met them at Union Station. At first they did not recognize him. 'He had grown a beard,' Michaels recalled. Their mother had died in the flu epidemic of 1918 and they had been living with their grandmother.[43] Michaels's story was not unique. Single-parent families comprised a significant minority in Toronto. In fact, nearly 20 per cent of the city's families had only one parent in 1931.[44] For young women like Michaels, her father's widower status had major consequences. Unlike other women her age, Michaels did not have much free time. She worked in retail at an Evangelical bookstore to supplement her father's wages, and, as she recalled with quiet resignation, 'I kept house for my father, so I *worked*. I was very busy. I didn't have much leisure time.' Her brother on the other hand enjoyed greater freedom. He was four years younger and still in school, which meant that Michaels was responsible for his care as well.

Childcare duties were important in families without stay-at-home caregivers. In all but a few households, paid childcare was an unheard-of expense. As Pat Mulligan asserted, 'there was no such thing as babysitting then.'[45] Joyce Cahill concurred: 'My mother,' she said, 'never had a babysitter even when she had the money.'[46] The cost of such services seemed frivolous when an older sibling would do the same job for free. Some young women accepted their roles and added responsibilities. Margaret Snowball was nine when her mother died in childbirth. It was 1932, and shortly thereafter her father lost his upholstery business. With a combination of great sadness and pride, Snowball remembered how her six older siblings worked to ensure the family survived. As Snowball explained to me about her eldest sister, 'She had a job at Penman's [in] menswear and she was a darling. It was her, she and my father who really raised us.'[47] This sister took up the role left empty by the death of their mother. As Snowball fondly recalled, she even used her wages to ensure her sisters had new clothes for celebrations. 'She'd say to us, "Go buy yourself a new Easter outfit."'

Other women's recollections indicate that elder sisters found such responsibilities burdensome. In 1932, Nell Moran turned eighteen and started to drive. She remembered her father encouraging her: 'Yeah, I started to drive then because he was a lousy driver. He hated it! ... And he was waiting for me to hurry up and get old enough so I could get [my licence].' She took her mother grocery shopping.[48] As the eldest child, Moran was also responsible for her younger siblings. Explaining this, she quipped, 'I'm the eldest of seven children so I was always carting children around.' On weekends and school holidays she was especially busy. Moran would take her siblings down to Toronto's beaches while her mother worked or tried to find time for herself. 'I always had a kid,' Moran repeated. '[Mother would] pack us a lunch and then we'd walk down the hill. That was quite a life, wasn't it? When you think of it, long walk down, long walk up too.' Though she was hesitant to describe this job as a responsibility, Moran did not seem particularly fond of her position. Her sisters remembered her aversion to this role. Younger sister Ivy Phillips was certain Moran lied about her day off to avoid domestic responsibilities.[49]

Though daughters were taking on greater economic roles, in most cases their brothers did not assume more domestic responsibilities. As in the Michaels household, the Tapp sisters recalled that their younger brother did very little. 'He was living great,' McLean explained, 'because Jim was uno-one-o. I don't think that Jim suffered at all.' When recalling Depression-era Montreal, one of Denyse Baillargeon's interviewees said: 'Little boys were like little kings,' when it came to domestic duties.[50] In families without daughters, however, the situation could be different. 'We're Italian,' Rocco Longo explained to me during our telephone interview. In the Depression, Longo and his parents lived within the city limits; however, they did not reside among other Italians. 'My mother didn't speak English,' explained Longo. 'She didn't have relationships with the neighbours, speaking over the back fence and such. I think she was pretty isolated sometimes.' Longo's mother did not have access to Italian neighbours or shopkeepers in north Toronto. Therefore, her son, who could speak English, ran some of the household errands. He recalled doing the grocery shopping, in particular. Each week he would buy fruit, vegetables, and live chickens from the 'Jewish market.' It was 'fifty cents for scrawny chickens and seventy-five cents for fat chickens,' and it cost an additional five cents if you wanted the Rabbi to take care of the 'unpleasant job of killing them.' He chose this option more frequently after he tried to bring two live birds home 'in the back seat of the car.'[51]

Though less typical, daughters often took over all domestic responsibilities in cases where their mothers deserted their families.[52] In 1929, when sisters Geraldine Windeatt and Helen Campbell were fifteen and seventeen years old, their mother left. This development caused quite a stir in their small suburban community of Weston, just outside Toronto. Rates of desertion had risen noticeably during the thirties, but this was usually due to the behaviour of fathers.[53] In 1931, single parents headed 20 per cent of families and lone women headed nearly 19 per cent of these Toronto homes.[54] During the heyday of scientific motherhood, which placed the responsibility for home and children squarely on the shoulders of mothers, social workers, child psychologists, and others argued that mothers were central to the 'building of character, citizenship, and nation.' Fathers had a shadowy presence, at best, in this discourse, and, therefore, a household without a mother was considered particularly errant.[55] For sisters Windeatt and Campbell, pictured here in one of the last photographs taken of the family (figure 8), the gossip and speculation that swirled around their community made them feel like outcasts. The changes that it brought to their lives exacerbated this feeling. In the late 1920s, their father worked in interior design at Reg Smith Blinds, but he suffered a 'nervous breakdown' after his wife left.[56] Thus his daughters had to take over all of the economic and domestic responsibilities in their home. Though she recalled 'too few jobs' in the Depression, Campbell found a job where her father had worked without much difficulty. When recalling Smith, Campbell said, 'He taught me everything I needed to know.' Later in the Depression she switched to a more responsible secretarial position and remembered that she was 'one of the ten highest-paid secretaries in Toronto.'[57] While Campbell earned wages, her younger sister quit school to assume all household duties, including cleaning, cooking, and caring for their ill father. As Windeatt's sister-in-law explained, 'Gerry took care of the house (figure 9). She was smart, but [she] had to look after the house when her mom left. She had a lot on her shoulders.' Being tied to the household did not offer Windeatt the same freedom her sister enjoyed. 'Helen had it best,' Nora Windeatt elaborated. 'I wish Gerry had done more, but she did not have the opportunities.' Really, running that household, 'what chance did she have?'[58]

Margaret Radforth's mother also left her family in the early 1920s. Her mother's desertion was not something she talked about freely, recalled her son Ian Radforth, but it certainly affected her life.[59] She was only twelve when her mother left, but Margaret was the eldest of four children. Consequently, as her son described it, she became a 'substitute mother' to her three siblings, particularly the youngest one, who was only three. When she was fifteen Margaret quit school and found work at a local chocolate factory. Her father's employment as a baker was steady and remained so throughout the Depression; however, the family had lost their mother's income from office cleaning. If they wanted greater economic stability then it was necessary for young Margaret to find employment. These responsibilities lasted well into the Depression and helped delay Margaret's marriage until 1937 (figure 10). At that time her

8   Sisters Helen Campbell (left) and Geraldine Windeatt (right) with their parents shortly before their mother left in 1929. Photo courtesy of Penny Srigley.

9   Working girls Geraldine Windeatt (left) and Nora Windeatt (right) in the early thirties. Photo courtesy of Frances Campbell Douglas.

10   Margaret and Sydney Radforth on their wedding day in 1937. Photo courtesy of Ian Radforth.

youngest sister Dorothy 'was seventeen and had just started in the work-force.' As Radforth surmised, this 'probably was a consideration, perhaps what mom and dad had been waiting for.'[60] Though daughters were taking on greater financial responsibility for their families, gendered divisions of labour within households tended to remain the same. This meant that, in most cases, daughters rather than sons helped with cooking, cleaning, and childcare. Moreover, in cases where mothers were absent because of employment, death, or desertion, daughters, particularly the eldest, often became substitute mothers.

The records of Toronto's Family Court offer one window into the effects of economic insecurities on families. The majority of cases brought to the court dealt with non-support on the part of husbands and fathers; nonetheless, as Joan Sangster and Marcus Klee have established, these cases often overlapped with problems of alcoholism, desertion, and abuse. The court records also reveal that the primary aim of judges, probation officers, and social workers was to preserve the family unit.[61] In fact, officials assumed that 'proper' family arrangements would cure most domestic problems. Thus, despite the increase in charges of assault and desertion in the thirties, the percentage of cases prosecuted declined substantially from 41 per cent in 1929 to 13 per cent in 1939. This pattern, notes Sangster, reflected 'the emphasis on placation and probation in Family Courts.'[62] Judges did not lack compassion but urged husbands to take their proper role: 'Go home and take the leadership in the house, act as a man.' This meant controlling their wives and 'protecting' them from the 'lust' of other men.[63] The court urged reconciliation and, as this example suggests, relied on a vocabulary of emasculation and male authority to bring men into line. This strategy constructed male power (physical and otherwise) as a normal attribute of healthy masculinity and proper family relationships. It also reflected broader societal notions of family roles, which treated male aggression casually. In a 1934 *Chatelaine* advertisement, a husband holds his clenched fist up with an angry face while his wife sits chastened below him. The caption reads '**MORE STOCKING RUNS**? YOU'LL *RUIN* ME, BABS.' By using the advertised product, the 'young bride learned how to cut down costly runs' but also placated her physically and verbally aggressive husband.[64] In fact, the normalization of male violence did little to encourage women to ask for help. Those who did report abuse often had to report it up to three times before the court took them seriously.[65] In the process, the court failed to protect women or to encourage them to seek shelter with state institutions or officials.

Acceptance of male power and dominance in the home fit uncomfortably with the helplessness caused by male joblessness. Toronto's City Council and Homeowner's Association were apprehensive that rampant unemployment was making men 'ill in mind and body.' In fact, they continued, 'the happiness and peace of our home life is almost destroyed through the enforced idleness of the breadwinners.'[66] Moreover, the 1930s was a period when, as the editor for *Chatelaine* noted, 'little irritations [could] grow into bitter misunderstandings and cruel words.' As a consequence, this writer continued, all women had a 'double duty to perform.' When husbands become 'touchy' and 'morose,' wives need to practise 'thoughtfulness and tenderness toward the men.'[67] Fictional accounts of the thirties frequently deal with the consequences of unemployment for fathers. In *Cabbagetown*, Myrla Patson's father descends into depression and insanity as he struggles with not having any work.[68] Similarly, in *The Stubborn Season*, Irene MacNeil's father finds solace in alcohol and is eventually killed by a car while walking Toronto's streets intoxicated.[69] In her analysis of fatherhood during the interwar years, Cynthia Comacchio points out that 'the provider role' was central to 'masculine identity and family relations, its loss could well disturb the father's accustomed status, straining relationships all round.'[70] Though most women did not want to represent their families as dysfunctional or their fathers as problem figures in their lives, the memories of Toronto's dutiful daughters reveal family troubles during the Depression that centred on both economic insecurity and male unemployment.[71]

For the Tapp sisters, downward economic mobility propelled their mother into the workplace, signalled the end of schooling and beginning of wage earning, and initiated their father's psychological decline. Margaret McLean, along with sisters Ivy Phillips and Joyce Cahill, recalled how depression and alcohol fundamentally altered their household. As McLean explained about her father's situation, after his gambling operation collapsed, 'Well he couldn't take it, couldn't take that being degraded and he had a mental breakdown.'[72] Phillips shared a similar memory with me: 'After he was caught or whatever you call it he went down and had a mental breakdown and then he was never the same. He was a different man.' 'Why was it so hard?' I queried. 'Going down, I guess ... because he was a very generous man when he had it.' George Tapp was no longer able to provide his wife with fur coats, purchase cars, or shower gifts on the community. He was unable to maintain his social standing or fulfil his role as breadwinner. As a consequence, he suffered psychologically. This kept him out of the workplace until the late 1930s.

Along with her father's depression, Ivy Phillips remembered alcoholism. Though things got difficult with money after his gambling operation was shut down, Phillips recalled that her father 'still drank his beer ... He was a drunk.' Tapp used to make his own beer down in the cellar of his home. In fact, before the police station was overhauled, he used to ply officers with it when they would 'raid' the house. As Phillips explained it, her father 'didn't grumble as long as he could get his beer ... but he changed. I mean, mentally he changed. He wasn't the same smart man' after his downfall. One day Phillips recalled sitting on the steps to the basement and watching her father with a mixture of fear and amazement. 'He was absolutely finished with the beer. So he smashed everything down in the cellar, all the bottles, everything he ever did.'[73]

Grace Michaels never claimed to have grown up in a controlling or abusive home. Her memories suggest, however, that such problems were part of her home life. Like many young women, Michaels's family duties curbed her leisure time; she also recalled how her father controlled what free time she had. On more than one occasion during our interview Michaels described how she 'didn't have a normal teen's life like they have now' because, she explained, 'my father looked on me as his wife and wanted to go everywhere I went and it kind of curtailed my teens.'[74] Whether such recollections point to suppressed or shameful issues of abuse, Michaels's memories relate how domestic space was a site of oppression for some dutiful daughters.

Two hours passed in my interview with Jean Jackson before she reflected upon the insecurities of her home life. During the thirties, Jackson had a nervous breakdown. She was only a teenager. At first she explained that she was 'worried about stupid things like every night mother would say, well not every night, but she'd say "We haven't any dessert because I can't afford to get dessert tonight" and I'd say, "But we *have* to have dessert."' Jackson would make a cake from available ingredients and tell her family: 'You can't eat it all tonight because we have to save it for tomorrow.' In reality, larger issues interrupted Jackson's sense of stability. 'To tell you the truth,' Jackson recounted later in our interview, 'my mother and father didn't get along very well. There was always quarrelling. I'm telling you this because it was true and it would have been far better you see in those days they stayed together which [was] hard on children. I found it very hard. I was just about a nervous wreck ... but that was the way it was and it would have been much better if they could have just each gone their own ways.' 'Other women' and money shortages were the source of much of this tension, and, as Jackson recalled about her role, 'you just automatically take sides but it really got to me I guess more than, I guess more than the rest [of my siblings].'[75] As the memories of women such as Phillips, Michaels, and Jackson indicate, some families experienced crises produced in part by Depression-era insecurities. In particular, male unemployment contributed to problems of mental breakdown, alcoholism, and marital discord.

In the thirties, male unemployment and economic uncertainty had various consequences for Toronto's families. Unlike in previous decades, Toronto's working daughters were often the only wage earners to find stable employment. This caused a significant change in household roles and responsibilities. Some families used crime to bolster their stability, but when this did not work, the women, particularly daughters, were forced to earn wages. Whether from their status as recent immigrants or due to discrimination in Toronto's labour market, for some families the Depression represented a continuation of insecurity. As such, during the thirties, daughters like Rose Edelist continued to provide for her family as she had done in previous decades. A daughter's wages provided important collateral in a city that had few jobs for Jewish men. Other daughters benefited from the support of their families as they finished their education; however, the employment they eventually found proved central to the well-being of their families as well.

Along with their economic roles, daughters also fulfilled important domestic responsibilities, including childcare, cooking, and cleaning. In fact, many found themselves in positions as substitute mothers when their own mothers were busy with wage-earning responsibilities, had passed away, or had left the family behind. That daughters recalled brothers having fewer domestic responsibilities points to the ways in which gendered divisions of labour persisted within households even as they were challenged by the primary wage-earning roles of young daughters. Also important to our understanding of the Depression is the glimpse that these women's memories provide into family dysfunction. The adjustments made within families to cope with the Depression did create crises for young women, both economic and social. They experienced ostracism in their communities and, in some cases, alcoholism, mental breakdown, and abuse. In the 1930s there were few avenues of support and almost no language for discussion of these problems. As chapter 3 shows, however, the city's workplaces could provide spaces of respite and opportunity, even in the midst of the Depression.

Chapter 3

Young Women's Job Options in an Urban Labour Market in the 1930s

On workday mornings in the 1930s, young wage-earning women from across Toronto left their homes and headed to work as domestics, teachers, clerical staff, and garment workers. Some of these women found their employment fun and exciting, remaining in their jobs for years; others found such responsibilities burdensome. Over the course of their wage-earning lives, many of them moved between jobs, leaving for promotion, in protest, for marriage, or for better work conditions. Norma Vineham began working in the factory at Dominion Silk Mills but was soon able to find a job in the company office as a file clerk. Anne Hinsta, who arrived in Toronto from Finland in 1929, worked as a domestic in north Toronto. She constantly looked for other work because living in meant she had to board her son with another Finnish family during the week. Though she took pride in her work, she also endured long hours and poor working conditions for little more than $20 a month. Nurse Dorothy Coles loved her job thoroughly. She fondly remembered her training at Toronto Western Hospital and the time she was able to spend with patients. Despite this, she scarcely regretted the requirement that she abandon her post when she married one of the hospital's doctors.[1] While these women's stories tell us something important about the job options available to young women in urban labour markets in the 1930s, they also point to the relationships between individual identities and employment choice. While factory work and domestic service employed women from a range of ethnic backgrounds, chiefly immigrant women, office jobs and professional service occupations like nursing were held, almost exclusively, by young working- and middle-class women of British descent who were unmarried.[2] As a generation of scholarship on racialized job markets suggests, paying attention to these complexities uncovers critical and otherwise hidden aspects of women's experiences.[3] This chapter examines young women's experiences in urban workplaces and considers, in particular, the hierarchies that shaped their job prospects and generated privilege and disadvantage in the 1930s. In domestic positions, in teaching, in clerical jobs, and in factory work, breadwinning daughters of different racial, ethnic, and religious backgrounds had distinct employment options. This gave some of them social and economic advantages over other women and even some men.

The importance of a critical analysis of the experiences and recollections of young women workers that considers individual identities is well illustrated by Claire Clarke's still painful memories of her work experiences. In our 2001 interview, Clarke remembered how she stood second in her graduating class in 1932, telling me 'I graduated at the top of my class ... you know I received the Timothy Eaton scholarship medal. The Jewish girl received the gold medal and I received the silver medal.' Equally evident all these years later was her disappointment that despite her impressive academic achievement, 'there was no [job] placement' for her. That was 'very unusual' she added, 'because during all my years at the school, in the summertime they would select girls and send them off to the parliament buildings to work. I was never selected.'[4] Like other girls her age, Clarke expected to find employment in order to help her family, who were living in a newly purchased home in a downtown Toronto neighbourhood.

In many respects, Clarke's work experiences confirm the findings of feminist historians who have examined how gender and class have shaped the employment of women workers in the early twentieth century. Wage earners like Clarke faced sexist job segregation; however, available jobs in Ontario's largest urban centre did not ensure young women a position of choice. Of the women employed in Toronto in the early years of the Depression, 27 per cent of them worked in personal service, 28 per cent in clerical occupations, 17 per cent in manufacturing (primarily in the textile industry), and 11 per cent in professional service occupations such as teaching and nursing.[5] By 1941, despite the onset of the war and the movement of women into non-traditional occupations, little had changed. Eighty-four per cent of employed women were involved in these sectors of the labour market.[6] This ghettoization denied women access to skilled jobs in the industrial sector and positions as administrators, principals, and doctors in offices and hospitals. It also legitimized lower earnings: women received on average one-third to one-half the earnings of men.[7] Hampered by these obstacles, Clarke was searching for work when the plight of the male breadwinner prompted widespread anti-feminist sentiment in the country's newspapers and sanctioned regulations that allowed employers in occupations in the civil service, nursing, and teaching to deny women employment after marriage. These discriminatory expectations about marital status and wage earning ensured, as Veronica Strong-Boag puts it, that women were 'defined and delimited, not so much by any lesser capacity for work or determination, or thought, but by patriarchal custom and male authority.'[8] Clarke undeniably lived in a society that valued the labour of men over women. She could not find work despite her vocational education. Nonetheless, sexism does not adequately explain Clarke's labour force experiences, especially as she was part of a cohort of young single women who were finding jobs in Depression-era Toronto. Significantly, when asked why she had difficulty securing employment, Clarke did not mention issues related to gender or class; instead, she exclaimed with great conviction, 'I am black in case you hadn't noticed?!' (figure 11).

Clarke's story, and her explicit racial explanation of her failure to find work in her field, as well as the work memories of the other women, Anglo-Celtic, European, and West-Indian Canadian, who are the subjects of this study, compel us to scrutinize more closely how race interacted with gender, class, and other variables to produce not only certain kinds of experiences, and women's memories of them, but also the complex identities that women workers forged in this period of economic stagnation. As Clarke's memories of racial discrimination and the differing memories of the other women central to this study suggest, we need to examine more closely how an individual's multiple identities influenced their lives in this particular time and place. In probing the individual stories of a diverse group of working women in Depression-era Toronto, I draw most explicitly on the scholarship of feminist historians whose work on immigrant, ethnic, black, and other racialized working-class women in North America has demonstrated the value of moving beyond static models of patriarchy that assume the primacy of gender as an explanatory factor in historical experience.[9] For some women at least, gender and class were not the only, nor necessarily the most important, social factors shaping their work experiences; nor did they prioritize them when remembering and trying to make sense of their past experiences.

Though a few men are recorded as domestic servants in the Depression, this occupation was overwhelmingly female in these years.[10] In 1931, more than 50 per cent of the women in personal service, which included jobs such as boarding-house keepers, waitresses, and general cooks, were domestics. Varpu Lindstrom's work on Finnish domestics makes

11   Claire Clarke with Katrina Srigley. Photo courtesy of Katrina Srigley.

the important observation that not all women accepted domestic work as negative and many of them worked collectively to maintain a positive image of housework and to resist employers who cast them as domestic slaves.[11] Nevertheless, this job had the lowest pay, the worst working conditions, and was typically the least desirable occupation for most wage earners. This meant that it was often a job ghetto for women who had no other employment options, particularly married and immigrant women. As Mabel Duncan noted in our 2001 interview, 'a lot of women went into housework because that was the only kind of work they could get if they were married.'[12]

The association between domestic service and immigrant women had a long history by the 1930s. Consistently since the early nineteenth century (and as early as the eighteenth century), the Canadian government worked to meet the demand for domestics by creating favourable conditions for immigration, including facilitating connections between workers, placement agencies, and steamship operators to draw young women from the British Isles, Scandinavia, and Western Europe to Canada.[13] Advertisements in Toronto's newspapers in the 1930s indicate the continued importance of this association, as well as age, to personal service occupations. Potential employers indicated a preference for certain ethnic groups that had a reputation for, or otherwise fit the image of, domestic service; they also used 'girl' to describe potential employees, indicating their desire for young and unmarried women and mobilizing hierarchies built on stereotypes of domestics as childlike.[14] Some of these ads used the following wording: 'Girl, Polish preferred, for Domestic Help'; 'Capable girl Russian or Polish preferred for general housework, no cooking, references, sleep out.' Similar ads appeared for German and Finnish women. Some advertisements emphasized religion: 'Domestic Help Wanted: Christian girl for general housework, with knowledge of cooking $5 weekly.'[15] Less well known is Claire Clarke's recollection that people from the United States living in Toronto requested black women for service as they were so closely associated with this occupation south of the border. Of course, desired applications and the available pool of employees were two different things, and whenever possible young women avoided domestic service, viewing it as a last resort.

Recollections of working conditions in domestic service make such reasoning clear. Diana MacFeeters's family had household help during the Depression. 'I remember,' she said, that 'my mother would interview them and they were live-in. Their magnificent pay was $25 a month,' but she quickly added, 'they got a uniform.'[16] When asked about the general feeling that conditions were poor for domestics, MacFeeters disagreed: 'You got all your food and lodging. You didn't have any other expenses ... unless you were sending money home to wherever you came from.' As historians have documented, many women were sending money home to family members, or supporting their own family who lived elsewhere in the city. That was true of Anne Hinsta, who worked at the Royal York and the Prince George hotels. In an interview conducted for labour historian Wayne Roberts in the 1980s, she described her position: 'I was a chamber maid and pay was small, but we used to get tips.' After her marriage in 1930 she stopped working, but when her husband lost his job in 1932 she headed out to find employment again. Her memory of that experience is noteworthy. 'They didn't have much work ... well they didn't have work at all ... we went on welfare ... city welfare, well I could not stand that. I started looking for a domestic job and I used to sit for days and days in the unemployment office. The ladies used to come and see you there if they want to pick you.'[17] Eventually, a woman from Forest Hill, a wealthy Toronto neighbourhood, hired both Hinsta and her husband, but not before she asked, '"Are you honest?"' As Hinsta remembered, 'That hurt my feelings and I said, "If there is anything we guarantee, it is that we are honest."' The couple were offered employment for $35 a month. Their two-year-old son Roy, however, was not welcome. With few employment options, they accepted the job and boarded their son for $25 a month elsewhere in the city.[18]

As a consequence of vacancies and a perceived shortage of acceptable workers, a tension emerged in the press between domestics who complained about working conditions and housewives who claimed that working-class women were shunning such jobs for a languid life on relief. In one editorial, signed 'ONE OF THOSE MOTHERS,' a self-identified homemaker in search of a domestic insisted that authorities compel working-class women to take on this job. Otherwise, 'how in the world can they succeed' in their role as household managers 'when so many homes are looking for help?' She claimed to be having a hard time finding a reliable girl despite the fact that she offered 'twenty-five dollars a month ... a good home, the best food, served at the same time the family [was] served, almost every night out, in addition to the regular full afternoon off each week and almost every Sunday afternoon [off].'[19] Economic disenfranchisement did not mean domestic servants accepted such perceptions of their work conditions without comment. They voiced their discontent in local newspapers. One critical domestic who wrote to the *Evening Telegram* compared her situation to slavery: 'The way domestics are treated in Toronto is shameful. My opinion is that free advertisements make it easier for people to exploit us. In most places there is work a plenty and skimmed milk, and the wage so small as to be not worth mentioning ... Cannot somebody act to cause an improvement? It's like buying and selling human beings.'[20] Another woman was so outraged by a cartoon published in the same newspaper depicting 'Mrs Toronto' as a kind employer willing to pay $20 for a maid but unable to find any willing takers that she wrote: 'I have answered every single advertisement for a housekeeper which appeared in the last nine months and the most I have been offered is 10 per month. The great majority offered me only a good home and perhaps a little pocket money. If I could get a pail of tar and some feathers I might be able to get along on this. How can anyone live decently on such wages?'[21]

Connie Lancaster has vivid memories of the difficulties of domestic service. After fleeing the conditions of the farm on which the Salvation Army had placed her in the 1920s as a young orphan from England, Lancaster found a domestic job. In our 2002 interview, she shared her story of those years with me: 'When I was eighteen my options were very limited, because of lack of education and I had no family to fall back on. I was homeless if I didn't make one, so I started as a domestic.'[22] But the dreadful work conditions meant she did not keep her first position for very long. 'It was a job; I had an awful time because I didn't know electricity when I came to the city ... I got $25 a month for keeping a fourteen-room house clean.' Although the literature on English immigrant women in Canada has said much about this sort of training, Lancaster received no help with the operation of household appliances. The first time she lit the stove she turned on the gas, went to find a match, and returned several minutes later. The subsequent explosion did not endear her to her employers. 'I lost my hair, my eyebrows, and the dust off the floor. I went up and the family said: "You could have blown us up!" But nobody told me.' She soon found a job at another home in the city.

Luckily for Lancaster, the Depression increased rather than decreased the demand for the household labour of certain groups of women, especially young, unmarried, white, and British-born ones. She found another job quickly. A *Chatelaine* journalist who covered this situation in a 1932 article marvelled that 'despite unemployment figures which have long passed the astonishing stage and almost leave one stupefied, superintendents of women's employment bureaus report that domestic service is the one class of job for which vacancies always outnumber suitable applicants.'[23] Indeed, as the cost of living decreased, more middle-class households could afford domestic help. Ron MacFeeters, a man from a middle-class Toronto family, remembers 'that a lot of small, really small, two- and three-bedroom houses ... had a funny little room off the kitchen called the maid's room. It would have a sink in it and room for a bed and I guess a chest of draws.'[24] Higher demand for domestics did not ease the job search of all women. The same *Chatelaine* writer noted that vacancies outnumbered 'suitable applicants.' Mrs Hinsta and other 'less suitable' women like her certainly remembered the lack of jobs. At the time, some domestics noted the exploitation of the situation with anger. 'Has it ever occurred to you, or anyone else,' she wrote, 'that a great number of Toronto's citizens (the average working class) who have not felt the inch of depression as others have, are taking a mean advantage of the present state of affairs?'[25] When they had the option, many women protested by refusing to take domestic jobs, irrespective of demand.

Not all people agreed with Toronto's housewives. Stories of poor wages, bad working conditions, and labour shortages did capture the attention of some people interested in reform. In 1932, Constance Templeton of *Chatelaine* magazine wrote an article which proposed that if the home 'were run on more businesslike lines, more women of the right type would be attracted to it.' Who was the right 'type' of woman? Well, Templeton noted, unlike in Europe, where wealthy houses required large staffs, most Canadian houses only required a 'cook general or houseworker.'[26] But these workers had to be trained, indeed certified, and given a regular routine much like a stenographer. That way, Canadian housewives would get trained women who knew what to expect at their workplace. Not surprisingly, these plans were never carried out, and domestic service remained a sector of the labour market in which married immigrant and non-Anglo women predominated and desirable bread-winning daughters were found in much lower numbers.[27]

In certain areas of the economy, such as office work, wages were more substantial and working conditions more favourable. As a consequence, young workers coveted these jobs. Clerical workers in the city's financial sector and in the offices of industry did not experience widespread slow-downs or job loss. Though it had been a male occupation until the early twentieth century, the feminization of clerical work, the expansion of the office, and the invention of the typewriter meant that more and more women were finding jobs in this area of the labour market by the 1930s.[28] Such shifts did not, however, eliminate gender divisions of labour within these spaces, which gave men access to higher-paying, more prestigious jobs. For instance, in 1931 men occupied more than twice as many accounting positions as women did, while 93 per cent of stenographers were women.[29] These differences were explained, in part, by the temporary nature of women's work. It was common practice, and in most offices obligatory, for women to leave work when they married. Matrimony meant the financial support of a husband and initiated greater household and family responsibilities from which wage earning would prove a distraction. Of those who worked in offices who were interviewed for this study 71 per cent left work when they married, while approximately 29 per cent did not marry or continued to work after they wed.[30] Mildred Johnston figured that it did not enter women's heads to work after marriage: 'I know women who had to work, but you see in those days we hadn't got to the place where women were tired of their homes.'[31] This explanation does not, of course, speak to those married women who did work for pay after marriage, but in general clerical occupations, unlike domestic service, were not open to women who were married.

Racial identities were an equally important determinant of access to office employment. Racist hiring practices and the implicit race designations for employment and employability are well captured by the stories shared by Claire Clarke and Violet Blackman. These Canadian women of West-Indian descent were single and between the ages of seventeen and forty during the Depression. They lived in a city that, unlike New York, had only a tiny black community that included three churches, Mr George's grocery store, mutual benefit and social organizations like the United Negro Improvement Association (UNIA), one medical doctor, and two lawyers.[32] Toronto's African-Canadian and West-Indian neighbourhoods were viable communities, but local businesses and workplaces could not provide women in the community with a range of jobs, or even a sufficient number of very low-paying ones. In this regard, white ethnic women had access to more jobs within their (larger) immigrant or ethnic communities than was the case for young women like Clarke and Blackman. As a result, they were compelled to search for jobs in mainstream white society where plenty of employers and businesses did not see them as viable workers.

Such views did not stop Claire Clarke from finishing her schooling, but after graduating, she could not find a job that required her skills in stenography and typing. 'I sent in applications, résumés and got one ... I got a very nice response from ACME and I was so happy they were very pleased with my résumé, and they invited me for an interview so I went for the interview but of course when they saw me.' In her effort to find work, Clarke also went to visit an influential and wealthy black professional, Mr Hubbard, and remembered being snubbed. With renewed anger, Clarke shared the incident with me: 'Well you might say he was a light coloured. He was married to a white so naturally he didn't have too much attachment to the black community. But he gave me an interview and he had just to tell me the white girls won't work with you. I got this from *him*!'[33] This recollection speaks to the tensions among blacks in a white-dominated world in which light-skinned black Canadians could lead considerably different lives by 'passing,' as Clarke called it. Though she was resentful about her own misfortunes, she never begrudged those who managed to get by as white. 'Why would I?' she said in a 2004 interview. 'Life was easier for them that way.'

Violet Blackman also had a clear sense of why she could not find employment in 1930s Toronto. Blackman, who had come to Toronto from Jamaica as a twenty-year-old in 1920, worked as a domestic during the Depression. When asked about employment options in the city, she responded with indignation and exasperation: 'You couldn't get office work and factory and hospital work and things like that! You couldn't because they would not give you the job ... because of the colour of your skin because you were black you couldn't. The only thing that you could get was a domestic.'[34] The irony of being able to find work in the intimate and private space of white people's homes but not in their businesses or classrooms, was not lost on these former working daughters; nor was the often subtle, insidious nature of racial discrimination in the Canadian context. Joseph Clarke recalled in a 1978 interview that racism 'got under your skin and you didn't know what the hell was irritating you,' except for when it came to employment.[35] 'It was the funniest thing,' Claire Clarke mused about blacks and whites in Depression-era Toronto. 'We mingled together, played together but we wouldn't work together at the time.'[36] Racism was not nearly as overt in Canada as in the United States. It was not spread across billboards in the city; it did not manifest itself in segregated fountains or washrooms or schools, but it had an equally powerful impact on opportunity and social acceptance. Clarke fit the profile of a dutiful working daughter. She also possessed important signifiers of middle-class status in Toronto: she had a secondary school education, her family owned their own home, and she and her sister took music lessons. However, the gender and class status that she shared with white women did not translate into the same employment opportunities for her. For Clarke, as well as for Blackman, race trumped education and marital status and other identities when she sought training and employment in Toronto's schools and workplaces.

When Mildred Johnston and Thelma Plunkett, single women of Scottish and English descent, landed office jobs in the city they were in their late teens. While Johnston chose not to marry and remained in an office throughout her working life, Thelma Plunkett left clerical work when she married. During our 2001 interview, Johnston, sitting tall and austere, her shoe heel rubbing methodically against her couch, remembered how she left school at eighteen to attend Shaw's business school to earn the requisite training in stenography and typing: 'I didn't go right through. I only went to the fourth form junior matriculation and then father asked me what I was going to do, and I said, "I guess I'll go and work in an office." So I went to Shaw's business college, and I got a good training there in business.' Job hierarchies within offices depended on skill and education. Secretaries who were expected to be stenographers and typists with a firm grasp of shorthand occupied the highest ranks, while clerks with filing responsibilities rounded out the bottom. The women themselves were well aware of these divisions. In discussing her employment as a secretary, Johnston, who is soft-spoken and of humble demeanour, confidently assured me: 'Though I don't consider myself a secretary, I was a darn good typist if I do say so myself.'[37]

Among the women in this study, the most popular school in Toronto for office training was Shaw's business school, which offered a range of courses and had locations all over the city. Advertisements appeared regularly in the city's newspapers, but only women who could afford school fees and books could take advantage of their offerings. Margaret McLean and others tell stories of education limited by the economic constraints of family responsibilities.[38] Malvern Collegiate was minutes from their home, but the Tapp family could not afford the cost of books. Phillips spoke movingly about her disappointment and envy: 'Well, I felt envious of the girls that went to Malvern and you'd see them the way they were dressed that bothered me. I hated going down that time of the morning and I had to pass all the girls all the kids going to Malvern ... I really *hated* it.'[39] The Tapp sisters went to Danforth Technical High School, which was located further away, but, as it turned out, they could not remain there either. In sharing this story with me, McLean began by saying, 'You speak of shame.' She continued: 'Ivy, my sister, and I we wanted to go to Danforth Tech, a high school. Ivy loved sewing. But, eventually mother said, "I can't buy your books so you will have to go and tell the principal that you are on relief." Well Ivy and I stood outside the principal's office and we couldn't go in. We just couldn't go in. And we went home and told mother and she said, "I'm sorry."'[40]

That young working-class women were acutely aware that family difficulties hurt their chances of earning the clerical training that would have given them access to better-paid jobs is evident not only by the stories that women shared with me but by their children, who grew up with their parents' Depression tales. Speaking of his mother Margaret and aunt Gladys, Ian Radforth understood well that these sisters had thought of extra education 'as something they couldn't afford to do.'[41] It was only after her marriage failed in the 1940s that Gladys eventually 'learned the superior skills' of shorthand and typing to become a secretary, but to do so she had to keep her clerking job while taking 'upgrading' courses at night and living cheaply in a rented room. During the Depression, the majority of young women and men did not finish high school, let alone complete a university degree or a business school diploma. In 1935, a help-wanted advertisement in the *Evening Telegram* requesting a 'stenographer and a dictaphone operator for [a] commercial office' stipulated that those without 'sufficient education' need not apply.[42] Access to a commercial education had an impact on job options, restricting access to employment in clerical occupations and to other jobs within the field.

At a time when jobs were scarce and employment still available in offices, it is interesting that far more young women than men enrolled in business schools for training in stenography, accounting, and typing. In fact, women occupied twice as many positions in business schools as men in 1930. In private business and commercial schools there were 3777 women and 1183 men enrolled in the city. In 1933, enrolment dropped substantially; however, women still occupied well over two-thirds of the positions: 1351 women and 540 men.[43] When asked about competing with men for jobs in offices or other places, Margaret McLean, who worked as a factory worker during the Depression, responded: 'Goodness no! Women were nothing until the war came!' Joyce Cahill, her sister, concurred: 'Yes, if a woman did it, then it was a job men wouldn't do.' Similarly, census analysts explained the greater than 10 per cent difference in female and male unemployment rates by pointing to 'the dissimilarity in the types of male and female employment.'[44]

The ironies of this disparity between male unemployment and female employment did not go unnoticed by Toronto's citizens. In the letter-to-the-editor section of Toronto's *Evening Telegram* a correspondent noted 'that if fifteen [were] waiting at a car stop to board the car, twelve [would] be well dressed girls, presumably office girls. Girls [were] in large numbers in offices. A large office looks more like a high-class school for stylish young ladies than a business office.'[45] The 'Goat,' the letter writer who had inspired this response, had written that he believed 'that many women, now employed in various vocations should not hold these positions in the face of so much unemployment,' but he was concerned that 'it might be a difficult matter to find a male sufficiently qualified to take the places.'[46] In Toronto's offices during the 1930s, men and women sat behind desks. They filed, typed, and tabulated. As these photographs of

Margaret Radforth with 'the girls' and office manager James Downie suggest, they also had some fun (figures 12, 13, 14). At times, their close proximity caused concern among those who feared that the presence of so many young working women signalled an end to male breadwinning, but men and women usually worked in different jobs. And notwithstanding tough economic times, men were unwilling to take or ineligible for many positions in the city's offices. Furthermore, these jobs were not open to all women in the 1930s. Young daughters who were single, had received an education, and were of British descent had the best chances of securing this employment.

After completing her schooling at Shaw's, Mildred Johnston hoped to find a job. 'For the first year I had a temporary [job] ... at the Faculty of Applied Science in the office there,' she recalled, 'but that only lasted till the end of June, the end of the university term proper.' After that, she noted with obvious disappointment, 'I tried to get a job and I couldn't get a job for love nor money.' Then came a call from Shaw's, who contacted her about a job. 'Because I was an Anglican you see they felt that I might apply for the job at the Anglican diocese on Jarvis.' As Johnston recalled her interview: '[The Bishop] wasn't in a good humour because the hospital in Iqaluit had just gone up in flames ... he scared me out of my wits. Anyway I came home and I said to my stepmother, I said, "Oh I do like the girl in the office, but goodness I don't know about the bishop; but they're going to phone me around 5:30 tonight" ... And the phone rang, "Could I come in in the morning?" Could I *come* in in the morning?! I was there before anybody,' remembered Johnston with incredulity.[47]

Landing a clerical position was an important economic and social achievement for young women in the context of the Depression. Clerical work, though hardly a ticket to prosperity, did give workers a degree of economic stability. In keeping with the minimum wage of $12.50 per week, Johnston's starting salary was $50 a month. This was significantly more than the wages of men who frequented relief lines or of women working as domestics or doing piecework. The latter earned as little as $3.80 per week.[48] Johnston shared with me an early story about the job that she would keep for forty-seven years: 'As soon as I got my first cheque, we were paid monthly, I ... paid board at home. Girls did in those days. I think I paid about $5 a week, and then as time went on and the salary increased, I increased it each time.' Johnston, like other dutiful daughters of her day, contributed a substantial portion of her wages to her family.

Clerical work might offer better conditions than domestic service or a job in a garment shop, but that did not mean all white-collar workers had good working conditions. Ruth Taylor, who clerked at Toronto General

12　The offices of Canadian General Insurance Company, Statistical Department, 13 May 1934. Photo courtesy of Ian Radforth

13   Office girls Lillian Walker, Jean McClelland, Margaret Radforth, and Beryl Bassingthwaite. Photo courtesy of Ian Radforth.

Insurance, was sometimes expected to work long hours, late into the night.[49] As chapter 4 explores in greater detail, this had disastrous consequences for Taylor. Thelma Plunkett also recalled poor working conditions in her first office job. Sitting on her sofa Plunkett vividly remembered her job at H. Brown Silk Company when she was nineteen: 'I worked there for five years and oh it was terrible the hours we had to put in ... I know one week I counted up and I had put in seventy-two hours!' She left her job as an invoice clerk, which paid $8 a week, on the advice of her doctor after toxic dye fumes made her faint.[50] She was not unemployed for long because she soon found a job at Aluminium Goods on York Street, in Toronto. Her story of the job interview effectively conveys

14   Office girls posing playfully with office manager Jack Downie. Photo courtesy of Ian Radforth.

the willingness of women to take advantage of opportunities to land better-paying positions:

> When I went in there was quite a group of people, and I thought, oh, I will never get the position ... but anyhow when I went in and was interviewed I told them the different machines that I could use and, but of course there weren't anything like computers then but there were comptometers ... and of course when he asked me I had to say that I didn't know how to use one ... so anyway at the end of the interview he said 'Would you go to comptometer school in the evening if we sent you and paid for it?' So I said 'oh yes'![51]

In a time of relative job scarcity, Thelma Plunkett transferred jobs, albeit unpleasant ones, with ease. Although she lacked the necessary comptometer skills, Plunkett acquired the job at Aluminium Goods and the company gave her money to attend a course in the evenings. It is interesting that her company was willing to pay for her to attend school in a time of hardship. This points to the fact that Plunkett was among the 'desirable workers' for these positions.[52] She accepted the job enthusiastically because, as she commented, 'I was lucky to have a job.' Indeed, Johnston and Plunkett were fortunate. Their access to education, their class, and their marital status made them suitable clerical workers. Still, as the experiences of women such as Claire Clarke clearly indicate, these identities did not ensure employment across the racial divide. Census analysts did note a significant number of second-generation Jewish and Italian women among clerical workers in the manufacturing industry in Toronto through the 1930s, which points to the fluidity of employment boundaries and the complicated identities which bestowed privilege in the form of employment access to the city's white single daughters.

Working in an industry that had long exploited its workers, female garment workers experienced greater vulnerability and insecurity than did clerical workers during the Depression. As H.H. Stevens's 1934 Royal Commission on Price Spreads highlights, the clothing industry, which employed 65 per cent of women in manufacturing in 1931, was an exploitative environment for wage earners.[53] Characterized by stiff economic competition and instability, workers dealt with chronically low wages, poor working conditions, and deskilling. In the dry, blunt words of the Royal Commission, 'the worker in the clothing industry can expect neither comfort nor security; in many cases he [sic] can indeed expect only hopeless poverty.'[54] Despite efforts to unionize garment workers during the interwar years, the position of a labourer in the needle trades remained precarious. Men maintained some control over the labour process because of their skilled positions as 'cutters and trimmers, machine operators, finishers and pressers.'[55] But, by the 1930s, women occupied very few skilled positions. Ready-made garments and piecework on sewing machines had replaced intricate hand sewing. In these low-paid positions, women were particularly vulnerable to mechanization and speed-ups.

Weak government regulations and the economic instability of the Depression exacerbated conditions. Several of the largest employers of women in Toronto increased hours and production requirements while simultaneously decreasing wages.[56] The Timothy Eaton Company's exploitative policies received considerable publicity because of the Royal Commission. In order to compensate for the economic decline of the 1930s, Eaton's decreased wages and increased production requirements so that, by 1933, a dressmaker who had earned $3.60 a dozen for her work on voile dresses in the late twenties now made only $1.75 for the same work. As Mrs Annie Wells testified, workers were being 'badgered, harassed,' and threatened with unemployment if they did not reach the expected production quota. By 1935, some women were earning as little as $6.00 to $7.00 a week despite the fact that $12.50 was the established minimum wage.[57]

Women workers faced specific barriers in their employment: vulnerable positions on the shop floor, male-centred unions, the masculinist culture of the labour movement, and the added burden of household responsibilities. Employment in the garment trade also had ethnic, religious, and class dimensions as it employed large numbers of immigrant women, particularly those who were Jewish. During the Depression, the Kensington Market area, situated on the border of Toronto's Spadina Avenue garment district, was the nucleus of this immigrant and working-class Jewish neighbourhood.[58] Here Yiddish was often the language of choice, and all became quiet as the sun set on Shabbat. Many women, married and single, helped support their families: mothers haggled in the marketplace to stretch limited budgets and daughters (and some married women) worked in the ready-made clothing industry.

Toronto's Jewish women workers included young women like Rose Edelist, who arrived on Baldwin Street in Kensington Market from Poland in the early twenties. During the Depression, she worked for several companies, each time changing jobs when conditions or wages worsened. She married in 1932 but continued to work until her daughter was born in 1935. The garment industry, along with jobs like domestic service, employed married women. When asked whether her marital status had forced her to abandon her job, Edelist stressed, instead, childcare responsibilities: 'Well, who was going to look after my child?' she asked in our 2002 interview.[59] Unable to afford childcare and without a large extended family, Edelist abandoned breadwinning until her husband opened a delicatessen on College Street. In this situation, Edelist's wage-earning options depended upon where she worked and the cost and responsibility of childcare. Her story also reminds us that many women worked in small family businesses that were more often seen as the husband's business. Nonetheless, Edelist's breadwinning experiences differed from those of single women who worked as teachers and nurses, as well as those of middle- and upper-class Jewish women who certainly faced discrimination in an Anglo-Protestant city. These latter women had greater economic security and could avoid the garment industry and find employment in other areas of Toronto's labour market.[60]

In the early 1930s, Edelist worked at the Walman Sportswear Company. She and her sister were the primary breadwinners in their family. At Walman, she joined a garment workers' union. As her story shows, she still has vivid memories of the strike that her union called in 1931:

The union wanted to have organized union shops. And then they called a strike and we had to leave. All my life I will never forget this strike. It was so terrible that the police protected the shops, and they treated the workers like garbage. It was so horrible. I tell you, I remember how they came so close by with the horses. The picketers they treated terrible. They protected the strike breakers. So you know even if you didn't believe in unions that made you believed in unions when you saw what was doing.[61]

When asked whether there was anyone who did not join the union, Edelist answered, 'the gentile girls didn't join because they were happy with their employment situation. They were in a shop that men worked so they made decent wages.'[62] Edelist insisted that she had no intention of being a scab. The shared ethnicity and class exploitation of many of Toronto's Jewish garment workers, and a shared history of social activism and of anti-Semitism, shaped their union involvement. Edelist's memories also suggest that while an activist heritage was certainly important, gentile women enjoyed access to jobs, which, in turn, gave them economic stability. They enjoyed the 'privilege' to reject unionization, if they wished, or move to other jobs rather than stay and fight.

By the 1930s, Toronto's Italian population, though not as large as it was after the Second World War, was the third-largest ethnic group in the city: they numbered roughly 13,000.[63] During the early twentieth century, an enclave of primarily sojourning men gradually became a settlement of Italian families: husbands, wives, children, and grandparents with a communal infrastructure replete with three parishes, grocery stores, and mutual aid societies.[64] Like Jewish women, Italian women frequently worked in the garment industry.[65] Mrs Bassi emigrated from Italy's north-eastern Friuli region to Toronto after the First World War. Many wage-earning Italian women took in piecework, but Mrs Bassi found a job in the garment district on Spadina, finishing men's suits.[66] There she encountered 'English women or Canadian women' who took advantage of her language difficulties by blaming any faulty workmanship on 'the immigrant.' To resist this treatment, Mrs Bassi drew upon the language skills of her husband and children. The story that her daughter, Evelina Bassi, shared with her interviewer confirms the impressive resourcefulness of immigrant women who had so little to work with:

She came home one night, and said 'I want you to tell me how to say a couple of words. That's not my job.' So she wrote it on a piece of paper, 'That's not my job.' So the next day when the jacket came back and she saw it wasn't hers she said, 'That's not my job!' She decided that she'd put, this was really clever, they had a punch clock, you know, and everybody had their own number, so she thought she is not going to fool me just because I can't speak. She thinks I'm stupid. So she put her number on every jacket.[67]

This memory of conflict underscores how language barriers and ethnic discrimination could shape Italian women's work experiences. Like many women in this industry, Mrs Bassi was married, suggesting that marital status was not always a determinant of employment, at least not if one was working in the 'right' job ghetto. Both Edelist's and Bassi's experiences also highlight some of the ways in which immigrant and ethnic working women of the Depression resisted and protested class exploitation and other forms of injustice, whether through unionization or smaller workplace protests.[68] More specifically, Mrs Bassi's story offers yet another challenge to the stereotypes of Italian women as reluctant wage earners and docile workers.

As Edelist's memories of union organizing suggest, Britishness also influenced employment options and job security in the garment industry. Nora Windeatt and Agnes Marks began their wage-earning careers as young single women in jobs similar to those of Edelist and Bassi, and they too earned meagre wages for long hours of work. In contrast, however, Windeatt and Marks did not remain in their positions on the shop floor. Both women became managers of their departments. Nora Windeatt immigrated to Toronto just before the Depression (figure 15). In May 1927, she arrived in Guelph, Ontario, from England. Having left her family behind, Windeatt had to support herself. With obvious pride, she explained how she did so. For a year, she worked in several positions including a house worker on a local farm and a food service employee in a hospital. As neither job appealed to her, and as she 'refused to clean other people's houses for a living,' she sought out different kinds of work.[69] Fairly soon she found a job at a hosiery company. Between 1929 and 1938, Nora Windeatt worked for Weldrest Hosiery in Mount Denis, a suburb of Toronto. Her first job at the company involved 'transferring the stamps onto the hosiery' for twenty-five cents an hour, not a task that Windeatt was particularly fond of doing. Fortunately, she added, 'it wasn't too long before I received a promotion.' She advanced from her position on the shop floor to a salaried position as head of fifty men and women in the finishing, mending, and boarding department.[70]

When Agnes Marks, a Canadian of English and Irish descent, began earning wages as a domestic, her family was on relief. At the age of sixteen, she abandoned personal service for a job sewing blinds at a curtain

15   Nora Windeatt shortly after her arrival in Canada in the early 1930s. Photo
courtesy of Nora Windeatt.

factory. It was 1935 and Marks was not happy with her wages or long hours, so when the International Ladies' Garment Workers' Union approached her to help unionize the factory, she was more than happy to help. They succeeded in unionizing her floor in 1936. Although justifiably proud of her accomplishment, Marks had no other union stories to share with me. Sitting in her Scarborough, Ontario, home, she told me, 'You see, I left the union shortly after they came. I was promoted to forelady and given $75 a month to oversee forty women.'[71]

Mabel Duncan was born in England and immigrated to Canada with her parents when she was four months old. Similar to Windeatt and Marks, she started work on the shop floor of a factory when she was in her early teens. Hayhoe Tea Company employed Duncan from 1921 to 1962. She never married. Recalling her first job in our 2001 interview, she laughed, perhaps a little self-consciously, and said, 'Well, I made boxes and packed jelly powders.' Not long after she started, the company mechanized their tea line. She explained: 'Well you know machines came in and they started to put ... tea in bags so when I left there, they had about four machines that they were using.'[72] Duncan left the shop floor because she was promoted. 'I got to the place where I was in charge of the female help.' By 1941 there were 17,993 women in the manufacturing sector, 340 of them forewomen.[73] Like Windeatt, Marks, and Duncan, forewomen made higher wages and had authority over men and women. Their experiences point to the possibility that, notwithstanding dominant patriarchal structures and sentiments, ambitious young white women of British descent could attain higher-status positions within manufacturing. They also indicate that ethnic and religious identities, along with language skills, worked concurrently to grant privileges to some women and exclusion for others in the garment industry.

Racial identity and social class also shaped access to white-collar work. During the Depression, as before it, women teachers entered a semi-professional world marked by a very clear gender hierarchy. Most women teachers worked at the elementary level, where they were paid less than their male colleagues who occupied the better-paying jobs in high school and administration. They received, on average, only 'two-thirds of the salaries offered to men' and were required to give up their positions at marriage or when their first child arrived.[74] When they left their classrooms, women teachers, much more so than men, could expect to have their behaviour scrutinized. While regular church attendance was a point in their favour, stepping out in the evening or taking a drink in public could result in harsh punishment, including dismissal.[75] Moreover, as this photograph

16   The staff of Oakwood Collegiate Institute, 1936. Photo courtesy of Alice Chrysler.

from Oakwood Collegiate shows us (figure 16), racial and class identities were also an important part of job access. The number of female teachers declined only slightly as a consequence of the Depression, from 2854 to 2811. Indeed, education offered rather stable and very privileged positions of employment, as only 0.03 per cent of working women in Toronto were teachers.[76] If women school teachers faced serious gender discrimination, unmarried white and British women, nevertheless, enjoyed privileges that did not extend to married women, black women, and even to most non-British immigrant or ethnic women.[77] In order to become teachers, they also had enjoyed access to Teacher's College or Normal School after high school. The individual experiences of Mary Chenhall and Dora Wattie, single, white Canadian women of English descent, provide the opportunity to explore this interesting convergence of gender discrimination with racial and class privilege.

Mary Chenhall, a sprightly ninety-year-old who still lived in her own apartment and drove her own car at the time of our interview, taught math at Markham District High School until she married in 1935. Sharing stories of her university education, Chenhall told the bitter tale of how she and other female classmates, arriving at their physics class at the University of Toronto one day, found the door locked and their profes-sor bellowing: 'Go away, you little Victoria angels! Go back to Vic and enrol in the Household Economics course! We don't want you in Math and Physics.'[78] It was with great pride that Chenhall recalled the success-ful completion of her degree. By the time she joined the teaching staff at Markham Collegiate in 1933, she had overcome a great deal of gender discrimination. Yet social class and Britishness also shaped her access to a relatively high-paying, stable teaching position. First of all, Chenhall had a university education. This was an advantage enjoyed by only four of the women interviewed for this study, which reflects the small percent-age of men and women enrolled in university during the Depression years.[79] In 1936, the *Annual Survey of Education* indicated that on average between 1920 and 1936 just 4 per cent of young men and 1.5 per cent of young women in Canada became university undergraduates.[80] University was not accessible to the majority of Canadians.[81] The Hall family could afford Chenhall's tuition and had the economic stability necessary to forgo her wages during her four-year degree program. They were never on relief. Mr Hall, who was employed in management at Bell Telephone, was never without work. 'It was a hard time, we were careful, but we al-ways had good food to eat,' Chenhall explained.[82]

Dora Wattie taught at Weston Collegiate throughout the 1930s, and her memories of those years certainly include examples of wage discrimination and cutbacks. These restrictions, which were largely a result of her gender, must, however, be balanced by a recognition of the advantages that she enjoyed. At one point noting that she had 'lost one hundred [dollars] when they cut the [teaching] salaries,' she said of women teachers like herself: 'We were just plain lucky, I had eighteen hundred dollars a year.'[83] In the midst of a severe depression, some fellow citizens were also keenly aware of teachers' privileges. Using the pseudonym 'Sock Em Board,' one writer to the *Telegram* complained that 'teachers have had no wage-cuts or staff reductions,' and added: 'Can't they be sports and take their medicine like the rest of us who have not had cuts but annihilation of wages to the tune of well on to 50 per cent, which may surprise them ... Teachers get an abundance of holidays and have only to ask for six months leave of absence for personal sickness and it is granted ... Their work is sure because there are always children to teach. So there is no depression in their class.'[84] Dora Wattie used her wages to help her father build a new house on Church Street in Weston (where she still lived at the time of our interview). Chuckling, she also related the following story: 'I had an extra hundred so I bought some stock in Palace Pier, lost every cent. I could have had units in the Maple Leaf Gardens, but I hadn't the second hundred!' In 1935, Wattie spent the summer travelling in Europe with friends: 'Can you imagine,' she exclaimed, 'it only cost three hundred and fifty dollars for two months!' Indeed, with a regular wage and the deflation of the Depression years, people like Wattie experienced a higher standard of living and, in some cases, upward class mobility. With a good salary they were able to consume much more at lower prices.[85] Dora Wattie's and Mary Chenhall's memories confirm that class and race privileges shaped women's employment options and economic stability. Both Chenhall and Wattie had families that supported their education. They were also single white women of British descent, as were most employed teachers working in an overwhelmingly Anglo-Protestant city.

When the women in this study made their way home at the end of their workdays, they brought wages that in most instances were essential to the well-being of their families. Understanding their role as a group of young wage-earning women in a city that was dealing with significant levels of male unemployment is important. On the one hand, their experiences and memories of them reveal a great deal about familiar themes in women's labour history, including female job ghettos, gender inequality in wages and salaries, and sex discrimination based on marital status. But the stories of the women who feature prominently in this study tell us more than that; they also reveal some of the ways in which racial identity, social class, and marital status created or sustained privilege and disadvantage.

In Toronto's labour market during the Depression domestic service continually occupied the lowest rung of the occupational ladder for women. It had the lowest pay and poorest working conditions and, despite a labour shortage, never appealed to the vast majority of Toronto's breadwinning daughters. It remained a job ghetto for women who had few other employment options. Clerical work on the other hand was a much more desirable occupation. It had greater social cachet and provided increased stability to women and their families. But, unlike in domestic service, fewer women had access to these jobs. Claire Clarke had all of the necessary qualifications: she was educated and single; her family owned their own home, an important class signifier, but she could not find a job. Certainly, Thelma Plunkett's gender ensured that she would not have the privilege of working in a high-status administrative job at Aluminium Goods Company, but it was more than luck that allowed her to transfer between clerical jobs with ease. Mildred Johnston found herself employed by the Anglican Church because Shaw's business school realized she had that religious affiliation. Both of these women also enjoyed a measure of economic stability that should not be discounted in our understanding of their wage-earning experiences. Rose Edelist and Mrs Bassi resisted their poor working conditions, challenging conceptions of ethnic women, Italian women in particular, as passive. Nora Windeatt, Agnes Marks, and Mabel Duncan, white women of British descent, entered the manufacturing industry on the shop floor, but within years they had higher-paying positions as managers of their departments. Dora Wattie and Mary Chenhall recognized and disliked the restrictions placed upon them because of their gender; but, in comparison with those for whom employment options were narrow, these women did not face the worst job prospects. Finally, and importantly, Claire Clarke and other West-Indian women attribute employment discrimination to the colour of their skin. Not only did these women not drive men out of work, at a time when rising numbers of men were unemployed: they held jobs that neither men, nor most Anglo-Celtic women in Toronto, considered palatable.

Chapter 4

Where Is a Woman Safe?
City Spaces, Workplaces,
and Households

When Marion Forsythe moved to the city to take an office job she knew that she needed to be careful about where and with whom she spent her time. The run-down areas of the city, any corners darkened by poverty or immigrants or nightfall, were to be avoided. It would also not be good to 'run around' with a crowd that was believed to indulge in the 'evil' delights of the city: alcohol, drugs, or prostitution. These proscriptions for danger were mobilized as cautionary tales for young Canadian women like Forsythe who, unlike the immoral young women cast as spectres of the city's 'girl problem,' were most deserving of protection from the dark and dangerous elements of urban space. Though the history of protection is as fraught with issues of conformity and coercion as that of regulation, women who were deemed good girls had a degree of latitude and freedom because of their respectability. They sometimes used this to their advantage. In other instances it put them in great danger, encouraging them to make presumptions about their safety, and hiding from view the places and situations in which they faced significant hazards. This chapter explores the meaning of dangerous and safe spaces for young working women in the 1930s; unlike most scholarship in the field, it uses women's memories of their experiences to highlight tension between perceptions and experiences of danger and safety. In the 1930s, as in other periods, some women were understood to be vulnerable, while others, it was said, brought trouble on themselves. Similarly, some spaces of the city were understood to be dangerous, while others were inherently and unquestionably safe. Young women's memories complicate our understanding of such conclusions.

Distinctions between good and bad girls were well worn by the 1930s. Judges, social workers, police, and others who reflected upon the relationship between danger and immorality for working girls in the Depression drew upon narratives of women as both victim and problem. As scholars Joan Sangster, Carolyn Strange, Judith Walkowitz, and others have shown, assessments of young women as good or bad girls were based on societal expectations about a young woman's behaviour that were rooted in subjectivities and normalized through legal, educational, and religious discourses.[1] Historians have faced significant methodological challenges trying to extricate women's experiences of danger and the consequences of good-and-bad-girl narratives for them from such sources. Nevertheless, as Franca Iacovetta and Wendy Mitchinson establish in their volume *On the Case*, the challenges of court records and police reports, social workers' assessments, and institutional documents should not discourage us from using them as sources for the voices of the disenfranchised, regulated, and victimized. We know a great deal more about women's experiences of danger in Upper Canada, or their regulation and protection through the courts as a consequence of such efforts.[2] This chapter builds on what these historians have done with case files, newspaper reports, and court records, but also integrates women's own memories of the danger they faced in Toronto in the 1930s. Good-and-bad-girl narratives did not play out equally for all women. Some good girls found themselves in horrible situations even though they were most respectable. Others faced great danger in their homes and workplaces even though such spaces were thought to be among the safest in the city.

Single, unemployed males who were congregating in city centres, riding the rods, and, as the situation in the relief camps in western Canada deteriorated, threatening Canadian society with their collectivization, have been the most consistent image associated with the breakdown of law and order during the Depression.[3] In Toronto, the police responded swiftly and sometimes violently to any protest or collective action on the part of the unemployed. For their part, young women threatened Canadian society by not conforming to notions of respectable womanhood and, by default, weakening the family. The rise of the eugenics movement and social-scientific explanations for behaviour kept some young female breadwinners in focus as a source of their own immorality in the thirties: in Toronto's courtrooms, a victim of rape could quickly become the cause of her own violation. She was poor, had been seen with men before, or was found in one of the city's disreputable neighbourhoods. In a 1935 issue of *Chatelaine*, Magistrate Margaret Patterson, the first woman magistrate in Toronto, wrote about this topic. Only a few girls were truly bad, Patterson noted, 'in the sense that they were lacking good qualities and were wicked, unprincipled, immoral, pernicious, unwholesome, corrupting and noxious.' Take Leta, for instance, 'a tall, dark, rather distinguished looking girl' who threw parties at her apartment with liquor and cigarettes. She faced Patterson for staging a hold-up.[4] There were also women, a good number according to Patterson, who 'for their own selfish ends deliberately encourage[d] the attentions of men whom they kn[e]w [were] married.'[5] But the majority were girls who 'drift[ed] in the avenue of least moral resistance and [had] no standards by which to measure their conduct.' These were the underprivileged, those young women who could be 'made good' again with the help of organizations such as the Salvation Army or institutions such as the Andrew Mercer Reformatory for females.[6] As Patterson's writing suggests, there was some discussion about the impact of hard times, broken homes, and poverty on young women's choices in the 1930s. Prostitutes or women who only wanted 'easy money' and 'craved silk stockings' did not become victims, but young women who otherwise might have claims to respectability were understood to suffer from dire economic need.[7] Florentine Lacasse, the protagonist in Gabriel Roy's classic *The Tin Flute*, or Hugh Garner's sympathetic rendering of Myrla Patson's descent from a bright young daughter to a sexually exploited domestic and waitress and finally to a prostitute in *Cabbagetown*, provide two poignant examples of this situation.[8] Relief levels troubled local women's organizations so much that they called an emergency meeting in October 1930 to discuss the situation of jobless women.[9] Existing schemes were insufficient, they asserted, to ensure that young women would not be tempted to find alternative, less appropriate means for fulfilling their needs. That same year, the Local Council of Women opened an unemployment bureau that placed women in available domestic jobs. They hoped this would provide young women with alternatives.[10] While raising money at a Women's Council of Action meeting in 1935, Miss Margaret Gould insisted that the YWCA wanted to help young women with basic needs. They were 'not asking for pocket money for the unemployed girl' but rather for an adequate sum to help provide 'toilet articles, clothing,' and other necessities.[11]

Irrespective of such efforts, protection and sympathy did not extend to all women. Indictment records from Ontario's Supreme Court reveal that women had to establish their morality before they would be recognized as true victims. Before pressing charges, a woman had to ask whether she would be cast as a bad girl. Would the reputation of her family suffer? After being raped, Grace Nelson had her home life scrutinized. She was residing in a rooming house with a girlfriend. 'Why wasn't she living at home with her family?' the defence lawyer asked. Nelson replied that she had left because 'there was a quarrel at home.'[12] Nelson was worried her parents might find out. 'Gee, you are not going to tell them this, are you? We got to keep this from them because mother is such nervous like ... It will only break up the home.' Pushing his assessment of her respectability further, the defence lawyer asked her how many times she had cried out, had she 'ever had connections with a man before? Did [she] suffer pain at the time' of the rape? Nelson had contracted gonorrhoea, which her doctor testified had not been present before the attack, but the defence lawyer was relentless when trying to tarnish her respectability.[13] To be sure, if the court protected women, it very rarely supported 'their sexual autonomy and complete freedom from all violence.'[14]

The formal and informal policing of women such as Nelson relied on similar notions of female morality. Vagrancy laws, instituted through the Criminal Code in 1892, were designed to regulate women's morality by controlling their presence in public. These laws made it illegal for a woman to be a 'common prostitute or night walker' or to be 'found in a public place and [unable], when required, [to] give a good account of herself.' The highest point for vagrancy charges in Toronto between 1920 and 1960 was 1931.[15] The Female Refugees Act (FRA) regulated women in a similar way, though its use could be even more far-reaching. Velma Demerson's story casts light on the punitive effects the FRA had on the lives of young working women. When Demerson landed in a Toronto courtroom, she had not been found in a bawdy house, nor was she walking the city's streets unable to give a good account of herself. Rather, she was sitting at her boyfriend's kitchen table eating breakfast. She was nevertheless charged under the FRA because her boyfriend was Harry Yip, a Chinese waiter working in downtown Toronto, and she was pregnant with his child. Demerson recalls her confusion and disbelief in her 2004 memoir, *Incorrigible*: 'I walk back and forth in this barred cell in shock. How could it be that a judge, knowing I'm pregnant, would refuse to allow me to marry the father of my child?'[16] Demerson was the classic 'bad' girl in need of reform. The FRA gave the courts leeway to charge women for behaviour that contravened accepted moral codes. Though the Act 'never mentioned race, its actual workings punished white women involved with men of colour.'[17] Demerson and Yip rarely spent time together outside of Yip's apartment unless it was late at night because of that fact.[18] By establishing a relationship with a Chinese man, Demerson was 'embark[ing] on a culturally unpopular course.' She knew that dating him was 'socially unacceptable.' She realized that there might be 'disapproving looks from passersby' but she did not care.[19] Couples like Yip and Demerson were also vilified in the city's newspapers. One 1935 headline read 'Yellow Kisses' and described the relationship between a white woman and Chinese man as a 'tragic example of the subtle lure and power of exotic passion.'[20] In another piece, reporters claimed that Toronto's police had rescued 'white girls for sale in ... one of the lowest and most vicious houses of degeneration.' Kipling may have argued 'east is east and west is west and never the twain shall meet,' but he was wrong, according to the article.[21] As Demerson explained it, she, like Yip, was a social misfit: 'He [was] an outcast by virtue of his race. But I [was] also the object of discrimination. Because of my mother's divorce I [was], like her, excluded from the world of stable, conforming families.'[22] Her mother read tea leaves and ran a boarding house on Church Street in Toronto. Her father lived in Nova Scotia with his new family and, Demerson concluded, did not love her. In fact, it was Demerson's father, who had 'social standing to protect,' who had reported her to police.[23]

Parents and people living in a young woman's community also monitored their respectability and behaviour.[24] Erma Frank's father controlled his daughter closely. Once when Frank came home late from a date on Toronto's waterfront, her father locked her out of the house. 'I heard the window go up and my father's voice. "Erma is that you?" Yes, papa,' Frank answered. '"Well you're not coming in here now!"'[25] Frank walked to the corner store and called her sister. As punishment for her late arrival, Frank was not permitted to return home and spent the night at her sister's house. This was until her date (apparently the voice of authority in this case) arrived the next day to explain that they had taken a moonlight cruise on the lake and that he had not put a hand on Erma.

For her part, Nell Moran found her behaviour scrutinized by a woman in her community. When Moran finished high school in the early 1930s a neighbour instructed her mother to send her to work. The 'young people in the neighbourhood ... we were running together, not *running* but just we played games.' But then 'the lady across the road, I told you, she decided that it was time that I got a job because I was always with a gang of boys.'[26] Not long after, Moran started to work full time.

If parents or neighbours did not successfully regulate the behaviour of young daughters, then Toronto's institutions would do that for them. As historians Carolyn Strange and Joan Sangster have shown, however, the protection of women 'has a troubled history' as it 'often slid into coercive surveillance, even stigmatizing incarceration.'[27] Certain organizations designed to 'protect' and 'rehabilitate' women were hardly better than jails. For her behaviour, Demerson was sent for one year to the Belmont House, a home for 'wayward women,' but shortly thereafter was transferred to the Andrew Mercer Reformatory for females. The Mercer was a 'house of correction' where women were expected to suffer for their sins. Demerson was locked in a small 'windowless enclosure' for twelve hours each day, given unpalatable food, and expected to toil for measly wages.[28] Organizations such as the Salvation Army were also involved in such efforts. While Connie Lancaster recalled that the Salvation Army 'looked after wayward mothers,' Sangster notes that the Army's 'efforts were suffused with moralism' and emphasized discipline and the expectation that a woman would find her way through connecting with Jesus Christ, which some women rejected.[29] In fact, young Grace Fife was reduced to tears when Magistrate Patterson sentenced her to two years with the Salvation Army. Fife was reported to have wailed that she would rather to be sent to jail, showing 'fear and hatred of the military saints.' One court reporter reflected that such outbursts were common in this particular court.[30]

City space was perceived as one of the greatest threats to young women, physically and morally; however, as the reactions of courts, parents, and organizations such as the Salvation Army suggest, a woman's right to protection rested far more on her ability to establish her own respectability than on her victimization or breach of established laws. Most women in this study did not discuss the type of experiences related by Demerson because they fit expectations for respectable working girls, but their memories reveal that even good women were in danger in the city.

Ruth Taylor's photograph first appeared in Toronto's newspapers on 6 November 1935. In one impression, the twenty-year-old office worker was shown leaning casually against a bridge railing, her fashionable belted dress loose and airy, seemingly perfect for a warm summer day.[31] Marion Forsythe recalled these images, which were spread across Toronto's newspapers to tell the tragic story of Taylor's murder: 'She was a nice-looking girl by her pictures. She had lovely dark hair.'[32] Friends and neighbours described Taylor in glowing terms: She was not a 'mixer' in any sense of the word. She attended church regularly. She was a 'good girl' and dutiful daughter who found herself in a horrible situation after working late at Toronto General Trusts, an insurance company in the downtown core. Taylor had been required to work into the evening one hectic day in November 1935, but, according to a work mate, she did not dilly-dally when she finished at ten o'clock. She headed directly for the eastbound streetcar that would take her home. The trip normally took a little over an hour, but the hockey game had just finished at Maple Leaf Gardens and Taylor boarded an eastbound 'hockey special' instead of her usual streetcar. This rerouted the car for fans to parking barns north and west of Taylor's home. Police surmised that Taylor alighted about two kilometres from her usual stop and decided to walk instead of waiting for the connecting car.[33] Only moments later, Taylor crossed paths with Harry O'Donnell, who struck her with a blunt object and dragged her into the nearby Gainsborough ravine where he raped and murdered her. 'Evidently he just mutilated her body. I hesitate to say,' explained Forsythe shaking her head, disbelief still evident on her face seventy years later.[34]

A murder like Ruth Taylor's reflected all too well the fear that dangerous, sexually insatiable predators lurked in the darkened corners of public space for young women.[35] 'It is a known fact that these immoral maniacs are constantly scouring parks and ravines for innocent prey,' the *Evening Telegram* reported in 1935.[36] 'Repeatedly,' noted *Hush*, a Toronto tabloid, 'there are vicious and revolting crimes perpetrated by sinister night time prowlers' against innocent children and young women.[37] As a young girl travelling downtown to school from her east-end home, Audrey MacMillan recalled her teacher warning her about strange men. 'Something was happening on the streetcars. Somebody was trying to stick needles in young girls. I remember [my teacher] saying people wanted young girls for immoral purposes, which chased us all to the dictionaries. Something we just knew, stay away from everybody on the streetcars and the street. Don't stand near a man.'[38] MacMillan's father told her that predators on streetcars 'used these girls for the white slave traffic.' But, as Macmillan recalled, learning this, 'she felt no more enlightened' about the hazards of the city. In a 1936 series of articles in *Hush*, 'Nancy,' a 'reformed harlot,' shared that her 'downfall definitely date[d]' from the day she left Women's Police Court after being convicted for drunkenness. Outside the court she had met a 'smart laddie in [a] grey felt hat' who offered a drink and friendship. Soon Nancy realized that 'Tom was nothing more than one of a select band of procurers in the white-slave traffic, a man who earned his despicable living making contacts with likely girls in the cities of Southern Ontario.'[39]

Fear of the white slave trade, though considerably dampened from the heated discussions of earlier decades, and the stranger lurking in dark corners provide examples of the dangers thought to lurk in Toronto for women. After Taylor's murder, Evelyn Smith refused to walk near the Gainsborough ravine. 'It's true,' explained Joyce Cahill, 'for a long time after that you just didn't go out alone and I remember being on the streetcar going past that place and always thinking ... of Ruth Taylor. Even to this day, I think of her in that ravine.'[40] When asked about how the murder made her feel, Mabel Duncan recalled, 'Well you were nervous being out at night.'[41] In response to such concerns, Toronto's ravines received a great deal of attention in the mid-thirties for their contribution to criminal activity. Just after Taylor's murder, Chief Constable Dennis Draper ordered a special report on 'perils near the Rosedale ravine' after complaints that they were poorly patrolled.[42] William Cattrell, who lived in Taylor's neighbourhood, presented a petition with 115 signatures to the Ratepayers' Association, which demanded 'the immediate filling in of the [Gainsborough] ravine, proper lighting and adequate police protection.'[43] In particular, the police needed to patrol ravines and parks more systematically between sunset and midnight 'to protect women and children.'[44] The Toronto Transit Commission (TTC) also came under fire. The petition demanded that streetcars not proceeding to typical terminals wait for those behind, particularly in stormy weather. Toronto's Board of Control asserted that the streetcar was a 'contributory factor' in Taylor's death as it 'compel[ed] passengers to vacate a car within a mile of its proper terminal at a late hour.'[45] Mrs M. Stevens also led a movement at the Board of Control meeting 'to request the city to erect a fence along the ravine, install street lights' and to urge the TTC to move its stopping place. 'That unprotected ravine,' Stevens claimed, 'is a menace to the womenfolk of our district and I am sure that if the city realized the fear in all our hearts, it would erect a wooden fence without delay, before someone else is made a victim.'[46] Toronto's Central Council of Ratepayers sought a new by-law that would compel 'owners, trustees or other responsible agents to keep clear from overgrowth, weeds, shrubs, bushes, and trees and also of shacks or unnecessary buildings, all vacant lots or area ravines' and to ensure that these areas were sufficiently lit.[47] Through such efforts citizens hoped that women, particularly respectable women such as Taylor, would be safer.

These actions did generate discussion about the harassment of women in public space. In 1935, several women came forward to share stories of incidents on Toronto's streets. The *Evening Telegram* reported that a young girl had been 'molested by a vulture only a few days before' Taylor's murder.[48] In response, women in the neighbourhood had formed a vigilante committee to find him, but they had no success. In another case, a villain named the 'Night Terror' had been lurking along Bloor Street in Toronto's upscale shopping district, 'call[ing] to women with strange, siren-like cries,' and when he captured their attention, he made lewd and inappropriate suggestions.[49] One reporter wondered why women did not report these crimes when they happened. After all, 'if Toronto women generally were in the habit of notifying police when chased or improperly approached by men, the tragic death of Miss Ruth Taylor might have been avoided.'[50] Women interviewed by the paper 'claim[ed that] reporting to police was futile and embarrassing.' One girl suggested that 'most girls just take that sort of thing as a problem of the modern world. You expected to have to watch for the odd man of the objectionable sort.' A young business woman reported that she had had 'half a dozen such experiences of men following [her], or passing lewd and suggestive remarks.' One man had grabbed her arm but she told him she would scream and he turned and ran. 'I didn't report it to the police,' she said. 'I suppose I should have done so.' Another business girl claimed she had been bothered three times by men as she went home late at night. She did not report these incidents to police. She claimed she did not want to worry her mother. 'I knew I couldn't avoid being out alone late. I sometimes have to work at night, just as Miss Taylor did, so what was the use?'[51] Placing the responsibility for such crimes on the shoulders of young women who did not report harassment did little to draw attention to or challenge the perils young working women faced. It also highlights the degree to which women felt that such events might reflect badly on their own respectability.

Ruth Taylor's murder had a profound impact on young working women because Taylor was a consummate 'good' girl. Taylor was a Protestant woman of British descent, a dutiful daughter, and sexually chaste. As Carolyn Strange and Tina Loo point out in their analysis of the true-crime version of the case, Taylor also had 'an iron-clad excuse for being out late.'[52] She was earning money to help support her family. She was a good employee. According to her department manager, 'Miss Taylor was a nice, quiet type of girl, who did her work efficiently.'[53] Moreover, she had worked overtime. Few women would have refused such a request in the thirties for fear of losing their jobs. Taylor's morality was also steadfast. Her family insisted that no matter how stormy the night might have been, Taylor would never have accepted a ride from a stranger. Olive Pickering, who attended young people's meetings at Hope United Church with Taylor, noted that she was 'gentle and lovable.' As for having a steady boyfriend, Miss Pickering said, 'Ruth just wasn't that kind.' In fact, Taylor was known to be shy around men and had no close male friends. The *Toronto Daily Star* interviewed a neighbour who, having seen Taylor with a young man two weeks before her murder, commented: 'It was the first time I had ever seen Ruth with a young man.'[54] At her funeral, Reverend Manuel said, 'We remember today ... a good girl, a girl well-known to our church.' Ruth 'was not a mixer in the modern sense of the word ... She was a girl of whose morality we are sure. Her character was unimpeachable. If ever there was an unprovoked attack on maidenly virtue, this was one.'[55] Her father's tribute to her was that 'she never knew sin.'[56] In characterizing Taylor in this way, police, the minister, her father, and the media affirmed Taylor's innocence, her right to vindication. And, unlike the murders of 'unrespectable or marginalized women,' the Taylor murder endured in working women's recollections as a cautionary tale.[57]

Apart from such tragic events, women recalled the city as a very safe place in the 1930s. As Jean Jackson explained it, 'Really no, I don't [remember crime]. I mean there wasn't anything happening like there is now. Not even in a very small way ... That is what is so different about the world today.'[58] Elizabeth Gammon had much the same recollection: 'Toronto was a very safe city really ... very middle class.'[59] As for murder, 'it was a major disaster when something like that happened. We were "Toronto the Good" in those days,' said Mildred Johnston.[60] The city's homes and the families they housed were at the heart of this 'good' city, but women's memories and the historical record reveal that they could be very perilous spaces for women in the 1930s, particularly as economic pressures heightened gender and generational tensions in families.[61]

The women in this study rarely discussed family violence explicitly. Nevertheless, as chapter 2 reveals, their memories do indicate, if in a guarded way, how family dysfunction shaped their lives. When women's recollections are joined with statistics from Toronto's Family Court and police records, the abuses and violence of the family home and the silences that underlay its acclamation as a safe place become more evident. Court records make it clear that domestic violence increased during the Depression. Wife assault, infidelity, drunkenness, and non-support preoccupied judges, social workers, and lawyers in these years. Between 1929 and 1939, reported occurrences of wife assault rose by nearly 50 per cent in Toronto, with the most precipitous increase occurring between 1934 and the end of the decade.[62] Toronto's homes were violent places, far more dangerous, in fact, than the city's public spaces. Unemployment, which challenged normative family relationships and also affected male self-worth, was recognized as central to this upswing in assault. In 1935, *Hush* reported that the legal system could no longer deal with the 'family fisticuffs and fireside squabbles among the happy homes of Montreal.' Problems had 'been swelling to the proportions of an epidemic and during the Depression, [had] been marked by a wave of wife beating, desertion, ill treatment of children and non-support,' stated one report published in *Hush*.[63] Such exposés fit uneasily with the prevailing familialism of these years. An article written by Judge J.F. McKinley in the same paper claimed to lift the 'veil [off of] unhappy domestic relations.' The judge argued that 'the backbone of any nation is the home,' and if the home was not stable it would cause children to lose 'respect for their parents and everything that is sacred in the home.'[64] Legal arbiters were not alone in this assumption; historical actors also embraced the idea that an 'intact family' and a 'forgiving wife' were the best for them and their children.[65]

As a consequence of such presumptions, women endured incredible violence in their homes at the hands of men they knew, but these stories never received the coverage Ruth Taylor's murder received.[66] In total eleven women were murdered in Toronto from 1929 to 1939: brothers, husbands, or boyfriends committed 90 per cent of these murders.[67] On 9 April 1930 at 9:30 in the morning, Walter Eley killed Ada La Brash while she lay in her bed. La Brash was 'shot through the back with a twelve-gauge double-barrelled shot-gun.'[68] Eley then sat on the floor and, using a fishing rod to press the trigger, killed himself. His motive: La Brash had threatened to leave him. In the same year, Helen McIntosh was shot and killed by her husband, who then turned the gun on himself. In 1933, Alfred Ellis, who 'had been quite downhearted owing to being out of employment ... fired a shot at his sweetheart Miss Muriel Jones.' He then shot himself through the head. Luckily, the bullet only grazed Miss Jones and, amazingly, Ellis survived as well. In 1931, Georgina Luxton, age thirty-five, died from three stab wounds in her back delivered by Walter Collins, a jilted lover who, police reported, could not handle that 'she had left him and gone to live with a Chinaman.'[69]

Many of these dangerous situations did not end up in the courts, young women and sometimes their parents being left to deal with the consequences. One evening, Margaret McLean decided she would accept a ride home from the son of a family friend. 'I knew he was sweet on me. Nobody much paid attention to him,' recalled McLean in 2001. 'I figured there would be no harm in getting a ride home.' As it turned out,

Jim had other intentions. Instead of driving her home, he veered off into a park, where he stopped the car and made his intentions clear. 'I screamed and fought and screamed. I got away and a nice couple offered to drive me home.' When McLean arrived home, she told her mother about her perilous experience. 'Mother took her umbrella and Nell (her older sister) along and went to Jim's home.' Mrs Tapp confronted Jim and his mother. 'She beat him over the head and told him if he ever touched one of her daughters again she would do far more damage.'[70] In this case, McLean's mother sought to punish the perpetrator and vindicate her daughter.

Though men most commonly perpetrated domestic abuse, women too could resort to violence against their supposed loved ones. In one case, James Donald was fatally stabbed with a bread knife in the hands of his wife, Mrs Elsie Brant. 'The couple had been drinking, and [Brant] claimed she struggled with her husband when he attacked her for being too talkative.'[71] The *Evening Telegram* reported that Brant 'acted very sullen,' and when 'told her husband was dead she didn't even cry.'[72] Brant claimed self-defence and the jury found her 'not guilty.' In another case, Alfred Haggett met his demise when his wife Violet stabbed him with a twelve-inch butcher knife. According to police, they had consumed a great deal of wine and Violet was enraged by her husband's role in the arrest of another man for theft. The jury found Haggett guilty and sentenced her to twenty years in prison for this crime. This was a very lengthy sentence for a woman; no other female perpetrator received such a lengthy sentence at the Supreme Court of Ontario during the 1930s. Indeed, the majority of women were found not guilty, like Elizabeth Lloyd, who allegedly shot and attempted to murder her husband Harold Lloyd.[73] Or they were given much shorter sentences, as in the case of Olga Bura, a resident of Montreal who travelled to Toronto in 1939 to confront her husband for desertion. She found him in the company of his niece Mary Watizka and attempted to murder them both. Bura was sentenced to fifteen months in the Mercer.[74]

While daughters most certainly witnessed domestic abuse, they were also its victims. In 1934, Mrs Bessie Derlick was charged with training her sixteen- and thirteen-year-old daughters to shoplift. This 'unnatural mother,' *Hush* reported, '[was] adept at the art of shoplifting, the specialty of the woman criminal' and 'weekly drew her toll from Toronto stores.'[75] Another one of the city's young women accused her mother of prostituting her to strange men. Apparently, Mrs Eileen Durvay, 'a drinker,' regularly had men over for parties and then would demand that her daughter strip for them.[76] According to *Hush,* Durvay also beat her daughter when she did not bring home enough money. As these stories suggest, the home could be a troubling place for working daughters. Domestic abuse was common in the thirties. These events did not, however, frighten most women away from heterosexual romance or marriage in the way that the Taylor murder made them afraid to walk alone at night.

In the 1930s, the workplace was no longer scrutinized as closely as it had been in previous decades as a site of moral and physical danger for women. In the late nineteenth century industrial surveys had stressed the sexual dangers of factories for women. For instance, the 1889 Royal Commission on the Relations of Labour and Capital focused a great deal on women's 'vulnerability to exploitation' in workplaces.[77] Analysts concluded that industrial establishments oppressed women and that steps must be taken to ensure that low wages, night work, and other characteristics of wage earning did not compromise female morality. By the Depression, the feminization of certain forms of employment and the economic importance of the female wage earner had dulled such concerns. As Frederick Lewis Allen said in his 1931 retrospective of the 1920s, 'as for the unmarried woman, she no longer ha[s] to explain why she work[s] in a shop or an office; it [is] idleness, nowadays, that ha[s] to be defended.'[78] If waged work had offered women 'a source of independent income' that freed them from dependence on their fathers, it also gave them the opportunity to provide their families with much-needed income. Having a job symbolized a working girl's diligence rather than a 'necessary evil of economic progress.'[79]

Despite such shifts, sometimes the workplace was a source of danger and harassment, particularly in a decade when many women could ill afford to lose their jobs. The Ruth Taylor murder shed some light on women's work conditions. On 9 November 1935, Eulalie Wilson's editorial appeared in the *Toronto Daily Star.* She wondered 'why so much night work in offices should be necessary when there [were] literally tens of thousands of people out of work?' Indeed, 'even a humble stenographer must wonder at a system which seems to require that office girls work until, say, close to midnight,' wrote Wilson.[80] Concerns were voiced at community meetings. The Central Ontario Women's Institute passed a resolution during their November 1935 meeting, which requested that the minister of welfare 'compel such places of business to supply their girl employees with their evening meal and a taxicab to their place of residence.'[81] Toronto's Central Council of Ratepayers 'sharply criticiz[ed]' the company for which Taylor worked. Why did Taylor have 'to work until such a late hour at night when there are so many Toronto girls unemployed, and why, having worked so late ... was [she] not sent home in a taxi where she would have been safe?'[82] Nevertheless, former working girls and men who remembered the crime seventy years later did not think Taylor's employer was at fault. Mabel Duncan said that 'nowadays there would be a big fuss about that but back in those days I don't think they would do anything about it. Nowadays I think they would send them home in a taxi if they kept them that long.'[83] Mr McClintock agreed and instead held Taylor partially responsible for her misfortunes. 'No they couldn't blame the company. She should have waited for the next streetcar. In those days that was not a thing that happened very often.' When I noted that the absence of criticism was quite interesting, McClintock raised his voice: 'Why would you consider the company to blame! The woman should have waited for the streetcar!'[84]

Hush magazine, noted for its exposés on employers who took advantage of young working girls, was not as quick to exonerate employers. They reported in July 1935: 'Terrible pitfalls and snares beset the path of the young girl who goes out into the world to earn her own living amid the fierce competition of a city like Toronto. She will find no lack of offers of employment from men who make it clear they like to be rewarded with services of an intimate nature.'[85] The economic conditions of the decade forced a good number of women into 'undignified employment,' the article continued. For instance, waitresses and stenographers find themselves hired only for their good looks. 'Employment managers soon get to know which of their clients are on the lookout for pretty girls ... Toronto and Montreal are literally filled with bosses young and old who make love to their stenographers.'[86] *Jack Canuck,* another populist weekly paper, echoed this concern. Alfred Dove, a forty-year-old mill manager, had a 'habit of focusing his attentions upon good looking mill girls under threat of firing them.' In one particular incident, Mrs Addison, a widow, declined 'to submit to lovemaking' and 'refused to be fired from her job.'[87] Instead, she managed to gather enough evidence from Dove's previous philandering to have him fired. In the restaurant where she worked behind the soda fountain, sixteen-year-old Velma Demerson finally gave into the persistent demands of a much older customer who wanted to take her out. During their date, he drove to a remote place and raped her, but she never told her family or the police.[88] Demerson's memories suggest that she well knew that reporting her situation to her parents or the police would not vindicate her but indeed would cast aspersions on her respectability.

Domestic workers toiled in particularly vulnerable positions. Unlike office or factory girls, who had co-workers they could sometimes turn to for support, domestic servants generally worked alone. In Toronto's homes, private spaces provided ample opportunity for sexual exploitation, but little attention was given to this fact in newspapers. In one case, a 'pretty housemaid' found herself the victim of 'naughty playboys,' who, upon hearing her employers were out of town, forced their way into the house. She managed to get away after putting up a good fight and yelling 'I'm not that kind of girl!'[89] Respectable working girls knew that they had to protect their sexual chastity at all costs. Domestics sometimes had to deal with the sexual advances of their male employers. If they lived in, they were particularly vulnerable because they had little avenue for escape. As mentioned previously, domestics themselves believed the way they were 'treated in Toronto' was 'shameful' and exploitative.[90] The economic conditions of the Depression gave people pause to wonder why there was a continual labour shortage in domestic service. This fact may have been less confusing had they considered issues of sexual harassment and abuse.

Women's recollections indicate that factory girls also experienced harassment. Joyce Cahill and Marg McLean talked about being a woman in Toronto during the Depression and about workplace harassment. 'Men were it!' noted McLean. 'When I was a young woman looking for work and that, you didn't [complain]; if you did, you lost your job. I walked out on one because I wouldn't let him molest me. Women had to be on her guard.' Her sister Joyce piped in 'Oh yeah!' 'We were brought up by a mother that said: "You say *no*!" We wouldn't but there were so many that probably did and that is the pity of [it]. They had nobody to protect them, either you did it or you didn't and you were out.' McLean's boss at Carleton Cards was fond of taking young women back to his office. When she was asked, McLean refused. 'I ran around the desk and he could not catch me so he gave up.' Later when someone finally spoke up, her boss had the audacity to ask McLean publicly if she thought he was capable of such behaviour. 'I yelled,' she recalled, 'I yelled! "You are, you are a dirty old man!" And then I quit. I went home and had to tell mother that I had left my job and she said: "I done right."'[91] While Toronto's editorial sections and tabloids occasionally raised concerns about women's safety at work prior to the thirties, the courts and police were surprisingly silent about such issues, focusing more closely on the stability of Toronto's homes and the economic conditions of the Depression. In fact, many women were vulnerable at work. With few avenues to successfully fend off economic insecurity and unwanted advances, deciding whether or not to comply with their boss's wishes was a difficult choice. Places thought to be safe for women in 1930s Toronto could be particularly dangerous. The silence about these situations indicates the powerful reverence of the home and respectable womanhood in women's memories and the public historical record. As elderly women who conceived of themselves and their families as respectable, they were unlikely to construe themselves as those 'sort[s] of girls.'[92]

The Depression did not bring exceptional changes to perceptions of the danger and safety of urban centres for single women. If the home and workplace were generally safe spaces, then the public areas of the city were not. The economic conditions of the decade and the effect they were having on Toronto's homes strengthened the veneration of 'normal' homes as sources of stability and 'broken' homes as promulgators of dysfunction and immorality. In an effort to protect 'good' women and reform 'bad' ones, the police, the courts, and organizations such as the YWCA all sought to bolster the family during the Depression. Such ideas about safety and danger made the murder of one working girl a particularly powerful cautionary tale, which, when analysed in connection with the experiences of single women, reveal the extent to which policing and protection in city space depended far more on a woman's respectability than on her victimization.

Fears about city space and conceptions of female morality cast a large shadow over other areas of Toronto where women faced danger. The conditions of the 1930s exacerbated family conflict by challenging male identities, encouraging desertion and wife assault. Moreover, breadwinning daughters whose earnings were so critical to their families were also vulnerable in workplaces where bosses knew many would comply with sexual requests in order to keep their jobs. In fact, women were not invulnerable to violence and harassment anywhere in Toronto. However, many of them successfully navigated the lines between respectability and danger as they sought to protect themselves in the city's homes, workplaces, courtrooms, and on its darkened streets. Moreover, as chapter 5 examines more closely, perceptions about the dangers of city space limited some, but not all, of working girls' options; in fact, most young women went out on the town, met and dated boys, and managed to maintain their respectability.

Chapter 5

The Rough 'n' Ready Spinsters' Club:
Working Women's Leisure
and Respectability

Though public space was a source of danger for young working women, and the Great Depression placed serious limitations on their free time and available money, they also found the time and space to have fun, consort with boys, and still be respectable and safe in urban centres during the 1930s. Norma Vineham had fond memories of her free time, much of which she spent with her older sister and closest friends. The girls called themselves the 'Rough 'n' Ready Spinsters' Club.' Their adventures together began at Sunday school under the tutelage of the 'precise and proper spinster lady, Miss Lillian Adams.'[1] On one particular weekend, the Club visited a cottage on Little Lake, north of Toronto. Using photographs to show what fun they had there, Vineham said with a mischievous grin: 'These were some of the boys that we waved to. Oh yes, we waved at all the boys. "Come see us!"'[2] (figures 17, 18).

As Vineham's story suggests, young working women enjoyed amusements that allowed them to express themselves by pushing at the boundaries of respectable feminine behaviour with humourous nicknames and by escaping the drudgery of work routines or difficulties at home with friends on weekends away.

Recreation and leisure are not topics typically associated with the Great Depression, but as this chapter demonstrates, Canadians in general and young women in particular continued to have fun at home, at church functions, in the city, and, like the Rough 'n' Ready Spinsters' Club, on road trips.[3] After decades of concern that working girls were using the home 'as a place of casual shelter where one stopped overnight on the way from the restaurant and the movie theatre to the office,' the Depression witnessed shifts in leisure activities toward home-based and affordable recreation.[4] In domestic spaces young women listened and danced to music played on the piano, gramophone, and radio. They also 'made do' with less money by entertaining themselves in inexpensive ways through church and community organizations. These places offered them a space to hone their debate, public-speaking, and organizational skills and, most importantly for many, to socialize with young men. At the same time, a wide range of commercial amusements, particularly movies and dancing, continued to capture the attention of wage-earning women. Fortunately for these young workers, by the 1930s mass entertainment had made leisure activities affordable and acceptable for all but the unemployed, the poor, or the puritanical.

Women's memories give new insight on the resistance of social reformers to the 'commercial amusement industry.'[5] When discussing their leisure time women did not mention the surveillance of middle-class associations like the YWCA or the Canadian Council on Child and Family Welfare, which were so vocal about the deleterious effects of public entertainment for working girls in previous years. This is not to say that young women who were more concerned with 'their pleasures than their reputations' did not continue to walk a fine line between sexual propriety and disrespectability; however, commercial amusements could be respectable, particularly when engaged in by women who followed cultural scripts of proper femininity.[6] The Rough 'n' Ready Spinsters' Club provides a good example of the ways in which certain young women could playfully adopt the very names and activities frequently attached to those who landed in the city's courtrooms or on the margins of acceptability. As Vineham explained, their Sunday School teacher, Miss Lillian Adams, 'didn't like the Rough 'n' Ready' aspect of the group's name. Adams would have been utterly disappointed in them 'if she'd seen [them] waving to the boys,' Vineham joked. She thought the girls 'should be proper … just so,' but this did not stop the girls from being '*ready* for anything!' exclaimed Vineham with great laughter.[7] In fact, the 'rough' part of their name did not apply to them, as none of these young office girls of British heritage would have been perceived as sexually available working-class girls or pathetic old spinsters as their nickname suggested. That, of course, was just the point. Narratives of feminine respectability did not cast all women equally. It was this flexibility that allowed young employed women to work with and around societal ideals to create space for kicking up their heels and having a good time.

People living on the margins of economic stability have always figured out ways to have fun with little or no money, but the Depression years made this important for a greater number of working women than it had

17   The Rough 'n' Ready Spinsters' Club. Clockwise from top: Norma Vineham, Dorothy Arnold, Kay Boyd, Irene Goodwin, Lillian Adams, Evelyn Hook, Gladys Davis, Grace Brown, Anna Neal. Photo courtesy of Norma Vineham.

18   From right to left Gladys Davis, Norma Vineham, and Anna Neal. In the distance 'the boys' they waved to. Photo courtesy of Norma Vineham.

before. In a time of economic insecurity, cost was important. 'We didn't have money in those days. You did things that didn't take money,' explained Grace Michaels. For instance, she elaborated, 'you'd go down to the beach [and] go on hikes.'[8] Such changes did not mean that working girls did not enjoy themselves, however. 'We made do,' but as Jean Jackson assured me, 'we didn't miss anything!'[9] The adage 'we made our own fun' fit ideals of hard work and personal sacrifice; they reflected a way of thinking about work and leisure common to those who lived through the thirties.

Home-based leisure activity, which often occurred in the living room, or front parlour as it was called then, provided one means through which young women 'made do' and still had fun. The piano, gramophone, and radio were popular forms of entertainment in working- and middle-class homes. Wilfred Wood explained: 'In practically every family there would be one or two people who could play the piano.' Wood's sister played 'so every couple of weeks she'd buy a new sheet of music, a new song would come out, and then we'd have a singsong around the piano; home entertainment.'[10] The gramophone and radio also allowed young people to listen to recordings of famous jazz artists like Louis Armstrong, 'crooners' like Rudy Vallee, and big-band players like Benny Goodman.[11] These records made a wider range of music accessible to a greater number of people and also allowed young workers to escape the world around them. Wood remembered these Depression-era songs well. '"I Can't Give You Anything but Love," that was a big one and very appropriate too.' These tunes evoked strong memories of the 1930s because, he continued, 'out of the Depression came a certain era of music.' He sang a few lines from 'Side by Side' to illustrate his point: '*We ain't got a barrel of money, we may look ragged and funny, but we travel along, singing a song, side by side.*' Music forged connections between people who had shared experiences. In 1977, Brigida Ely recalled that she did not have time to go to the movies in the Depression, 'maybe one time a year.' As Ely explained it, when her husband came home from work he often went out again to 'night school, [to] learn English a bit.' However, in this immigrant household they did listen to Italian music on the gramophone for fun, something that made them feel at home in Anglo-Protestant Toronto.[12] The music also offered relief from hard times and, perhaps, the struggle of fitting in at work. In Norma Vineham's household, they used to listen to music in the living room at the parties she and her sister hosted after church. 'On Sunday night we'd go to church and then we'd come back to our place. Maybe twenty or so young people would come back,' said Vineham.

'There was one fellow that I knew he played the piano in the orchestra and he went to the same church. And then another one he played and they would come back. My Dad was always there. He never came and mingled with us but he'd just say hello. He always said, "As long as you behave yourselves, it's good to come back [after church]."'[13] Together the group would sing and dance 'everything from soup to nuts. All the latest music and so on, once in a while we'd sing a hymn, but more often the groovy music,' recalled Vineham with laughter.

The family living room was also a respectable place for a woman to entertain her beau. Courting straddled both public and private spaces. It often involved initial encounters at church, dance halls, movie houses, and amusement parks, which led to the porch or, after a while, the living room. The front parlour was sufficiently public to entertain a non-family member but private enough for meetings to escape the censure that a public rendezvous might. Here parents could monitor and restrict behaviour, or so they thought. As Jean Jackson recalled, 'I remember Beryl (her sister) and her boyfriend and Morris, my husband, we would come in from wherever we were and sit in the living room … Once we decided that we were going to see who could wait the longest,' Jackson continued. Young couples did their best to steal a few kisses under the watchful eye of parents. Jackson and her sister tried to outlast one another, hoping the other couple would say 'good night' first. They could always hear their father. 'He would walk around upstairs and you could hear him at the top of the stairs. I knew he was looking down' to make sure there was no 'funny business,' remembered Jackson with a smile.[14] The Tapp sisters have similar memories. They would sit with their boyfriends while their mother sat in the kitchen. Every once in a while they would hear her clear her throat or shake her newspaper. Cahill recalled, laughing as she explained, 'we were in the living room necking!'[15] In some Toronto families, the home was the only approved place for young women to socialize with young men. Italian women recalled these expectations and the ways they dealt with them. Mrs DeZorzi, who immigrated to Toronto from northern Italy in the early twentieth century, recalled the strictness of some families in these years: 'Oh, in some parts at least of the south a girl c[ouldn]'t go out with a boy and if they go out once, they better get married.' In courtship, young women 'couldn't do a lot,' but as DeZorzi explained it with a chuckle, when parents 'weren't there you would do it anyway!'[16] In her interview with Enrico Cumbo, Mrs Chiara Pillo explained that 'Italian families were very, very strict about dating and friends' but her parents were more liberal: 'Our father trusted us as long as we didn't run wild.'[17] The family of Johnny Lombardi's wife was Sicilian. In order to court her he had to learn about 'Sicilian Old World tradition.' There were 'different ways of showing respect' for the woman and the family, Lombardi noted. For instance, 'you did not sit beside a girl without having someone beside you. Put your arms around her, you would never do that!' In addition, 'if you were asked into the house for tea you were never alone without parents.'[18] Some women found Italian cultural traditions that tied male honour with female chastity or shame to be limiting.[19] For second- and third-generation Italian women, socializing could become a delicate balancing act between the gender precepts that had been important for their mothers, their roles as vital income earners for their families, and their desires. To do so they sometimes arranged clandestine meetings and had their boyfriends drop them off several blocks away from home. These stories affirm, as Franca Iacovetta and Donna Gabbaccia caution, that it is important not to generalize about Italian culture or its impact on women. Like their contemporaries, these women sometimes challenged precepts of respectable behaviour in order to fulfil their own desires.[20]

Religious associations have long provided an important source of leisure activity for young women.[21] The connection between faith and free time had roots in the social gospel movement that began at the end of the nineteenth century.[22] The YWCA, Canadian Girls in Training, and Young People's societies were expressions of this development. These organizations were particularly popular among the women in this study. Run informally out of Toronto's churches, they typically drew young women and men from the surrounding neighbourhood; participation was not dependent on involvement in the church congregation but was designed to appeal to young people by uniting non-denominational activity with religious and moral training.[23] As Neil Semple points out in his study of Canadian Methodism, Young People's Societies provided an avenue for the church to draw more young people into its fold.[24] After the war and the onset of the Depression, it was particularly important to show the relevance of the church to society. Grace Michaels remembered well, and was proud of, how the youth group from Forward Baptist Church helped the unemployed in the 1930s. She spent some of her free time handing out hot dogs at the Yonge Street Mission.[25]

Whatever the perceived purpose of such organizations in the 1930s, it is undeniable that Christianity dominated the religious landscape of

Toronto during these years.[26] In 1931, 92 per cent of the city's citizens were Christian. Of that group, 68 per cent were affiliated with the Anglican, Presbyterian, and United churches and 14 per cent with the Roman Catholic Church. Toronto also had a substantial Jewish community; over 45,000 people claimed Judaism as their religion in the 1931 decennial census.[27] Whatever their faith, nearly 100 per cent of Torontonians claimed a religion, a clear indication of its importance in the city.[28] According to Toronto's Mayor James 'Jimmy' Simpson, who spoke on Ladies' Night at the Rosedale Men's Club, 'no matter what the activity of the city, it [was] the better if influenced by religion.'[29]

If organizations and the mayor saw religious influence in this manner, women more often recalled church-based groups as a source of fellowship, self-affirmation, and a place to meet young men. At Grace Carmen United Church, Norma Vineham enjoyed the sense of community church activities provided. 'You see,' offered Vineham, 'it was in the church where I grew up.'[30] In particular, Vineham recalled her lead role in the *New Minister Drama*, a play put on by the church to raise money during the Depression (figure 19) The plot revolved around a church congregation welcoming a new, young, and single minister to their community. 'We had the gossipy ladies auxiliary and the young ladies swooning over the new minister. It was great fun,' said Vineham with a chuckle.[31] Vineham's character 'landed' the new minister. The show was a huge success and they were asked to run it longer than they had expected. For Lois Wilson, whose family belonged to the Church of Latter Day Saints, church was 'where [she] got [her] social activities. It wasn't just ours. All my friends talked about it,' she recalled. 'Friday nights were activity nights. Sometimes we would have meetings. Some nights kids learned to debate.' Her sister, June Pugseley, who participated in the joint interview, affirmed, 'it was a good night Friday.'[32] Mildred Johnston also remembered that most of her free time was taken up with events at the Anglican Church. Along with other young women, Johnston participated in a 'scripture union, which [was] a Bible reading society' that drew women from different Christian denominations. 'We used to have get-togethers and that sort of thing ... and we used to go out [to] hospitals and visit people.' 'Really,' Johnston concluded, 'my life has all been church related.'[33] Audrey Sewell belonged to a group called the Young Ladies Dorcas at Forward Baptist Church in Toronto. As she recalled it, 'Dorcas was a woman in the Bible who died and I guess it was Peter that brought her back to life.'[34] In keeping with the spirit of Dorcas, who was known for her skills as a seamstress, this group did a lot of hand work. During such leisure activities young women developed

19 The cast of the 'New Minister Drama,' Grace Carmen United Church, mid-thirties. Photo courtesy of Norma Vineham.

organizational and public-speaking skills, learned from the Bible, enjoyed fellowship, and, through plays like the *New Minister Drama*, acted out familiar discourses of marriage and heterosexuality.

Church-based recreation also functioned to bring together young, unattached women and men who dated and sometimes married. 'I could sing in the choir. So that was the good part, a big part of my life. We had fun. We sang in different places. We went out of town to sing in the choir,' said Vineham. The choir leader had a cottage on one of Toronto's islands, where they used to gather. On one evening, Vineham had an escort. 'This young man in the choir asked me if I'd like to sail over in the boat he and his brother had built. I said "yes." Well, it was a beautiful day and we sailed over to the island.' Unfortunately, on their return calm winds trapped them in the eastern gap. 'We had to row back. Yes. Yes! And the thing was he didn't have any lights for the boat and it was getting darker!'[35] Vineham ended up with blisters on her hands and had to phone her father because they were late. Helen Wilks and her friends sought out the company of young men through these groups. 'When I was about eighteen or so (1935) there were a lot of girls' clubs. You would have a meeting and then have a party so you could invite boys. The boys were a bunch of lounge lizards. They had no money but at least you got a date out of it.'[36] Thelma Plunkett attended the Baptist Church in Weston (a Toronto suburb) during the Depression. 'You asked me about the social,' she commented, 'well the thing was it was so late when I would get home with all these long hours [of work].' However, 'on Wednesday night they would have prayer meetings and I would go to these meetings if I got home in time.' For Plunkett it was important to relate that she met her husband at one of the meetings. She explained: 'My husband was there, of course he wasn't my husband then, but he was there.' When one of the meetings drew to a close, a friend of Plunkett's husband said, '"Why don't you give Thelma a ride home?" So anyhow,' Plunkett related, 'he did and that was when we started going together.'[37] They were married in the early years of the Second World War.

At the same time, church could also be a source of self-identity and cultural affirmation for young working women. Three churches in the city were generally recognized as black churches: the African Methodist Episcopalian (AME), British Methodist Episcopalian (BME), and the First Baptist Churches. These churches, now demolished, once stood in the heart of downtown Toronto. In the interwar years, as Claire Clarke recalled, they had an important function among black Torontonians: 'The church was very instrumental in the life of the community as a whole because whether West Indian, Canadian, or American, all people went to church.'[38] Indeed, outside of church a cohesive community of black Canadians did not really exist in the 1930s. Instead class status, skin colour, and nationality divided people. Canadian-born blacks tended to have greater economic stability and cultural integration than West-Indian ·and American-born blacks. This, Clarke recalled, gave the former group a sense of superiority that she felt they used against those from other countries. Church activities muted these divisions.

Though some people, particularly those from the West Indies, were Anglican, the majority of Toronto's black population attended the Methodist or Baptist churches. This was in part because racism kept them out of Toronto's 'white' churches. When Clarke's father first arrived in Toronto from Barbados, he attended an Anglican church, but he soon found it necessary to join the BME church. '[My father] and a few of the other black men came from Sydney, Nova Scotia; a lot of them from the islands landed at Halifax and worked in [the mines].' Once in Toronto, Clarke explained, 'they used to attend one church particularly, St Phillips [Anglican] Church,' but a 'point of racism' encouraged them to find another church. As Clarke put it, 'these fellas were mostly, you knew they were blacks. They were not light-skinned or anything.' Unfortunately, when they attended church, Clarke continued, 'the white ladies would pull themselves away until one day, one Sunday, the minister got up in the pulpit and said, "Do you think it would not be proper if you went to your *own* churches?" His name was Robinson, Reverend Robinson at St Phillips Anglican Church. I suppose he had to do something because his membership was probably giving him a hard time.'[39] Such explicit racism was not the only reason for the formation of all-black congregations. They also provided a place where young women could benefit from mentors and socialize with other young people.

In 1937, a Young Men's Bible Class was formed at the Baptist Church, which drew members from the BME and AME churches as well. As June Braithwaite clarified, 'I was part of the Young People's, Young Men's Bible Class ... it was called the young men's' but women went too. The group met on Sunday afternoons. They would 'sing Negro Spirituals at the different churches, interracial, interreligious, you know.' One of the main functions of the group, Daniel Braithwaite recalled, was to 'spread some joy and also some harmony and friendship with young people in the community.'[40] Madame Leona Brewton led the group. Brewton and her husband had migrated from the United States to Canada in the early twentieth century. Soon after, in 1924, Brewton opened a hairdressing and beauty salon, the Brewton Comfort Shop, on Yonge Street. Her husband was a podiatrist.[41]

Brewton's organization of leisure activities and her impact on Toronto's young black women were great indeed. Brewton challenged recurring images of black economic and social inferiority, which were common in Toronto schools and workplaces and which had been reaffirmed for young women who tried unsuccessfully to find work. Rella Braithwaite, who was in her early twenties when she first became involved with the Young Men's Bible Class, explained to her interviewer Diana Braithwaite: 'I can see her now, I really [can], she was quite a role model as far as I was concerned ... because I wasn't used to black women being business women.' Braithwaite continued, 'She lived in *north* Toronto which was quite something because the majority of the black families were in the centre of the city [and] she had a white maid, which was really a little different.'[42] According to Braithwaite she used to drive 'around in her big faux fur that she wore. She was quite a humanitarian and she was always getting young people gathered together.' Brewton also made an indelible impression on Claire Clarke, who insisted that her story was one of the great untold histories of interwar Toronto. 'Madame Brewton you know she was a pillar of the black community. She was a woman [who] gave back to the community' even though 'she didn't earn her living from the community because her business was strictly with the Hadassah [women].' Clarke elaborated, saying that Brewton 'provided a platform for speakers for young people to debate and she'd bring in speakers like the Rabbi Fineberg and Rabbi Eisendrath.' In doing so she forged alliances between the Jewish and black communities, something Clarke respects to this day. 'She did wonderful work but you never hear about [her]. Young blacks today, they don't know these people,' Clarke added.[43]

Toronto's synagogues, particularly larger ones such as Holy Blossom, also had youth organizations. Joe Soren's middle-class family lived in the west end of Toronto in an Anglo-Protestant region of the city. As he recalled, 'In the thirties, we would go only on the High Holidays ... because there was no synagogue around where we were.'[44] Rose Edelist lived close to available synagogues around Toronto's Kensington Market, but she had neither the time nor the energy on a Friday evening or Saturday to observe the Jewish sabbath or to attend meetings organized for afterward. 'Well I tell you, I was worn out' at the end of the week, Edelist said.[45] Workers who observed the Christian day of rest enjoyed a time off on Sundays, which gave them greater time and energy to attend services and connect with their religious communities. Through her work in the garment industry, Edelist was involved in a Toronto union. In 'the interwar period the Jewish unions served as vital social and cultural centres'; however, unlike men who used the Labour Lyceum and union halls to socialize, women did not typically use these venues for recreation.[46] Edelist attended the occasional lecture held by her union, but in general she did not participate in social activities. Women had domestic responsibilities and, Ruth Frager argues, union-hall activities appealed little to them anyway.[47]

While police, parents, and social workers rarely questioned home- and church-based recreation, the diversions of public space, namely amusement parks, movie houses, and dance halls, drew more attention. As chapter 4 highlighted, women in public space who behaved in ways that contravened moral codes could find themselves in Toronto's courtrooms charged for being vagrant or incorrigible. Nevertheless, pronouncements about the ill effects of public entertainment did not stop women from having fun. The majority of them thoroughly enjoyed the city's commercial offerings, but they did so by carefully choosing where and with whom they socialized.

Toronto's waterfront was the location of numerous places of entertainment: the Toronto islands, the Canadian National Exhibition (CNE), and Sunnyside Amusement Park. Mike Filey's photographic collections make clear the fact that numerous generations of Torontonians have enjoyed these lakeside amusements.[48] Hanlan's Point on the Toronto Islands was a particularly popular destination in the 1930s. As Audrey Byers explained, 'We went to Hanlan's Point. They had a live orchestra there. It was great but you had to take the ferry over.'[49] Along with dancing, the islands also drew young women interested in sports. 'There was quite a stadium at the islands,' Mabel Duncan recalled. 'They used to have ballgames and then it was quite a thing to go over there and walk from one island to another' (figures 20, 21, 22).[50] Families and community groups also went to the islands for picnics and for swimming. The MacMillans, like sisters Geraldine Windeatt and Helen Campbell pictured here, used to 'take a picnic lunch and ... [they] always took a bathing suit.'[51] Ethnically based picnics were also common. 'They would have a special day for the Scots, one for the Irish, one for the Germans, one for the Italians. I guess there was a pavilion,' recalled Margaret Lawson.[52] Often church and community groups organized these functions. For instance, the Fame Friulani Club sponsored annual picnics for citizens from the Friuli region of northeast Italy.[53] Even the economic difficulties

20   Geraldine Windeatt and Helen Campbell with family friends at Hanlan's Point, Toronto Islands, in the mid-thirties. Photo courtesy of Penny Srigley.

21   Nora and Geraldine Windeatt swimming at Toronto's beaches in the late
thirties. Photo courtesy of Penny Srigley.

22   Nora and James Windeatt at Toronto's beaches in the late thirties. Photo
courtesy of Nora Windeatt.

of the Depression did not stop the annual picnic of Toronto's 'Italian Colony,' held at the CNE, reported the editors of *Toronto Women*.[54]

The CNE and the Sunnyside Amusement Park were also popular destinations for young working women. While most of them recalled these venues as sources of childhood amusement, some also remembered them as places to go with friends or on a date. During the CNE's annual two-week run in Toronto in late summer, the energy and excitement of the fair, its midway, food, exhibits, and rides, swept young people away. Mildred Johnston, like many other women, recalled the free food given out to young people; one year she won a contest. 'I remember going to the Exhibition. I always went to the Exhibition ... and there was a little contest and [my friends and I] got into it and I won ten pounds of sugar. Well was I greeted with great enthusiasm at home!'[55] Audrey MacMillan recalled her older sisters dressing up to go to the CNE. 'Oh, you got really dressed up. My sisters always went on Labour Day. You didn't wear your summer clothes. You officially went into your autumn clothing. They always had new clothes to wear, completely, to wear at the Exhibition with their boyfriends on Labour Day.'[56]

Opened in 1922 as part of the Toronto Harbour Commission's plans to revitalize the waterfront, Sunnyside Amusement Park became the 'playground of Toronto' in the interwar years. There young women ate Downy Flake donuts, drank Honeydew, swam in Lake Ontario, or rode the Flyer roller coaster, which reportedly 'would read sixty miles per hour when coming home' after new cars were installed in 1933.[57] The city's working girls could also be found strolling the boardwalk with friends or a beau. Sunnyside, like the CNE, was a destination for couples. Audrey MacMillan recalled that her sisters 'went down to the Easter Parade at Sunnyside. I think they had boyfriends, probably the same men they married ... They were in the Easter Parade and they were actually in the [news].' Every Easter young women participated in a parade along the boardwalk. Before Sunnyside opened in 1922, 'fashion-conscious Torontonians had frequently participated in Easter parades along the old wooden boardwalk.' When the Harbour Commission built a new walkway on the south side of Lakeshore Boulevard, this provided 'Torontonians [with] a very special place to hold the annual Easter parade.'[58] Widely documented in Toronto's dailies, this event, unofficially organized by the Harbour Commission, was an exhibition of pretty women and new clothing styles that continued throughout the thirties.[59] Unlike their working-class sisters, whose names sometimes landed in the paper because of vagrancy charges received while strolling on the city's streets, Torontonians celebrated this type of walking.

Movie theatres were a relatively new but well-loved source of leisure time in the 1930s. In fact, the Depression has been called the 'golden age' of film because of the universal popularity of motion pictures in that decade.[60] In Toronto in 1934, the city's eighty-nine theatres drew 19,242,000 patrons, more than thirty times the city's population.[61] Entire pages of Toronto's daily newspapers provided advertisements for the latest films. Billboards lined the walls outside neighbourhood and downtown theatres with beautiful women, heads tipped back, leaning into the embraces of the decade's leading men; their headlines and images enticed young women inside as successfully as the show windows at Eaton's department store. In Toronto, working women found an almost endless number of venues at a range of costs, whether they desired entertainment in the 'majestic downtown picture palaces' like Loew's Uptown or Shea's or in the smaller community theatres, such as the Ideal or the Victory.[62] Early 'silent dramas ... had removed the movies' lower-class stigma.'[63] This had encouraged the building of a range of both expensive and inexpensive movie houses in Toronto. Mildred Johnson recalled Shea's. 'Oh yes! Oh that was nice. That was a treat if you went to one of the big theatres: Shea's, Loew's downtown or uptown theatre. But, there were many little neighbourhood theatres. I mean there might be in three or four blocks two theatres, two neighbourhood theatres.'[64]

Affordability was central to the motion picture industry's heyday during the 1930s. At five to twenty cents per show, movies were an inexpensive pastime for the lean Depression years.[65] If a young woman could not afford to go dancing or to attend the pricier movie houses downtown, she could probably afford a movie at her local theatre. Mabel Duncan recalled the release of *Gone With the Wind*, but she did not see it in 1939. 'You see we could only go to the local theatres because it was cheaper. We never went downtown to the theatres because it cost too much.' Margaret Lawson said, 'I went to the movies [but] first you had to have money to get in and hopefully a nickel to spend' on candy and other treats. If you did not have much money then you 'could go to the Ideal. We weren't supposed to go there. It was on the south side of the tracks ... I remember seeing Val Kee Man Shu and being scared to death. You know, the yellow peril.'[66] Much like newspapers and other forms of media, in the 1930s, North American films employed racist images of the Orient, particularly those that construed Asian men as a threat to white womanhood.[67] Even Velma Demerson, who was punished for her relationship with Harry Yip, recalled walking on the other side of the street to avoid a Chinese man carrying laundry when she was young.[68] Joyce Cahill would leave the door of the laundromat open when she delivered her family's laundry in the Depression. 'I'd open the door and hear cling, cling and then you'd hear swish, swish, swish, swish and you knew the mad Chinese man was coming up.' Her sister explained further: 'You had fear because they were so silent and different.'[69] The racist images in the movies that young women watched perpetuated such fears.

While the movies promulgated racism, they also (at least until the New Production Code, or Hays Code, took effect) exposed young women to female movie stars who were among the most independent and sexually liberated leading ladies of the twentieth century. As Lary May points out in *Screening Out the Past*, the motion picture industry was central to a revolution in North American morals and attitudes.[70] The early Depression years saw a revolutionary representation of women, which captured the attention of movie critics. Despite preoccupations with love themes during these years, 'marriage suffer[ed] a particular anemia on screen.'[71] This was due in no small part, critics thought, to the dearth of female characters who reflected respectable femininity. In his exposé of motion pictures, Henry Forman reported that Greta Garbo, who 'had at least touched on the shady side of life' had not been 'portrayed [as] what might be regarded as a good woman' in any film.[72] Moreover, Norma Shearer had had only 'mediocre' success until 'she came along as the reckless girl in *Divorcée*.' In this film Shearer declared, when dissatisfied with the restrictions of a traditional marriage, 'Why can't a woman be more like a man?'[73] Forman further notes that Shearer, in the movies she made after 1930 (*Strangers May Kiss, A Free Soul, Private Lives*, and *Strange Interlude*), was 'ravishing and revealing, almost a torch bearer for the double standard.'[74] Though love relationships with men continued to be a dominant theme and married women were typically portrayed as happier than single women, these leading ladies did not necessarily choose marriage or sexual chastity. For instance, in her 1930 film *Morocco*, Marlene Dietrich chose 'her sexual attraction to Gary Cooper over marriage to a devoted and wealthy Adolphe Menjou.'[75] In another film, *Blonde Venus* (1932), Dietrich assumed the primary responsibilities for her family's needs. Despite such disruptions of standard codes of femininity, during the Depression and for the first and only time in film history, 'women achieved top box office parity with men accounting for at least half of each year's top ten stars in films which drew record audiences numbering as high as ninety million each week.'[76] While affirming heterosexual romance, these films also challenged traditional values, particularly those rooted in female sexual propriety.

Nora Windeatt recalled admiring actresses Myrna Loy and Simone Simone, while Elizabeth Gammon recalled film stars Gary Cooper and Barbara Stanwyck.[77] One nineteen-year-old interviewed for a 1930s study claimed, 'I am wearing my hair with a view to getting the same entrancing effect that Greta Garbo gets with hers.'[78] Another college girl said that after watching the movie *Wild Party*, there was 'nothing [to] be done about it': her mother had to buy her a 'sleeveless jumper dress' just like that worn by Clara Bow.[79] Indeed, movies 'existed to put the star over, to capitalize on the image, and sometimes to advance the image.'[80] In 1939, MGM produced a promotional film called *Hollywood – Style Center of the World*. The production detailed the 'film industry's gift of fashion to the masses' that had allowed even farm girls to be aware of the latest styles.[81] This is not to say that working girls passively consumed movies. To be sure, they decided which movies they wanted to watch and those they wanted to avoid. In fact, as Nan Enstad argues, the movie 'gaze created a possibility for women's desires.'[82] The cinema exposed young women to a world of glamour, wealth, and beauty, which were sources of fantasy and social identification. 'For the first time in history, human beings had the privilege of sitting in the dark and looking at the faces of other human beings, often beautiful ones, thirty feet high and lit up with emotion.'[83] They did so to get outside themselves and indulge in a world of wealth and luxury.[84] Producers wanted their audiences to enjoy their movie-going experiences, to create stars and story lines that would bring people back week after week.

Perspectives about the effect of motion pictures on the Depression generation varied. Some contemporary observers thought that movies 'infus[ed] romance into a dull world and thereby add compensation to the ordinary routine of life,' and others were certain that movies had a harmful influence on the lives of people, encouraging crime, delinquency, and weakening moral standards.[85] There were various attempts to create a regulatory system for films in Canada. Motion pictures garnered attention as early as 1929; 'talkies ... [and] film subjects that emphasize[d] violation of law, underworld life ... sex problems and nudity' were a problem, movie censors charged.[86] In order to protect the innocence of young people, 'all of the provincial governments censored movies,' but no formal legislation was ever enacted.[87] After the Depression had taken hold, the Canadian Council on Child and Family Welfare (CCCFW) published a series of bulletins that dealt with 'the problem of the constructive use of the leisure time of millions of Canadians.'[88] Of particular concern was the 'tremendous increase in the motion picture industry and professional sports' that was taking advantage of the 'de-moralizing effects of disappointment in the search for work.'[89] Through their bulletins, the CCCFW wanted to promote the 'constructive utiliza-tion of leisure time in which self-activity in sport, hobbies, and other phases of recreation [had] a central place.'[90] This, the CCCFW hoped, would shift attention away from amusements like movie theatres and promote healthier applications for body and mind. Perhaps most influ-ential was the New Production Code, or Hays Code. Leading film studios in the United States accepted the code in 1930 and formally imposed it in 1934. This move was 'meant to silence, once and for all, those many vociferous critics of the film industry' by eradicating 'the kinds of ex-cesses and sagging moral standards' that had been seen on the screen. In particular, the code changed representations of 'crime, brutality and sex.'[91] Remembering these restrictions, film star Mae West said, 'We weren't even allowed to wiggle when we sang.'[92] Henceforth, women who transgressed sexual norms could never be heroines, and they typically relinquished their careers for a husband. Those who did not lost their men, forever becoming spinsters. Such regulations changed the poten-tial of feature films for offering young women alternative scripts to dominant notions of femininity and did little to quell their passion for movies.

In our 1998 interview, Helen Campbell exclaimed, 'I was dance crazy!'[93] With this declaration, Campbell captured both the fears of social com-mentators, who claimed that the 'modern "indecent dance" was "an of-fence against womanly purity,"' and the passion of working women for this leisure activity.[94] Dancing was also Ethel Watson's favourite pastime: 'I loved it! All the girls did.'[95] Dancing 'bedazzled the single working woman.'[96] By the Depression years, critics of dance halls, including those in the Moral and Social Reform Council of Canada, had worried about the dance craze for close to thirty years. Though the police 'were closely watch[ing]' the public dance halls, Chief Constable Draper rarely com-mented on them in his annual reports.[97] Indeed, regulators seemed to be fighting a losing battle. After a long week of work, thousands of young women in Toronto were captivated by the whirl and energy of the dance floor and the beat of the orchestra which could be found at the Palais Royale or in the warm evening air of the newly opened Palace Pier.

The city offered working women many dancing spots with a range of costs. Dorothy Coles did not have much time for dancing. 'When you're in nursing and you're working and ... on duty from seven to seven ... seven days a week, there is not an awful lot of time.' But if you liked dancing, Coles recalled, there were a lot of 'very nice dance halls ... one or two were formal ... there was the Old Mill, we still have the Old Mill, and there was the Silver Slipper and the Top Hat [Club Esquire until 1939], which was formal'(figure 23).[98] The Palais Royale was 'where you went and your friends would go and you would meet new friends there. There were a lot of dance bands and then later on big bands came along, like Bert Niosi and Guy Lombardo,' explained Wilfred Wood.[99]

The majority of dance halls were not exceptionally costly. For instance, in October 1932, the Embassy Club offered free admission to see the Bert Niosi Orchestra if you arrived between 6:30 and 8:30. After this time, the entry fee rose to one dollar a person.[100] The Palace Pier also cost two dollars per couple on Friday and Saturday nights to see the popular bands of Count Basie and his orchestra and Cab Calloway and his Hi-De-Ho Orchestra, but the first one thousand tickets for each night often sold for one dollar.[101] The Palais Royale was often a cheaper option. As Sydney Palmer recalled about this dance hall, 'I think it was four tickets for a quarter. They did not charge you to go in, but you had to buy tickets to get on the dance floor. Every time you asked a girl to dance you had to get a person at the gate to get entrance to the floor. The dance floor was terrazzo and they sprinkled wax powder. You could really go flying.'[102] Called jitney dancing, this pay-as-you-dance system was a 'sure-fire way to impress the girls.' In fact, as Paul Young explains in his popular history of Ontario dance pavilions, jitney dance tickets hanging conspicuously from breast pockets were 'the finishing touch to a young man's wardrobe.'[103]

Joe Soren did not have memories to share about the Palais Royale. He said, 'I am not that familiar with the Palais Royale; we stayed more with the hotels and the better night clubs actually.' Wealthier young women and their beaux danced at locations such as the King Edward Hotel or Casa Loma. As Soren explained, 'It was fabulous. You used to pay a buck to go in or something. When we used to have these big dances at the King Edward or the Royal York, you used to buy a corsage for the girlfriend for a buck. You paid two dollars [and] you had top orchestras playing at the ballrooms ... [I] had a tail suit and a top hat.'[104] You did not go alone to these events and you typically danced with your girlfriend or wife, Soren explained to me. At Casa Loma, couples could have dinner in the Palm Room and dance to music played by the internationally renowned Casa Loma Orchestra. Rand Sparling, whose father's architectural firm, Sparling Services, designed such well-known Toronto landmarks as the Imperial Tower and the original Granite Club, attended

23   Posing at home before attending a dance at the Empress Hotel, 26 October 1935. Photo courtesy of Ian Radforth.

dances at Casa Loma.[105] On one evening in particular, he recalled dancing with Mrs Theresa Small, the widow of Toronto theatre tycoon, and millionaire Ambrose Small, who had mysteriously disappeared in 1919. 'She was down at Casa Loma dancing ... and my father was going to have a dance with her,' but she said to him '"I am not dancing with you tonight; send my boy over." That was me. So I went over and I had a dance with her.'[106] Wealthy young women such as Miss Norah Findlay were given debutante balls at Toronto hotels. The *Evening Telegram* reported in November 1929 that Findlay had 'the distinction of being the first Toronto debutante to have the superb new Royal York ballroom as the setting for her coming-out party.'[107] Over 300 guests attended the function meant to signal Miss Findlay's readiness for suitors. The vast majority of young women did not have the social standing or wealth necessary for a debutante ball at one of Toronto's expensive hotels, but the Depression does not seem to have dampened the pleasure they took in dancing at the city's less glamorous dance halls.

As with other forms of leisure activity, questions of respectability shaped women's memories and experiences of dancing. Toronto's working women recalled that some dance spots officially prohibited jitterbugging and alcohol. As Audrey Byers explained about dance restrictions, 'Just once we started to sort of jitterbug and I guess it was a bouncer he came and tapped my husband on the shoulder. You weren't supposed to break away I suppose.'[108] Confining dancers to waltzes or two-steps ensured structured body positions and discouraged close physical contact.[109] 'It was the style of dancing ("whirling") that so bothered observers,' points out Cynthia Comacchio in her study of interwar leisure. Particularly questionable were those dances that 'involved close bodily contact in darkened rooms, such "fevered" dances as the tango, the fox trot,' or worse, 'the "uncivilized" strains of jazz and other "Negro" music.'[110] Nell Moran recalled enjoying the Palais Royale immensely: 'Oh, it was a great dance floor. Good bands. Good bands.' But Moran continued: 'We didn't do any goofy dancing. We didn't drink.' Her husband Jack Moran had a slightly different perspective: 'People used to take their own booze in a brown paper bag.' But, countered Nell, '*we* didn't drink in those days.'[111]

Helen Wilks loved to dance but not at the Palais Royale. Wilks attended dances with one of her first boyfriends at the University of Toronto. 'I was pinned by him,' Wilks recalled, 'except that his family wouldn't go for it.' As for dance clubs such as the Palais Royale, Wilks responded, 'We (she and her sister) didn't go to those. Those weren't for our class.'

Working women such as Wilks read codes of respectability through the setting of the dance and the social class and behaviour of those who attended. As to who did frequent 'those' dance halls, Wilks elaborated: 'At the worst time in the Depression when things were really bad we got a job, Marie and I got a job at ... the peapicking plant.' The sisters worked, Wilks said, with 'beautiful, beautiful young girls, I mean pretty but they had mouths like stevedores. They could curse with the best of them. They used to go to the Palais Royale and called it the Bucket of Blood.'[112]

Ruth Fowler often attended dances north of the city, where she worked as a school teacher. These venues were not unseemly, but as a teacher she had to take care with whom she danced. One night she attended a dance with a beau: 'The chap I had been going with had gone with a friend to Sutton and that was the only place that they could have anything to drink.' Fowler danced with him once that evening. 'The only time I danced with him was in the Paul Jones ... when you stop you dance with the person opposite you.' Fowler continued: 'I could smell his breath, or someone else told me [about his breath]. I never went out with him again. I was afraid to just because he made that one mistake you know.' She added a little wistfully: 'Oh, he could sing and it was my first romance, you know. So, it was finished. I was afraid I'd get fired.'[113] Rose Edelist took dancing classes one evening a week in the early years of the Depression. Edelist loved to dance and to read, though she had limited time and money. 'This was my hobby,' she said.[114] Nearby her home in Kensington Market was a place that gave dance lessons. 'It was tap dancing. Then this was in style, tapping with the heels, tapping with the toes.' She took the lessons but did not frequent Toronto's dance halls. As she explained, 'I didn't think it was right for a girl to go to the dances by themselves.' She met her husband in 1930 but they still did not dance. 'My husband wasn't very fond of dancing and we couldn't afford it,' she related.

While no ethnic enclave had a monopoly on dancing, couples were denied access to dance halls in Toronto because of their racial identity. For instance, black Torontonians were not welcome at the Palais Royale. When Count Basie, a popular black American big-band player, was performing at the dance hall in 1939, the youth of the Toronto United Negro Improvement Association (UNIA) decided to picket the establishment. They did not have success, and Joseph Clarke felt they had wasted their time. 'I thought it was more important to demonstrate down at city hall that we should get jobs that we were qualified for, even a sit-in in the mayor's office [rather] than picketing a dance hall.'[115] However, such racism did not mean that young African or West-Indian Canadian women did not dance.

In a city that offered little acceptance, economic, political, or social, to African Canadians, American Blacks, or West Indians, an association like the UNIA offered community connection, political voice, and cultural affirmation.[116] Friday and Saturday night dances were particularly popular events. Rella Braithwaite started attending when she arrived in Toronto in 1936. 'I went there to meetings and also the Saturday night jump session when they played records, and even then the floors used to shake when the young ones were dancing.'[117] Braithwaite recalled that 'the older women figures [were] quite active in assisting the young and, you know, sort of looking after things for the evening, taking tickets at the door.' As Claire Clarke explained, 'We had mentors, very good mentors especially the women. You know, looking back today … everybody thinks that these women from the West Indies were shall we say uneducated.' But, continued Clarke, 'they're very wrong because the traits and the things I learned from those women … For instance, one lady she was from Guyana. She taught me how to recite and talk, which has stood me in good stead to this day.'[118] This mentor also taught Clarke 'how to do of all things the Scottish sword dance you know they cross the swords and you dance over these swords and stuff and I performed! I had a beautiful outfit you know. You see!' added Clarke, with great laughter. 'We didn't just learn all things that were racial; we learned about other cultures.' These stage experiences also provided the opportunity for self-expression. Clearly taking pleasure in these memories, Clarke continued to talk about the importance of such activities. 'We always wanted to do plays. We were always performing. I suppose it was the time that we could express ourselves and be our own selves …. It didn't take much to give us a sense of belonging.'[119] Having the opportunity to participate in 'plays and … dances and socials and … programs every Sunday afternoon' gave Daniel Braithwaite 'confidence in being in the public.' The UNIA 'was an atmosphere to develop and see that we could put on things the same that others kids could put on things.'[120] As Clarke further explained, 'Oh yes … my whole outlook on life is governed by the Marcus Garvey affiliation and that has set the pattern of life my outlook even to this day. You see, in my youth that was the only thing that gave hope to people like myself. We had something to look forward to, to build our hopes on a better, what you would call a better share of life. We could, you know among ourselves, find strength in living the kind of life we lived in Toronto at that time.[121]

The UNIA initiated countless opportunities for fun, learning, and collegiality. It also represented an important defence against the racial discrimination that limited the access of blacks to other centres of leisure activity. 'The only outlet [we] didn't have,' explained Claire, 'was one that would give [us] a reasonable livelihood. Had there been proper employment opportunities, Toronto would have seen a different community, a black community.' Other people, Europeans, 'and even the Jewish people could blend in working with other people. Blacks, you definitely stuck out like a sore thumb.'[122]

The amusements that women like Norma Vineham recalled reflect the hardships of the Depression decade. Economy was a priority in the financially strapped thirties, and women, whose wages were essential to family well-being, had to reduce their spending. Thus, many made do with less than they might have in other decades; however, this did not dampen their fun. Family-based amusements were particularly popular. In the living rooms of Toronto's homes, the gramophone, piano, or radio entertained young women and their families. That they enjoyed these amusements in private space made them unquestionably acceptable, so much so that even intimate heterosexual contact often escaped the censure of parents. In similar ways, the religious underpinnings of church-based leisure activities made them popular and respectable for young women during the Depression. The function of church-based leisure activity did not fundamentally change in the Depression; however, in this financially strapped decade churches provided cheap entertainment and were sources of fellowship and community for Toronto's single women. Young People's Societies provided a place in which public activities and private ideals were joined successfully. Young women and men not only met one another for Bible study but also arranged social activities that included dates, parties, dances, and weekends away. In important ways, church groups also offered the opportunity to challenge racial inequality through community cohesion and performance.

The public amusements that were cause for concern in the early twentieth century continued to raise red flags among parents, social workers, and the courts in the 1930s. The women in this study did not refer directly to such restrictions; however, the mores of feminine respectability that such groups promoted had resonance. In the 1930s, they considered where, with whom, for how long, and at what time of day they participated in certain leisure activities. Nevertheless, this chapter verifies that leisure was not simply about perpetuating or confirming dominant norms. Within their leisure time, working girls created ways and means to engage in the activities they desired while consciously and unconsciously monitoring their respectability and dealing with money shortages and racial discrimination.

Conclusion

With the onset of the Second World War, Canada's economy roared into action and prosperity returned to many of Toronto's families. Men, previously unemployed, suddenly had an abundant number of choices for work and obligations to serve in the war effort. This shift did not push young women out of the workforce; instead it expanded their job opportunities in unprecedented ways, especially in non-feminized industrial sectors. The war also ended Claire Clarke's 'ten dark years.' By 1939, Clarke was fed up with persistent rejection and underemployment. She 'went right to the top. I can't believe I did that,' said Clarke with laughter. 'I went right to Ottawa.'[1] She sent a letter to Miss Saunders at the offices of Canada's Secretary of State outlining her training, her achievements, and her inability to find work. Soon after Clarke found clerical employment in Toronto working for the Canadian Navy. Here she finally used her training and, most importantly, was able to contribute wages to her family's needs. Her mother had been right. The day had arrived when she could use her education. Clarke remembers her first day with great fondness. She had never been saluted before and took immense pleasure in the rituals of her new workplace. In the Depression, Toronto's labour market held no such promise for her; like other young daughters, she had to take whatever work she could find. By focusing on the economic instability of the decade, its concomitant unemployment, and the impact it had on men, young and old, we have missed an important piece of the historical puzzle. Young daughters were essential to the labour market and family economies of urban centres during the Great Depression. Never before had so many families relied on the wages of young daughters to survive, daughters who became the primary breadwinners rather than supplementary wage earners to their fathers and brothers.

What were the consequences of such changes for Toronto's young women? The 1930s altered their life choices, shaped their economic and social positions within their families, subjected them to danger and harassment, yet also created the possibility of independence and adventure, and opened up access to the city's commercial amusements. Their stories remind us of the power of Britishness and other sources of identity to bestow privilege and generate disadvantage in these years. They also provide us with a unique window into the burdens and pleasures of the Depression era for them.

In the 1930s, no less than in previous decades, Toronto was a magnet for working women. Unlike the economy of nearby Hamilton, which relied heavily on the steel industry, Toronto had a diversified economy. Young single women of British heritage had little trouble finding jobs in light industry, particularly as textile workers, in the offices of finance, insurance, and manufacturing, in schools, hospitals, and in the city's homes. During the Depression, these sectors of the economy proved far more resilient than areas dominated by men. As a consequence, young daughters became an integral part of Toronto's family economies and its workplaces. Such economic responsibilities affected these workers in distinct ways. When Margaret Gairns finally found the teaching job she wanted at Lawrence Park Collegiate, her parents' retirement was secured. Rose Edelist's job as a skilled garment worker ensured that her family could immigrate from Europe to Toronto and then survive the difficult Depression years. Ivy Phillips's work and the employment of her sisters guaranteed that her mother could put food on the table. While such positions did create a context for independence and adventure, young women also found such responsibilities disruptive. Many were particularly upset by lost schooling opportunities, as they had to choose wage earning over an education. This stood out in the memories as a particularly poignant sacrifice of these years. The Great Depression also delayed marriage because of societal restrictions on women's work after marriage in all but the lowest-paid domestic and factory jobs. Most women negotiated these sacrifices in individual and culturally specific ways. Some of them returned to school in later years, while others did not have the opportunity. Many young workers waited to marry until their family was in a better economic position. Some of them never married, which was often a hardship and sometimes a choice based on individual desire. Still other women realized that their marital status would not give them access to jobs, which their racial and ethnic background denied them. Whatever the case, young workers made choices as dutiful daughters who were responsible for the economic well-being of their families. They remember these years with sadness – looking to the importance of education in today's society as an indication of what could have been – but also with pride. They endured difficult times and only needed to look to the achievements of their grandchildren and others in younger generations to determine the value of their experiences.

While fathers and brothers struggled with unemployment, daughters took jobs to ensure that their families had food, clothes, and shelter. Despite such responsibilities, in most families young women played important roles in their families as substitute mothers, taking up domestic responsibilities and caring for younger siblings. Some young women found such duties onerous. This strained family relations, creating lasting bitterness between siblings that seeped into recollections, as well as fierce loyalty and appreciation, particularly as fathers, unable to fulfil their roles as breadwinners, abandoned their families or disappeared into the foggy and grey worlds of alcoholism and depression. Though far less typical, mothers also left their families, no longer able to cope with making ends meet or in search of greater fulfilment. Such changes only added to the upheaval of the decade for the city's young women and emphasized the importance of their wage earning.

In Toronto's labour market, young daughters typically filled 'women's' jobs that men were unwilling or unable to occupy, as domestics, clerical workers, factory girls, teachers, and nurses. A gendered labour market created both disadvantages and privileges in these women's lives. They had lower wages than men and very limited or no access to jobs with power and privilege, as lawyers, doctors, principals, business managers, and the like. This study confirms these findings. As Claire Clarke and other women's recollections reveal, there is, however, more to 'the story.' Racial and ethnic identities, social class, and religion also determined whether women found and kept employment in these years. Moreover, while married women faced significant limitations in the job market, single women between the ages of fifteen and thirty-five found more jobs in the 1930s than they ever had before. As this study suggests, the gendered labour market was not unified but variegated and uneven, and job options were determined in ways that gave women of British descent, who were unmarried and had access to schooling, the freedom to apply for relatively high-paying, stable positions as teachers, clerical workers, and managers, while immigrant, ethnic, black, poor, and married women faced narrower and less lucrative options. Women did not accept their workplace disadvantages passively; domestics wrote letters to the editor;

women such as Rose Edelist joined unions; and Claire Clarke challenged
the racism of the white and Protestant establishment. However, understanding their positions in the labour market of 1930s Toronto requires
attention to their individual stories.

If the positions of working girls in Toronto's homes and workplaces
was a vital part of the Depression economy, their movement through
public space continued to be a source of concern for middle-class organizations, the police, parents, and women themselves. These assessments
were based on culturally derived ideas about good and bad girls. The
murder of breadwinning daughter Ruth Taylor became a disturbing cautionary tale on the safety of Toronto for working women, heightening
fears of attacks by strange men and of places such as the city's ravines.
Women's memories and the documentary record nevertheless indicate
that the home and the workplace could be greater sources of harassment, abuse, and violence for young women than public space. Yet
the enduring and reinforced veneration of the home and family in the
1930s meant that little attention was paid to these places as locations
of danger.

Toronto's working daughters took up pronouncements about the perils of public space in individually and culturally varied ways. Some young
women were as adventurous as their flapper predecessors; they were, like
Luella Luno, excited about the freedom of the city. For all but the most
destitute and strait-laced, wages provided young breadwinners with access to Toronto's movie houses, to cheap ready-made clothing, and to
the city's amusement parks. The economic constraints of the decade
meant that they made do with home entertainment like playing the
piano or listening to the gramophone or radio, but they still had a great
deal of fun. As in previous decades, religion was also crucial to sociability.
Church-based youth organizations offered cost-effective and respectable
sources of leisure for young working women. At young people's groups,
working girls met and made friends, danced, and went away on weekend
excursions. These groups were also an important source of identity and
fellowship.

When working girls foxtrotted their way across the city's dance floors,
enjoyed the spectacle of Hollywood movies, or strolled on the boardwalk
at Sunnyside Amusement Park they participated in a public leisure culture which was by the 1930s a permanent and acceptable fixture of
Toronto's urban space. Consequently, young women could and did find
ways to enjoy these entertainments without compromising their respectability or placing themselves in significant danger.

Breadwinning Daughters is about women such as Norma Vineham, Claire Clarke, Rose Edelist, and Helen Wilks: young, single wage earners for whom Depression-era Toronto offered both responsibility and delight. It draws most explicitly on women's memories to give breadth to a historiography dominated by the stories of men, the unemployed, and the powerful, and to permit us to enter the homes and workplaces of Toronto in ways that the documentary record does not allow. Without these recollections, I could neither have interpreted women's lives in the same manner nor considered their experiences as individuals and as a group. Of course, this study does not offer the final word on the Depression. It should represent the beginning of Depression-era studies that consider women, identity, and experience. There remains much to be done on issues of resistance and protest, domestic violence, and the stories of Aboriginal women and women of colour.

Notes

Introduction

1 Norma Vineham, interview with Katrina Srigley, Toronto, Ontario, 27 October 1997. Unless otherwise indicated, Katrina Srigley conducted all interviews.

2 Margaret Gairns, interview, Toronto, Ontario, 12 November 2002; Rose Edelist, interview, Toronto, Ontario, 23 January 2002; Claire Clarke, interview, Toronto, Ontario, 15 May 2001.

3 In Toronto between 1931 and 1941 the number of women fourteen years of age and over reported as being gainfully occupied rose by 21 per cent. Census, 1941, vol. VII, 1102. In 1931, 72 per cent of the city's female workers were between the ages of fifteen and thirty-five, and 84 per cent of them were single. Many women who were doing piecework from their homes, performing domestic work (inside and outside their homes), and helping with family businesses would have been missed during census counting, and it is, therefore, likely that statistics underestimate the extent of women's involvement in the labour market. Canada, Census, 1931, vol. VI, 22, 1172. These numbers, and all numbers in this study, should be perceived as estimates, particularly because the classification of data shifted from census to census.

4 The overwhelming majority of employed women worked in 'women's jobs' throughout these years. Of the 79,120 women reported as employed in 1931, 27 per cent worked in personal service, 28 per cent in clerical occupations, 17 per cent in manufacturing, and 12 per cent in professional service occupations such as teaching and nursing. Census, 1931, vol. VII, 226–37. By 1941, despite the onset of the war and the movement of women into non-traditional occupations, little had changed; 84 per cent of employed

women were involved in these sectors of the labour market. Canada, Census, 1941, vol. VII, 218–20. This presents yet another challenge to theories about women as a 'reserve army of labour.' In 1976, Ruth Milkman questioned this theory with her study of the 1930s,'Women's Work and the Economic Crisis: Some Lessons of the Great Depression,' *Radical Review of Political Economics* 8, 71 (1976): 71–97; *Gender at Work: The Dynamics of Job Segregation during World War Two* (Urbana: University of Illinois Press, 1987).

5 Alice Kessler-Harris, *Out to Work: A History of Wage-Earning Women in the United States*, 20th anniversary ed. (New York: Oxford University Press, 2003), 251.

6 I completed 54 interviews with women, 29 interviews with men, and listened to 29 interviews drawn from other collections. The majority of the women interviewed for this study were between the ages of 15 and 25, single, and living with their parents during the 1930s. In keeping with demographic patterns prevalent in Toronto at the time, 64 per cent of interviewees were white and of British ancestry, while 36 per cent were from the city's smaller Italian, Jewish, West-Indian, and African-Canadian communities. I contacted interviewees through retirement homes in Toronto and area. I hung posters in these facilities. Activity directors helped me set up meetings or schedule information sessions where I spoke about my project and met potential participants. I also placed advertisements in local and national newspapers, church and community bulletins. Interview questions addressed experiences of family, schooling, neighbourhood, wage earning, leisure, and danger. Participants responded on biographical information sheets and in conversations recorded by tape. Most interviews lasted between 1½ and 3 hours. Some included multiple visits. In all cases, interviewees had the option to remain anonymous. When confidentiality was desired, I have used different names.

7 Mrinalina Sinha, 'Mapping the Imperial Social Formation: A Modest Proposal for Feminist History,' *Signs* 25, 4 (Summer 2000): 1077; Kerry Abel, *Changing Places: History, Community, and Identity in Northeastern Ontario* (Montreal and Kingston: McGill-Queen's University Press, 2006), xxii–xxiii; Kathleen Canning, 'Gender History, Meanings, and Metanarratives,' in *Gender History and Practice: Historical Perspectives on Bodies, Class, and Citizenship* (Ithaca and London: Cornell University Press, 2006), 21. See also Elizabeth Thompson, 'Public and Private in Middle-Eastern Women's History,' *Journal of Women's History* 15, 1 (Spring 2003): 52–68.

8 Karen Hagemann, *Frauenalltag und Männerpolitik: Alltagsleben und gesellschaftliches Handeln von Arbeiterfrauen in der Weimarer Republik* (Bonn: Verlag J.H.W. Dietz Nachf., 1990); Franca Iacovetta, *Such Hardworking People: Italian*

Immigrants in Postwar Toronto (Montreal and Kingston: McGill-Queen's University Press, 1992); Selina Todd, *Young Women, Work, and Family in England, 1918–1950* (London: Oxford University Press, 2005).

9 See Barry Broadfoot, *Ten Lost Years: Memories of Canadians Who Survived the Depression* (Toronto: Doubleday, 1973).

10 Denise Baillargeon, *Making Do: Women, Family and Home in Montreal during the Great Depression*, trans. Yvonne Klein (Waterloo, ON: Wilfred Laurier University Press, 1999); *Ménagères au temps de la crise* (Montreal: Éditions de Remue-Ménage, 1991); 'If You Had No Money, You Had No Trouble, Did You?' Montreal Working-Class Housewives during the Great Depression,' in Wendy Mitchinson et al., eds, *Canadian Women: A Reader* (Toronto: Harcourt Brace, 1996), 251–68; 'Beyond Romance: Courtship and Marriage in Montréal between the Wars,' in Veronica Strong-Boag, Adele Perry, and Mona Gleason, eds, *Rethinking Canada: The Promise of Women's History*, 4th ed. (Toronto: University of Toronto Press, 2002), 203–20; Patricia Bird, 'Hamilton Working Women in the Period of the Great Depression,' *Atlantis* 8, 2 (1982): 125–36; Christina Bye, 'I Like to Hoe My Own Row: A Saskatchewan Farm Woman's Notions about Work and Womanhood during the Great Depression,' *Frontiers* 26, 3 (2005): 135–67; Lara Campbell, 'Respectable Citizens of Canada: Gender, Family, and Unemployment in The Great Depression, Ontario' (PhD dissertation, Queen's University, 2002); Margaret Hobbs, 'Gendering Work and Welfare: Women's Relationships to Wage-Work and Social Policy during the Great Depression' (PhD dissertation, University of Toronto, 1995); Hobbs, 'Equality and Difference: Feminism and the Defence of Women Workers during the Great Depression,' *Labour/Le Travail* 32 (Fall 1993), 201–23; Katrina Srigley, 'In Case You Hadn't Noticed!? Race, Ethnicity and Women's Wage-Earning in a Depression-Era City,' *Labour/Le Travail* 55 (Spring 2005): 69–105; 'Clothing Stories: Consumption, Identity, and Desire in Depression-Era Toronto,' *Journal of Women's History* 19, 1 (2007): 82–104; 'Stories of Strife?: Memories of the Great Depression,' *Oral History Forum*, forthcoming.

11 Lorne Brown, *When Freedom Was Lost: The Unemployed, the Agitator and the State* (Montreal-Buffalo: Black Rose Books, 1987); L.M. Grayson and Michael Bliss, *The Wretched of Canada: Letters to R.B. Bennett, 1930–1935* (Toronto: University of Toronto Press, 1971); Michiel Horn, *The Dirty Thirties: Canadians in the Great Depression* (Toronto: Copp Clark, 1972); *The Great Depression of the 1930s in Canada* (Ottawa: Canadian Historical Association Booklet #39, 1984); Ronald Liversedge, *Recollections of the On to Ottawa Trek*, ed. Victor Hoar (Toronto: McClelland and Stewart, 1973); Wayne Roberts, 'Hobos and Songsters: Working-Class Culture,' *Oral History Forum/Forum*

d'histoire orale 7 (1984): 24–7; John Thompson and Allen Seager, *Canada 1922–1939: Decades of Discord* (Toronto: McClelland and Stewart, 1985), 175–6.

12　Margaret Hillyard-Little, *No Car, No Radio, No Liquor Permit: The Moral Regulation of Single Mothers in Ontario, 1920–1997* (Toronto: Oxford University Press, 1998); James Struthers, *The Limits of Affluence: Welfare in Ontario, 1920–1970* (Toronto: University of Toronto Press, 1994); Struthers, *No Fault of Their Own: Unemployment and the Canadian Welfare State, 1914–1941* (Toronto: University of Toronto Press, 1983). See also Nancy Christie, *Engendering the State: Family, Work, and Welfare in Canada* (Toronto: University of Toronto Press, 2000); Dorothy Chunn, *From Punishment to Doing Good: Family Courts and Socialized Justice in Ontario, 1880–1940* (Toronto: University of Toronto Press, 1992); Alvin Finkel, *Business and Social Reform in the Thirties* (Toronto: James Lorimer, 1979).

13　Veronica Strong-Boag, *The New Day Recalled: Lives of Girls and Women in English Canada, 1919–1939* (Toronto: Copp Clark Pitman, 1988); Susan Porter-Benson, *Household Accounts: Working-Class Family Economies in the United States* (New York: Cornell University Press, 2007); Tamara Myers, *Caught: Montreal's Modern Girls and the Law, 1869–1945* (Toronto: University of Toronto Press, 2006).

14　Paul Thompson, *The Voice of the Past: Oral History*, 2nd ed. (Oxford: Oxford University Press, 1988), 2.

15　Dionne Brand, *No Burden to Carry: Narratives of Black Working Women in Ontario, 1920s–1950s* (Toronto: Women's Press, 1991); Marlene Epp, *Women without Men: Mennonite Refugees of the Second World War* (Toronto: University of Toronto Press, 2000); Ruth Frager, *Sweatshop Strife: Class, Ethnicity, and Gender in the Jewish Labour Movement of Toronto, 1900–1939* (Toronto: University of Toronto Press, 1993); Jan Gross, *Neighbours: The Destruction of the Jewish Community in Jedwabne, Poland* (Princeton: Princeton University Press, 2001); Iacovetta, *Such Hardworking People*; Varpu Lindstrom, *Defiant Sisters: A Social History of Finnish Women in Canada, 1890–1930* (Toronto: Multicultural History Society of Ontario, 1988); Thomas Klubock, 'History and Memory in Neoliberal Chile: Patricio Guzman's Obstinate Memory and the Battle of Chile,' *Radical History Review* 85 (2003): 272–82; Kristina R. Llewellyn, 'Productive Tensions: Feminist Readings for Women Teachers' Oral Histories,' *Oral History Forum/Forum d'histoire orale* 23 (2003): 89–112; Joan Sangster, 'Telling Our Stories: Feminist Debates and the Use of Oral History,' in Robert Perks and Alistair Thomson, eds, *The Oral History Reader* (New York: Routledge, 1998), 87–100.

16 Franca Iacovetta, 'Gendering Trans/National Historiographies: Feminists Rewriting Canadian History,' *Journal of Women's History* 19, 1 (Spring 2007): 210.

17 In 1931, Toronto's population was 631,207, and its five largest racial and ethnic groupings included 510,432 citizens of British heritage, 13,015 Italians, 45,305 Hebrews, 10,869 French, and 9343 Germans. Groups such as the Polish and the Dutch numbered between 5000 and 9000, while African Canadians, Russians, Greeks, and Ukrainians registered between 1000 and 5000 in the decennial census for the 1930s. Census, 1931, vol. IV, 912–13; Census, 1941, vol. IV, 156.

18 Patricia Hill-Collins, *Black Feminist Thought, Knowledge, Consciousness, and the Politics of Empowerment* (Boston: Unwin Hyman, 1990).

19 Jennifer Brown, *Strangers in Blood: Fur Trade Company Families in Indian Country* (Vancouver: University of British Columbia Press, 1980); Sylvia Van Kirk, *Many Tender Ties: Women in Fur Trade Society in Western Canada, 1670–1870* (Winnipeg: Watson and Dwyer, 1980).

20 See Hobbs, 'Gendering Work and Welfare'; 'Equality and Difference'; Linda Kealey, *Enlisting Women for the Cause: Women, Labour, and the Left in Canada, 1890–1920* (Toronto: University of Toronto Press, 1998); Kealey, ed., *A Not Unreasonable Claim: Women and Reform in Canada, 1890–1920* (Toronto: Canadian Women's Educational Press, 1979); Kealey and Joan Sangster, *Beyond the Vote: Canadian Women and Politics* (Toronto: University of Toronto Press, 1989); Meg Luxton, *More Than a Labour of Love* (Toronto: Women's Press, 1980); Margaret McCallum, 'Keeping Women in Their Place: The Minimum Wage in Canada, 1910–1925,' *Labour/Le Travail* 17 (1986), 29–56; Joan Sangster, 'The 1907 Bell Telephone Strike: Organizing Women Workers,' *Labour/Le Travail* 3 (1978), 109–30; *Dreams of Equality: Women and the Canadian Left, 1920–1950* (Toronto: McClelland and Stewart, 1989); *Earning Respect: The Lives of Working Women in Small Town Ontario, 1920–1960* (Toronto: University of Toronto Press, 1995).

21 Bettina Bradbury, *Working Families: Age, Gender, and Daily Survival in Industrializing Montreal* (Oxford: Oxford University Press, 1993); Brand, *No Burden To Carry*; Frager, *Sweatshop Strife*; Lindstrom, *Defiant Sisters*; Iacovetta, *Such Hardworking People*; Joy Parr, *The Gender of Breadwinners: Women, Men, and Change in Two Industrial Towns, 1880–1950* (Toronto: University of Toronto Press, 1990); Carolyn Strange, *Toronto's Girl Problem: The Perils and Pleasures of the City, 1880–1930* (Toronto: University of Toronto Press, 1995).

22 See Julie Guard, 'Authenticity on the Line: Women Workers, Native "Scabs," and the Multi-Ethnic Politics of Identity in a Left-Led Strike in Cold War

Canada,' *Journal of Women's History* 15, 4 (Winter 2004), 117–40; Franca
Iacovetta and Donna Gabaccia, *Women, Gender, and Transnational Lives:
Italian Workers of the World* (Toronto: University of Toronto Press, 2002);
Iacovetta, 'Feminist Transnational Labour History'; Donna Gabaccia, Franca
Iacovetta, and Fraser Ottanelli, 'Labouring across National Borders: Class,
Gender and Militancy in the Proletarian Mass Migration,' *International Labor
and Working Class History*, 66 (2004), 57–77.

23 Anne McClintock, *Imperial Leather: Race, Gender and Sexuality in the Colonial
Contest* (New York: Routledge, 1995), 5. For some Canadian scholarship that
has engaged with questions of race see Constance Backhouse, *Colour Coded:
A Legal History of Racism in Canada, 1900–1950* (Toronto: University of
Toronto Press, 1999); Carl E. James, *Seeing Ourselves: Exploring Ethnicity, Race
and Culture*, 3rd ed. (Toronto: Thomson Educational, 2003); Carl E. James
and Adrienne Shadd, eds, *Talking about Identity: Encounters in Race, Ethnicity,
and Language* (Toronto: Between the Lines, 2001); Carl E. James,
Experiencing Difference (Halifax: Fernwood, 2000); Adele Perry, *On the Edge of
Empire: Gender, Race, and the Making of British Columbia, 1849–1871* (Toronto:
University of Toronto Press, 2001); Sherene Razack, *Looking White People in
the Eye: Gender, Race, and Culture in Courtrooms and Classrooms* (Toronto:
University of Toronto Press, 1998); Elizabeth Vibert, 'Real Men Hunt
Buffalo: Masculinity, Race and Class in British Fur Traders' Narratives,'
Gender and History 8, 1 (1996): 4–21.

24 Ann Stoler quoted in Catherine Hall and Sonya Rose, eds, *At Home with the
Empire: Metropolitan Culture and the Imperial World* (Cambridge: Cambridge
University Press, 2006), 20, 22.

25 ·For an excellent review of shifts in the field of oral history see Alistair
Thomson, 'Four Paradigm Transformations in Oral History,' *Oral History
Review* 34, 1 (2007): 49–71. On memory see, for instance: Susan A. Crane,
'Writing the Individual Back into Collective Memory,' *American Historical
Review* 102, 5 (December 1997): 1372–85; Julie Cruikshank, *Life Lived Like a
Story: Life Stories of Three Yukon Native Elders* (Vancouver: University of British
Columbia Press, 1990); *The Social Life of Stories: Narrative and Knowledge in
Yukon Territory* (Lincoln: University of Nebraska Press, 1998); Paula Draper,
'Surviving Their Survival: Women, Memory and the Holocaust,' in Epp,
Iacovetta, and Swyripa, eds, *Sisters or Strangers? Immigrant, Ethnic and
Racialized Women in Canadian History* (Toronto: University of Toronto Press,
2004), 399–414; Epp, *Women without Men;* Maurice Halbwachs, *The Collective
Memory*, trans. Francis J. Ditter, Jr, and Vida Yazdi Ditter (New York: Harper

and Row, 1980); *On Collective Memory*, trans. Lewis A. Coser (Chicago: University of Chicago Press, 1992); Pierre Nora, 'Between Memory and History: Les Lieux de Mémoire,' *Representations* 26 (Spring 1989): 7–24; Luisa Passerini, *Fascism in Popular Memory: The Cultural Experience of the Turin Working Class* (Cambridge: Cambridge University Press, 1987); Passerini, 'Mythbiography in Oral History,' in Raphael Samuel and Paul Thompson, eds, *The Myths We Live By* (London: Routledge, 1990): 49–60; Passerini, 'Work Ideology and Consensus under Italian Fascism,' in Robert Perks and Alistair Thomson, eds, *The Oral History Reader* (New York: Routledge, 2000); Alessandro Portelli, *The Death of Luigi Trastulli, and Others Stories: Form and Meaning in Oral History* (New York: State University of New York Press, 1991); *The Battle of Valle Giulia: Oral History and the Art of Dialogue* (Madison: University of Wisconsin Press, 1997); *The Order Has Been Carried Out: History, Memory, and Meaning of a Nazi Massacre in Rome* (New York: Palgrave Macmillan, 2003); Roy Rosenzweig and David Thelen, *The Presence of the Past: Popular Uses of History in American Life* (New York: Columbia University Press, 1998).

26 Detailed field notes recorded before, during, and after the interview that reflect upon the interview context are the best method for considering the shared process of memory generation. See Sherna Berger Gluck and Daphne Patai, *Women's Words: The Feminist Practice of Oral History* (New York: Routledge, 1991); Robert Georges and Michael Owen Jones, *People Studying People: The Human Element in Fieldwork* (Berkeley and Los Angeles: University of California Press, 1980); Trevor Lummis, *Listening to History: The Authenticity of Oral Evidence* (London: Hutchinson, 1987); Donald Ritchie, *Doing Oral History: A Practical Guide*, 2nd ed. (New York: Oxford University Press, 2003); Thompson, *The Voice of the Past*; Valerie Raleigh Yow, *Recording Oral History: A Guide for the Humanities and Social Sciences* (New York: Altamira Press, 2005).

27 Fred Allison, 'Remembering a Vietnam War Firefight: Changing Perspectives over Time,' *Oral History Review* 31, 2 (2004): 69–83.

28 Joanna Bornat, 'Oral History as a Social Movement: Reminiscences and Older People,' in Robert Perks and Alistair Thomson, eds, *The Oral History Reader* (New York: Routledge, 1998), 201; Thompson, *The Voice of the Past*, 59.

29 Enrico Cumbo, '"As the twig is bent, the tree's inclined": Growing Up Italian in Toronto, 1905–1940' (PhD dissertation, University of Toronto, 1996).

30 Toronto's unemployment rate was 16.7 per cent in 1931 compared with the national average of 18.87 per cent. In comparison, Hamilton's unemployment rate was just over 20 per cent in 1931. Census, 1931, vol. VI, 1268.

31 In 1931, the average cost for rent, fuel, food, and lighting was $900 per year. In Toronto during the same year the average male wage earner brought home $1262 and the average female wage earner $728. 'Prices in Canada and Other Countries,' *Labour Gazette* (Ottawa 1933), 6–7; Census, 1931, vol. V, 25.

32 The Royal York Hotel, Maple Leaf Gardens, Eaton's College Street, and the Customs Building near the harbour were finished by 1932 and there was no other major building until the war years. James Lemon, *Toronto since 1918: An Illustrated History* (Toronto: James Lorimer, 1985), 60, 76.

33 Ethel Bird, interview, Toronto, Ontario, 26 February 2002; Agnes Marks, interview, Toronto, Ontario, 11 December 2001.

34 Audrey Macmillan, interview, Barrie, Ontario, 7 February 2002.

35 In 1930 Bennett introduced the Unemployment Relief Act. This earmarked $20 million for unemployment relief. However, four-fifths of this money was to be used to expand work projects not for direct relief. Even this amount, which was considered substantial in 1930, was not nearly sufficient to cover the needs of Torontonians. Pierre Berton, *The Great Depression, 1929–1939* (Toronto: McClelland and Stewart, 1990), 58, 76.

36 Harry Cassidy's study on unemployment, published in 1933, claimed that relief should be provided but only in a way that a man's dignity could be maintained. This meant that relief recipients should not simply be given charity. See Harry Cassidy, *Unemployment and Relief in Ontario, 1929–1932* (Toronto: J.M. Dent, 1933); Lemon, *Toronto since 1918,* 60.

37 Marks, interview. For more on the demoralizing experience of visiting the House of Industry see Arthur Lendrum, 'On Relief,' *Maclean's,* 1 April 1933, 9, 41. See also Hugh Garner, *Cabbagetown* (Toronto: McGraw-Hill Ryerson, 1968), 69–71; Hillyard-Little, *No Car, No Radio, No Liquor Permit.*

38 Marcus Klee, 'Between the Scylla and Charybdis of Anarchy and Despotism: The State, Capital, and the Working Class in the Great Depression, Toronto, 1929–1940' (PhD dissertation, Queen's University, 1998), 57, 69. Interestingly, Klee notes that though relief recipients received inadequate food and rental relief, unlike the working poor they did have access to adequate medical services.

1: Young Working Women in a Depression-Era World

1 See, for example, Nan Enstad, *Ladies of Labor, Girls of Adventure: Working Women, Popular Culture, and Labor Politics at the Turn of the Twentieth Century*

(New York: Columbia University Press, 1999); Kathy Peiss, *Cheap Amusements: Working Women and Leisure in Turn-of-the-Century New York* (Philadelphia: Temple University Press, 1986); Joanne Meyerowitz, *Women Adrift: Independent Wage Earners in Chicago, 1880–1930* (Chicago: University of Chicago Press, 1988); Ruth Milkman, *Women, Work and Protest: A Century of Women's Labor History* (Boston: Routledge and Kegan Paul, 1985); Carolyn Strange, *Toronto's Girl Problem: The Perils and Pleasures of the City, 1880–1930* (Toronto: University of Toronto Press, 1995); Martha Vicinus, *Independent Women: Work and Community for Single Women, 1850–1920* (London: Routledge, 1985).

2 Veronica Strong-Boag, *The New Day Recalled: Lives of Girls and Women in English Canada, 1919–1939* (Toronto: Copp Clark Pitman, 1988).

3 See for example: Tamara Myers, *Caught: Montreal's Modern Girls and the Law, 1869–1945* (Toronto: University of Toronto Press, 2006); Joy Parr, *The Gender of Breadwinners: Women, Men, and Change in Two Industrial Towns, 1880–1950* (Toronto: University of Toronto Press, 1990); Susan Porter-Benson, *Household Accounts: Working-Class Family Economies in the United States* (New York: Cornell University Press, 2007); Joan Sangster, *Regulating Girls and Women: Sexuality, Family, and the Law in Ontario, 1920–1960* (Toronto: Oxford University Press, 2001); Sangster, *Earning Respect: The Lives of Working Women in Small Town Ontario, 1920–1960* (Toronto: University of Toronto Press, 1995); Strong-Boag, *New Day Recalled*; Selina Todd, *Young Women, Work, and Family in England, 1918–1950* (London: Oxford University Press, 2005).

4 Census, 1931, vol. XIII, 491. Between 1921 and 1941 the numerical discrepancy between the sexes in urban centres widened from just over 20,000 to nearly 26,000. Census, 1941, vol. II, 231. See also Census, 1931, vol. XIII, 77; Census, 1931, vol. I, 384; Census, 1941, vol. I, 432–3, 436.

5 Marion Forsythe, interview, Toronto, Ontario, 13 March 2002; Luella Luno, interview, Stroud, Ontario, 23 February 2001.

6 Cynthia Comacchio, 'History of Us: Social Science, History, and the Relations of Family in Canada,' *Labour/Le Travail* 46 (Fall 2000), 167; Chunn, *From Punishment to Doing Good*, 36. Linda Gordon also draws a direct connection between the Depression and increasing fears about the collapse of the 'conventional' family. *Heroes of Their Own Lives: The Politics and History of Family Violence, Boston 1880–1960* (New York: Penguin, 1988), 22.

7 Forsythe, interview.

8 Richard Dennis: 'Apartment Housing in Canada, 1900–1940,' *Urban History Review* 26, 2 (March 1998), 17; '"Zoning" before Zoning: The Regulation of Apartment Housing in Early Twentieth Century Winnipeg and Toronto,'

Planning Perspectives 15 (2000), 268; 'Morley Callaghan and the Moral Geography of Toronto,' *British Journal of Canadian Studies* 14, 1 (1999): 35–51; 'Territorial Maneuvers: Space and Place in Canadian Cities,' *International Journal of Canadian Studies* 24 (2001): 217–26.

9 Strong-Boag, *New Day Recalled*, 13; Census, 1931, vol. XIII, 158. As Suzanne Morton points out in her article on Halifax, in the interwar years particularly, perceptions about what marriage meant for the roles of men and women crossed class boundaries. Suzanne Morton, 'The June Bride as the Working-Class Bride: Getting Married in a Halifax Working-Class Neighbourhood in the 1920s,' in Bettina Bradbury, ed., *Canadian Family History*, 2nd ed. (Toronto: Irwin, 2000), 360–79.

10 Alice Kessler-Harris, 'Gender Ideology in Historical Reconstruction: A Case Study from the 1930s,' *Gender and History* 1, 1 (Spring 1989): 31–49; Margaret Hobbs, 'Rethinking Antifeminism in the 1930s: Gender Crisis or Workplace Justice? A Response to Alice Kessler-Harris,' *Gender and History* 5, 1 (Spring 1993): 4–15; Alice Kessler-Harris, 'Reply to Hobbs,' *Gender and History* 5, 1 (Spring 1993), 16–19. See also Margaret Hobbs, 'Gendering Work and Welfare: Women's Relationships to Wage-Work and Social Policy during the Great Depression' (PhD dissertation, University of Toronto, 1995); Lois Scharf, *To Work and to Wed: Female Employment, Feminism, and the Great Depression* (Westport, CT: Greenwood Press, 1980).

11 *Evening Telegram*, 9 November 1935, 12; 19 February 1936, 4. .

12 *Toronto Daily Star*, 20 March 1939, 23.

13 Merderic Martin, 'Go Home Young Women,' *Chatelaine*, September 1933, 10.

14 Cited in Ruth Frager, *Sweatshop Strife: Class, Ethnicity, and Gender in the Jewish Labour Movement of Toronto, 1900–1939* (Toronto: University of Toronto Press, 1993), 113.

15 Edward Mann, interview, Richmond Hill, Ontario, 21 March 2002; See also Edward Mann, *A Mann for All Seasons: A Memoir* (Toronto: Lugus, 1996). The CCF, formed in 1933, was a national social democratic party 'dedicated to "eradicating capitalism" by gradual reforms and constitutional methods.' Craig Heron, *The Canadian Labour Movement: A Short History*, 2nd ed. (Toronto: James Lorimer, 1996), 67–8.

16 Alison Prentice et al., *Canadian Women: A History* (Toronto: Harcourt Brace, 1996), 205.

17 Dorothy Livesay, *Right Hand Life Hand: A True Life of the Thirties: Paris, Toronto, Montreal, the West and Vancouver. Love Politics, the Depression and Feminism* (Toronto: Porcepic, 1977), 115.

18 Census, 1931, vol. XIII, 18.

19 Archives of Ontario (OA), RG7-12-0-320, Miss Lavyne Bast to Premier
    Hepburn, 8 May 1935; OA, RG7-12-0-383.1, Miss Asselin, Renfrew to Hon.
    David Croll, Minister of Labour, 7 January 1936. Cited in Christie,
    Engendering the State, 207.
20 *Evening Telegram*, 12 December 1929, 6.
21 Wilfred Wood, interview, Toronto, Ontario, 27 November 2001.
22 Ontario Archives (OA), Anne Hinsta, interview, Wayne Roberts' Collection,
    Ontario Archives Sound Room, 1972.
23 Helen Campbell, interview, Toronto, Ontario, 14 July 1997.
24 In her study of socialist women Linda Kealey finds a similar pattern of
    support for the domestic roles of women. See Linda Kealey, 'Canadian
    Socialism and the Woman Question, 1900–1914,' *Labour/Le Travail* 13
    (Spring 1984): 77–100; Linda Kealey, *Enlisting Women for the Cause: Women,
    Labour, and the Left in Canada, 1890–1920* (Toronto: University of Toronto
    Press, 1998). For the British context see Pamela Graves, *Labour Women:
    Women in British Working-Class Politics, 1918–1939* (Cambridge: Cambridge
    University Press, 1994).
25 Audrey Macmillan, interview, Barrie, Ontario, 7 February 2002.
26 Ivy Phillips, interview, Toronto, Ontario, 22 March 2002.
27 Mary Macnamara, interview, Maple, Ontario, 15 December 2001.
28 Thelma Plunkett, interview, Toronto, Ontario, 3 November 1997.
29 Barbara Burman and Carole Turbin, eds, *Material Strategies: Dress and Gender
    in Historical Perspective* (Oxford: Blackwell, 2003), 5. See also Joanne Eicher,
    ed., *Dress and Ethnicity* (Oxford: Berg, 1995); Carroll Smith-Rosenberg, 'The
    New Woman as Androgyne: Sexual Disorder and Gender Crisis, 1870–1936,'
    in *Disorderly Conduct: Visions of Gender in Victorian America* (New York: Oxford
    University Press, 1985), 245–96; Mariana Valverde, 'The Love of Finery:
    Fashion and the Fallen Woman in Nineteenth-Century Social Discourse,'
    Victorian Studies 32, 2 (Winter 1989), 169–88.
30 Vineham, interview.
31 Chris Cotter, *Toronto between the Wars: Life in the City, 1919–1939* (Toronto:
    Firefly, 2004), 65; Alison Lurie, *The Language of Clothes* (Toronto: Random
    House, 1981), 77–8.
32 *Evening Telegram*, 8 January 1932, 10.
33 *Evening Telegram*, 1 May 1936, 10.
34 *Evening Telegram*, 10 May 1935, 11.
35 *Evening Telegram*, 2 January 1931, 10.
36 Claire Clarke, interview, Toronto, Ontario, 2000; 2006.
37 Macmillan, interview.
38 Mabel Duncan, interview, Toronto, Ontario, 23 November 2001.

39 Cynthia Wright, '"Feminine Trifles of Vast Importance": Writing Gender into the History of Consumption,' in Franca Iacovetta and Mariana Valverde, eds, *Gender Conflicts: New Essays in Women's History* (Toronto: University of Toronto Press, 1992), 232.

40 Jane Gaskell, 'Education and Job Opportunities for Women: Patterns of Enrolment and Economic Returns,' in Naomi Hersom and Dorothy Smith, eds, *Women and the Canadian Labour Force* (Ottawa: Social Science and Humanities Research Council, 1982), 295; Canada, Dominion Bureau of Statistics, *Annual Survey of Education* (Ottawa 1930), ix. For more on schooling regulations in Ontario see Canada, Census, 1921, vol. II, xx. The situation was worse for francophone women in Quebec. See Clio Collective, *Quebec Women: A History*, trans. Roger Gannon and Rosalind Gill (Toronto: The Women's Press, 1987), 241–2.

41 On women, gender, and education see Alison Prentice, *The History of Women and Education in Canada* (Toronto: Canadian Scholar's Press, 1992); Ruby Heap and Alison Prentice, *Gender and Education in Ontario: An Historical Reader* (Toronto: Canadian Scholar's Press, 1991).

42 Veronica Strong-Boag, *Janey Canuck: Women in Canada, 1919–1939* (Ottawa: Canadian Historical Association, 1994), 5; Craig Heron, 'The High School and the Household Economy in Working-Class Hamilton, 1890–1940,' *Historical Studies in Education* 7, 2 (1995): 217–59. In 1931, 98 per cent of 10–14-year-old boys attended school while only 47 per cent of 15–19-year-olds attended. Census, 1931, vol. III, 906–907. In 1921, school attendance dropped from 92 per cent (girls and boys) for 10–14-year-olds to 28 per cent for girls and 24 per cent for boys. Census, 1921, vol. II, 698. In 1941, the pattern was similar to that of 1931 with a drop from 98 per cent attendance to 45 per cent attendance for girls and 47 per cent attendance for boys aged 15–19. Census, 1941, vol. III, 679.

43 Vineham, interview.

44 Phillips, interview.

45 Helen Wilks, interview, Toronto, Ontario, 31 May 2000.

46 Claire Clarke, interview, Toronto, Ontario, 15 May 2001.

47 Statistics Canada, *Selected Marriage Statistics, 1921–1990* (Ottawa, 1992), 10. The majority of women in Toronto were unmarried. Census, 1931, vol. II, 292. This was also the case in 1941. Census, 1941, vol. III, 120; In Toronto weddings declined substantially over the thirties and were particularly low during the worst years of the Depression. Ontario, *Sessional Papers*, 1929–1939.

48 Ethel Bird, interview, Toronto, Ontario, 26 February 2002.

49 Alice Chrysler, interview, Toronto, Ontario, 23 May 2002.

50 Margaret and Bill Lawson, interview, Toronto, Ontario, 18 November 1999.
51 Bill Pearson with Margie Pearson, interview, Toronto, Ontario, 14 March 2002.
52 Strong-Boag, *New Day Recalled*, 46.
53 Kathryn McPherson, *Bedside Matters: The Transformation of Canadian Nursing, 1900–1990* (Toronto: Oxford University Press, 1996). See also Deborah Gorham, *Caring and Curing: Historical Perspectives on Women and Healing in Canada* (Ottawa: Ottawa University Press, 1994); Diana Mansell, *Forging the Future: A History of Nursing in Canada* (Ann Arbor, MI: Thomas Press, 2004); Susan Reverby, *Ordered to Care: The Dilemma of American Nursing, 1850–1945* (New York: Cambridge University Press, 1987).
54 Elizabeth Gammon, interview, Toronto, Ontario, 11 December 2001.
55 Strong-Boag, *New Day Recalled*, 103.
56 Nan Robins, 'I Would Rather Have Beauty Than Brains,' *Chatelaine*, February 1931, 3.
57 Connie Lancaster, interview, Toronto, Ontario, 11 March 2002.
58 Forsythe, interview.
59 Nora Windeatt, interview, Reading, Pennsylvania, 3 June 1997.
60 Norma Hall, interview, Toronto, Ontario, 3 December 1998.
61 Alice H. Parsons,'Careers or Marriage?' *Canadian Home Journal* (June 1938), 63. Cited in Strong-Boag, *New Day Recalled*, 13.

2: Breadwinning Girls and Substitute Mothers: Negotiating Family Responsibilities

1 Vineham, interview, 1997.
2 Census, 1931, vol. XII, 48–50; Census, 1931, vol. V, 990; Census, 1931, vol. V, 1355; Census, 1941, vol. I, 873.
3 Emphasis on the relationship between mothers and their children was particularly strong in scientific and medical discourse during the 1930s. For more on this see Katherine Arnup, *Education for Motherhood: Advice for Mothers in Twentieth-Century Canada* (Toronto: University of Toronto Press, 1994); 'Raising the Dionne Quintuplets: Lessons for Modern Mothers,' *The Journal of Canadian Studies* 29 (1994–5): 65–85; Cynthia Comacchio, *Nations Are Built of Babies: Saving Ontario's Mothers and Children* (Montreal and Kingston: McGill-Queen's University Press, 1993); 'Another Brick in the Wall: Toward a History of the Welfare State in Canada,' *left history* 1, 1 (Spring 1993), 103–8; 'Beneath the Sentimental Veil: Families and Family History in Canada,' *Labour/Le Travail* 33 (Spring 1994): 279–302; 'A Postscript for Father: Defining a New Fatherhood in Interwar Canada,'

Canadian Historical Review 78, 3 (1997): 385–408; *Infinite Bonds of Family: Domesticity in Canada, 1890–1940* (Toronto: University of Toronto Press, 1999); Seth Koven and Sonya Michel, eds, *Mothers of a New World: Maternalist Politics and the Origins of Welfare States* (New York: Routledge, 1993).

4 Census, 1931, vol. XII, 104; Census, 1931, vol. V, 725–6. See also Heron, 'The High School and the Household Economy.'

5 Alice Kessler-Harris, *Out to Work: A History of Wage-Earning Women in the United States*, 20th anniversary ed. (New York: Oxford University Press, 2003), 252. See also Comacchio, 'Beneath the Sentimental Veil,' 279; Tania Das Gupta, 'Families of Native People, Immigrants, and People of Colour,' in Nancy Mandell and Ann Duffy, eds, *Canadian Families: Diversity, Conflict and Change* (Toronto: Harcourt Brace, 1995), 141–74; Enaskhi Dua, 'Beyond Diversity: Exploring the Ways in which the Discourse of Race Has Shaped the Institution of the Nuclear Family,' in Enakshi Dua, ed., *Scratching the Surface. Canadian Anti-Racist Feminist Thought* (Toronto: Women's Press, 1999), 237–60.

6 Citing the study conducted by the Social Service Council of Canada, one *Chatelaine* writer wondered whether family life was disintegrating. Byrne Hope Saunders, 'Is Family Life on the Wane?' *Chatelaine,* June 1930, 16. Toronto's Chief Constable Dennis Draper connected increasing youth crime to the disintegration of the family in his annual reports on crime in 1936 and 1938. City of Toronto Archives (CTA), Draper, *Annual Report,* 1936, 22; CTA, Draper, *Annual Report,* 1938, 27.

7 CTA, Draper, *Annual Report,* 1935, 22; See also *Toronto Daily Star,* 23 March 1938, 4.

8 CTA, Civic Unemployment Relief Committee, Report and Recommendations, City of Toronto, 38–9. See also Margaret Hobbs, 'Gendering Work and Welfare: Women's Relationships to Wage-Work and Social Policy during the Great Depression' (PhD dissertation, University of Toronto, 1995); Joan Sangster, *Regulating Girls and Women: Sexuality, Family, and the Law in Ontario, 1920–1960* (Toronto: Oxford University Press, 2001), 102.

9 *Hush,* 13 November 1930, 13; *Hush,* 16 December 1933, 2; *Hush,* 16 October 1930, 1, 5. Unlike scandal sheets today, *Hush* and its competitor *Jack Canuck,* while prone to rhetorical exaggeration, were dedicated to covering the news as it occurred in the courtrooms, on the streets, and in the homes of Canada's cities. Both papers have a decidedly working-class slant to their coverage of events, always anxious to champion the 'little' guy and dethrone big business. For more on these newspapers see Susan E. Houston, '"A little steam, a little sizzle and a little sleaze": English Language Tabloids in the Interwar Period,'

Papers of the Bibliographical Society of Canada 40, 1 (Spring 2002): 37–59; Frank Rasky, 'Canada's Scandalous Scandal Sheets,' *Liberty* 31, 9 (1954): 17–80; Carolyn Strange and Tina Loo, 'The Moral of the Story: Gender and Murder in Canadian True Crime Magazines of the 1940s,' in Margaret Thornton, ed., *Romancing the Tomes: Popular Culture, Law and Feminism* (London: Cavendish, 2002), 221–39; Strange and Loo, 'From Hewers of Wood to Producers of Pulp: True Crime in Canadian Pulp Magazines of the 1940s,' *Journal of Canadian Studies* 37, 2 (Summer 2002): 11–32.

10 Sangster, *Regulating Girls and Women*, 92.

11 Jennifer Stephen, 'Deploying Discourses of Employability and Domesticity: Women's Employment and Training Policies and the Formation of the Canadian Welfare State, 1935–1947' (PhD dissertation, University of Toronto, 2000), 126; *Pick One Intelligent Girl: Employability, Domesticity, and the Gendering of Canada's Welfare State, 1939–1947* (Toronto: University of Toronto Press, 2007).

12 As Bettina Bradbury has noted, decisions about secondary wage earners were 'never made in an ideological or economic vacuum, they represented a complex and often unconscious balance between basic need, existing ideology, and practise regarding gender roles, the structure of the economy, and the particularly economic conjuncture.' Bradbury, 'Gender at Work at Home: Family Decisions, the Labour Market and Girls' Contributions to the Family Income,' in Bradbury, ed., *Canadian Family History* (Toronto: Irwin, 2000), 178. See also Elizabeth Ewen, *Immigrant Women in the Land of Dollars: Life and Culture on the Lower East Side, 1890–1925* (New York: Monthly Review Press, 1985); Lesley Woodcock-Tentler, *Wage-Earning Women: Industrial Work and Family Life in the United States, 1900–1930* (Oxford: Oxford University Press, 1979).

13 Bradbury, 'Gender at Work,' 192.

14 With the exception of two families, everyone interviewed for this study who had brothers recalled that their brothers earned wages in this manner, or not at all. For more on the labour market advantages women enjoyed during the Depression see Kessler-Harris, 'Some Benefits of Labour Segregation in a Decade of Depression,' in *Out to Work*, 250–72.

15 Helen Gregory MacGill, 'The Jobless Woman,' *Chatelaine*, September 1930, 5.

16 Phillips, interview.

17 Census, 1931, vol. XII, 196. In 1931, this was the average yearly earning of conductors and motormen of streetcars in Ontario.

18 McLean and Cahill, interview, 2002. For an advertisement for and cost of the Durant and similar cars see *Toronto Daily Star*, 2 January 1931, 13; *Toronto*

Daily Star, 28 August 1931; *Toronto Daily Star*, 9 March 1933; *Toronto Daily Star*, 10 March 1933.

19 CTA, Dennis Draper, *Chief Constable's Annual Report* (Toronto: Carswell, 1938), 8. CTA, Draper, *Annual Report*, 1936, 9. Gambling was never totally outlawed in Ontario; this was due in part to class perspectives on what constituted improper behaviour. As Suzanne Morton points out, important class distinctions sanctioned daytime betting at the Queen's Plate or the Ontario Jockey Club while censuring working man's betting done in the evening through bookies or at bingo parlors. Crackdowns on gambling were also characteristic of other Canadian cities during the Depression. In 1931, Vancouver had an increase in prosecutions against sweepstake holders. In 1938 indictments increased in Halifax, and in 1935 Quebec's Premier Taschereau demanded that police crack down on gambling houses and that people convicted should receive jail time not just the usual fines. Suzanne Morton, *At Odds: Gambling and Canadians, 1919–1969* (Toronto: University of Toronto Press, 2003), 10–12.

20 Margaret Lawson and Bill Lawson, interview, Toronto, Ontario, 18 November 1999. Mr Lawson recalled children grabbing pieces of coal that fell from the trains.

21 Lara Campbell, 'Respectable Citizens of Canada: Gender, Family, and Unemployment in The Great Depression, Ontario' (PhD dissertation, Queen's University, 2002), 199–204. For a fictional version of this situation see Hugh Garner, *Cabbagetown* (Toronto: McGraw-Hill Ryerson, 1968), 84–6. See also John Bullen, 'Hidden Workers: Child Labour and the Family Economy in Late Nineteenth-Century Urban Ontario,' in Bettina Bradbury ed., *Canadian Family History*, 2nd ed. (Toronto: Irwin, 2000), 199–219; Ellen Ross, *Love and Toil: Motherhood in Outcast London, 1870–1918* (Oxford: Oxford University Press, 1993).

22 McLean and Cahill, interview; Phillips, interview.

23 Phillips, interview.

24 McLean and Cahill, interview.

25 McLean and Cahill, interview.

26 Clarke, interview, 2001.

27 The Depression virtually halted immigration to Canada for families such as the Edelists. In fact, immigration to Canada fell by nearly 60 per cent between 1930 and 1931, reaching its lowest point in 1935. Donald Avery, *Reluctant Host: Canada's Response to Immigrant Workers, 1896–1994* (Toronto: McClelland and Stewart, 1985), 11. For more on these issues see Irving Abella and Harold Troper, *None Is Too Many: Canada and the Jews of Europe, 1933–1948* (Toronto: Key Porter Books, 2000); Irving Abella, *A Coat of Many*

Colours: Two Centuries of Jewish Life in Canada (Toronto: Key Porter Books,
1999); Pierre Berton, *The Great Depression, 1929–1939* (Toronto: McClelland
and Stewart, 1990), 138–42; Lita-Rose Betcherman, *The Swastika and the
Maple Leaf: Fascist Movements in Canada in the Thirties* (Toronto: Fitzhenry
and Whiteside, 1975); Franca Iacovetta, Roberto Perin, and Angelo
Principe, *Enemies Within: Italian and Other Internees in Canada and Abroad*
(Toronto: University of Toronto Press, 2000); Barbara Roberts, *Whence They
Came: Deportation from Canada, 1900–1935* (Ottawa: University of Ottawa
Press, 1988); Martin Robin, *Shades of Right: Nativist and Fascist Politics in
Canada, 1920–1940* (Toronto: University of Toronto Press, 1991). Charlotte
Whitton is a particularly apt example of such a government official. See
Berton, *The Great Depression*; Jim Struthers, 'A Profession in Crisis: Charlotte
Whitton and Canadian Social Work in the 1930s,' in Allan Moscovitch and
Jim Albert, eds, *The Benevolent State: The Growth of Welfare in Canada*
(Toronto: Garamond, 1987), 111–25.
28 Edelist, interview.
29 Margaret Gairns, interview, Toronto, Ontario, 12 November 2002.
30 Christine Beckett, 'Lives Lived,' *Globe and Mail*, 9 February 2005, A18.
31 Gairns, interview.
32 *Evening Telegram*, 20 May 1935, 35.
33 Census, 1931, vol. V, 456, 458, 446. Canada, Dominion Bureau of Statistics,
Annual Survey of Education, 1936, ix.
34 Gairns, interview.
35 Canada, Department of Labour, *Labour Gazette*, January 1932, 93; 'Prices in
Canada and Other Countries, 1932,' *Labour Gazette* (Ottawa, 1933), 6–9.
36 Isabel Turnbull Dingman, 'Can She Manage Alone?' *Chatelaine*, April 1932,
12.
37 Helen Gregory MacGill, 'What of the Wage-Earning Wife?' *Chatelaine*,
March 1930, 9.
38 For more on marital status and teaching see Erin Phillips and Paul Phillips,
Women's Work: Inequality in the Labour Market (Toronto: James Lorimer,
1983), 28; Beth Light and Ruth Pierson, *No Easy Road: Women in Canada,
1920s to 1960s* (Toronto: New Hogtown Press, 1990), 209. See also Alison
Prentice, 'Themes in the Early History of the Women's Teachers'
Association of Toronto,' in Paula Bourne, ed., *Women's Paid and Unpaid
Work: Historical and Contemporary Perspectives* (Toronto: New Hogtown Press,
1985), 97–120; for the American experience see Lois Scharf, *To Work and to
Wed: Female Employment, Feminism, and the Great Depression* (Westport, CT:
Greenwood Press, 1980), 66–85.
39 Dora Wattie, interview, Toronto, Ontario, 23 November 1997.

40 Mary Chenhall and Pat Mulligan, interview, Toronto, Ontario, 12 December 2001; Mary Chenhall, *Memoirs: Forever in My Heart* (Toronto, 1998).

41 Joy Parr, *The Gender of Breadwinners: Women, Men, and Change in Two Industrial Towns, 1880–1950* (Toronto: University of Toronto Press, 1990). In Montreal and Peterborough, Denyse Baillargeon and Joan Sangster reach similar conclusions. Denise Baillargeon, *Making Do: Women, Family and Home in Montreal during the Great Depression*, trans. Yvonne Klein (Waterloo, ON: Wilfred Laurier University Press, 1999); Sangster, *Earning Respect: The Lives of Working Women in Small Town Ontario, 1920–1960* (Toronto: University of Toronto Press, 1995).

42 Parr, *The Gender of Breadwinners*, 85. As scholars such as Neil Sutherland have shown, the domestic work of daughters has been important to families in various periods in Canadian history. See Neil Sutherland, 'Introduction: Children and Families Enter History's Main Stream,' *Canadian Historical Review* 78, 3 (September 1997): 379; *Children in English Canadian Society: Framing the Twentieth-Century Consensus* (Toronto: University of Toronto Press, 1976); *Growing Up: Childhood in English Canada from the Great War to the Age of Television* (Toronto: University of Toronto Press, 1997).

43 Grace Michaels, interview, Toronto, Ontario, 29 November 2001.

44 Census, 1931, vol. V, 1355. For more on this topic see Marcus Klee, 'Between the Scylla and Charybdis of Anarchy and Despotism: The State, Capital, and the Working Class in the Great Depression, Toronto, 1929–1940' (PhD dissertation, Queen's University, 1998).

45 Mulligan and Chenhall, interview.

46 McLean and Cahill, interview.

47 Margaret Snowball, interview, Toronto, Ontario, 26 February 2002.

48 Nell Moran, interview, Toronto, Ontario, 31 January 2002.

49 McLean and Cahill, interview; Phillips, interview.

50 Baillargeon, *Making Do*, 42.

51 Rocco Longo, interview, Toronto, Ontario, 15 February 2002. I interviewed Mr Longo twice on the phone.

52 On the history of broken families see Nancy Christie and Michael Gauvreau, eds, *Mapping the Margins: The Family and Social Discipline in Canada, 1700–1975* (Montreal and Kingston: McGill-Queen's University Press, 2004).

53 As Klee notes, cases in the Family Court rarely dealt with one issue; alcoholism and abuse were often tied to non-support; nevertheless, this cause was most consistently cited. Klee, 'Between the Scylla and Charybdis,' 94; Sangster, *Regulating Girls and Women*, 78.

54 Only 0.02 per cent of families had divorced males living with their children. Census, 1931, vol. V, 1355–6.

55 Cynthia Comacchio, 'A Postscript for Father: Defining a New Fatherhood in Interwar Canada,' *Canadian Historical Review* 78, 3 (1997): 388.
56 Frances Campbell Douglas, interview, 24 December 2000.
57 Helen Campbell, interview.
58 Windeatt, interview.
59 Ian Radforth, interview, Toronto, Ontario, 22 December 2003.
60 Ian Radforth, email correspondence, 5 April 2005.
61 Sangster, *Regulating Girls and Women*, 73–4; Klee, 'Between the Scylla and Charybdis.'
62 Sangster, *Regulating Girls and Women*, 77.
63 Ibid., 81.
64 *Chatelaine*, February, 1934, 32. Emphasis and capitalization in text.
65 Sangster, *Regulating Girls and Women*, 76–7.
66 Campbell, 'Respectable Citizens of Canada,' 241.
67 Byrne Hope Sanders, 'The Editor's Own Page for February,' *Chatelaine*, February 1932, 4. See also Light and Pierson, *No Easy Road*, 135, 155.
68 Garner, *Cabbagetown*, 218–19.
69 Lauren B. Davis, *The Stubborn Season* (Toronto: Harper Flamingo, 2002), 154–8.
70 Comacchio, 'A Postscript for Father,' 394–5.
71 As Marlene Epp's work on Mennonite rape victims has demonstrated so well, in these cases meanings must be teased out of memories through silences, disaffected explanations, and, sometimes, complete denial. See Marlene Epp, 'The Memory of Violence: Soviet and East European Mennonite Refugees and Rape in the Second World War,' *Journal of Women's History* 9, 1 (1997): 58–87; Marlene Epp, *Women without Men: Mennonite Refugees of the Second World War* (Toronto: University of Toronto Press, 2000).
72 McLean and Cahill, interview.
73 Phillips, interview.
74 Michaels, interview.
75 Jean Jackson, interview, Toronto, Ontario, 15 May 2002.

3: Young Women's Job Options in an Urban Labour Market in the 1930s

1 OA, Hinsta, interview, Wayne Roberts; Dorothy Coles, interview, Toronto, Ontario, 15 March 2001.
2 In Ontario, 85 per cent of women in professional service occupations such as nursing and teaching were from the British Isles. Census, 1931, vol. VII, 951. As census analysts explained it, 'native (meaning Canadian women of British descent) Canadians ... [were] in a position to acquire the necessary education for a profession. Census, 1931, vol. XII, 716.

3 On this theme see Nancy A. Hewitt, *Southern Discomfort: Women's Activism in Tampa Florida, 1880–1920s* (Urbana: University of Illinois Press, 2001); Tera W. Hunter, *To 'Joy My Freedom: Southern Black Women's Lives and Labors after the Civil War* (Cambridge, MA: Harvard University Press, 1997).
4 Clarke, interview, 2001.
5 Of the 79,120 women reported as employed in 1931, 21,263 worked in personal service, 21,959 in clerical occupations, 13,352 in manufacturing, and 9172 in professional service. These broad areas of occupation were further divided into categories such as teaching, domestic service, and stenography. Census, 1931, vol. VII, 226–37.
6 Census, 1941, vol. VII, 218–20. For a discussion of gender-based job segregation in the American context see Ruth Milkman, *Gender at Work: The Dynamics of Job Segregation during World War Two* (Chicago: University of Illinois Press, 1987). In this important study of job segregation in the U.S. electrical and auto industry, Milkman asserts that employment discrimination based on sex was a consequence of industrialization rather than a natural division based on family responsibility. Once established, she claims this division was intractable and did not respond to the jump in women's employment in the 1930s and 1940s.
7 In Ontario in 1931, women earned on average $636 per year, while men earned $1005. By 1941 the situation was worse: women earned on average $574 per year, while men earned $1112, 49 per cent more. Census, 1941, vol. I, 801.
8 Veronica Strong-Boag, *The New Day Recalled: Lives of Girls and Women in English Canada, 1919–1939* (Toronto: Copp Clark Pitman, 1988), 3.
9 See Antoinette Burton, *Burdens of History: British Feminists, Indian Women, and Imperial Culture, 1865–1915* (Chapel Hill: University of North Carolina Press, 1994); Ruth Frager, *Sweatshop Strife: Class, Ethnicity, and Gender in the Jewish Labour Movement of Toronto, 1900–1939* (Toronto: University of Toronto Press, 1993); Nancy Hewitt, 'Beyond the Search for Sisterhood: American Women's History in the 1980s,' *Social History* 10 (October 1985): 299–322; Hewitt, *Southern Discomfort*; Evelyn Brooks Higginbotham, 'African American Women's History and the Meta-language of Race,' *Signs* (1992): 251–74; Hunter, *To 'Joy My Freedom*; Franca Iacovetta, *Such Hardworking People: Italian Immigrants in Postwar Toronto* (Montreal and Kingston: McGill-Queen's University Press, 1992); Jacqueline Jones, 'Race and Gender in Modern America,' *Reviews in American History* (March 1998): 220–38; Gerda Lerner, 'Reconceptualizing Difference among Women,' *Journal of Women's History* 1 (Winter 1990): 106–22; Varpu Lindstrom, *Defiant Sisters: A Social History of Finnish Women in Canada, 1890–1930* (Toronto: Multicultural

History Society of Ontario, 1988); Joy Parr, *The Gender of Breadwinners: Women, Men, and Change in Two Industrial Towns, 1880–1950* (Toronto: University of Toronto Press, 1990); Elizabeth V. Spelman, *Inessential Woman: Problems of Exclusion in Feminist Thought* (Boston: Beacon Press, 1988); Carolyn Strange, 'Wounded Womanhood and Dead Men: Chivalry and the Trials of Clara Ford and Carrie Davies,' in Franca Iacovetta and Marianna Valverde, eds, *Gender Conflicts: New Essays in Women's History* (Toronto: University of Toronto Press, 1992), 149–88.

10 Census, 1941, vol. VII, 1106. There were 10,758 female and 741 male domestics noted in Toronto in 1931. Census, 1931, vol. VII, 236. I could find no other indication of these men in the historical record; however, one man who worked as a launderer during the Depression did write an editorial in the *Evening Telegram* which discusses his job loss in the 'old–fashioned trade' of blacksmithing and his subsequent employment in an occupation for which his 'wife showed [him] the fine points.' He had been doing it for four months, quite 'fanc[ied]' hand laundering, and figured he was 'ready anytime to go into a contest against the best fancy work laundresses in the world.' *Evening Telegram*, 23 July 1932, 15.

11 Census, 1941, vol. VII, 1106; Lindstrom, *Defiant Sisters*; Lindstrom, '"I Won't Be a Slave!": Finnish Domestics in Canada, 1911–1930,' in Franca Iacovetta, Paula Draper, and Robert Ventresca, eds, *A Nation of Immigrants: Women, Workers, and Communities in Canadian History, 1840s–1960s* (Toronto: University of Toronto Press, 1998), 166–85.

12 Duncan, interview.

13 On the ongoing and historical connection between immigration and domestic service see Marilyn Barber, *Immigrant Domestic Servants in Canada* (Ottawa: Canadian Historical Association Press, 1991); Lindstrom, *Defiant Sisters*; Susan McClelland, 'Nanny Abuse: Why Ottawa Played Along,' *The Walrus*, March 2005, 42–9; Makeda Silvera, *Silenced*, 2nd ed. (Toronto: Sister Vision Press, 1989). See also Magda Fahrni, '"Ruffled" Mistresses and "Discontented" Maids: Respectability and the Case of Domestic Service, 1880–1914,' *Labour/Le Travail* 39 (1997): 69–97.

14 The Brigit stereotype associated with Irish domestics is a good example of this. See, for example, Barber, *Immigrant Domestic Servants*; Lorna R. McLean and Marilyn Barber, 'In Search of Comfort and Independence: Irish Immigrant Domestic Servants Encounter the Courts, Jails and Asylums in 19th century Ontario,' in Marlene Epp, Franca Iacovetta, and Frances Swyripa, eds, *Sisters or Strangers? Immigrant, Ethnic, and Racialized Women in Canadian History* (Toronto: University of Toronto Press, 2004): 133–60.

15 *Evening Telegram*, 29 January 1935, 30.

16 Ron and Diana MacFeeters, interview, Toronto, Ontario, 14 March 2002.

17 OA, Hinsta, interview by Wayne Roberts.

18 Hinsta does not indicate where she boarded her son Roy; however, she does say that boarding was common because so many Finnish women were domestics and Finnish men were off working in the bush. Hinsta, interview. On this see Lindstrom, *Defiant Sisters*; Ian Radforth, *Bushworkers and Bosses: Logging in Northern Ontario, 1900–1980* (Toronto: University of Toronto Press, 1987).

19 *Evening Telegram*, 7 February 1935, 6; capitalization in text.

20 *Evening Telegram*, 30 April 1935, 6.

21 *Evening Telegram*, 23 April 1935, 6. The cartoon was published in the *Evening Telegram* on 18 April 1935.

22 Connie Lancaster, interview, Toronto, Ontario, 11 March 2002. Eventually Lancaster became a nurse with the Salvation Army. She worked in Toronto at the Grace Hospital.

23 Constance Templeton, 'Can Domestic Service Be Run on a Business Basis?' *Chatelaine*, December 1932, 17.

24 MacFeeters, interview.

25 *Evening Telegram*, 29 August 1932, 6.

26 Templeton, 'Can Domestic Service?' 17.

27 In New York during the 1930s, training schools were organized for domestics by community associations like the Urban League and funded by the federal government. The School of Household Work was one of the better-known schools. Ultimately, Brenda Clegg concludes, despite their innovation such schools did little if anything to improve the working conditions of black domestics in New York during the Depression. Brenda Clegg, 'Black Female Domestics during the Great Depression in New York City, 1930–1940' (PhD dissertation, University of Michigan, 1983), 137.

28 Graham Lowe, *Women in the Administrative Revolution: The Feminization of Clerical Work* (Toronto: University of Toronto Press, 1987). For a discussion of the American context see Margery Davies, *Women's Place Is at the Typewriter: Office Work and Office Workers, 1870–1982* (Philadelphia: Temple University Press, 1982).

29 Of the people employed as accountants and bookkeepers in Toronto in 1931, 3124 were women and 9520 were men. In 1941 little had changed. Men held 10,124 of the positions and women occupied 4124 of them. In stenography there was a similar pattern. In 1931, 10,843 stenographers were women and 758 were men. In 1941, women and men held 12,888 and 659 positions respectively. Census, 1941, vol. VII, 1106.

30 Fourteen women in my study were clerical workers. Ten left their jobs when they married. Two did not marry and two continued to work after marriage.

Neither of these women found this to be exceptional, though Helen Campbell did explain that she was a *private* secretary. She obviously felt this was an important factor in legitimizing her position as a married office worker. Campbell, interview.

31 Mildred Johnston, interview, Toronto, Ontario, 28 February 2002.

32 B.J. Spencer Pitt was a well-known lawyer and important role model for young West-Indian and African-Canadian women and men during this time. Violet Blackman, interview with H. Casimir (Multicultural History Society of Ontario [MHSO], BLA-6894-BLA, 15 January 1979); Daniel Braithwaite, interview with Diana Braithwaite (MHSO, BLA-5124-BRA, BLA-7986-BRA, 23 September 1981); Rella Braithwaite, interview with Diana Braithwaite (MHSO, BLA-7987-BRA, 26 July 1981); Clarke, interview, 2001; J.E. Clarke, interview with Diana Braithwaite (MHSO, BLA-5122-CLA, 1 August 1978); Dawn Moore, *Who's Who in Black Canada* (Toronto: D. Williams, 2002), 81.

33 Clarke, interview; 2001; interview, Toronto, Ontario, 28 April 2004. For Canadian discussions of such tensions see Dionne Brand, *No Burden to Carry: Narratives of Black Working Women in Ontario, 1920s–1950s* (Toronto: Women's Press, 1991); Keith S. Henry, *Black Politics in Toronto since WWI* (Toronto: MHSO, 1981), 6; Harry Gairey, *A Black Man's Toronto, 1914–1980*, ed. Donna Hill (Toronto: MHSO, 1981), 14; James and Shadd, eds, *Talking about Identity.*

34 Blackman, interview. Brand, *No Burden to Carry*, 37–8.

35 J.E. Clarke, interview with Diana Braithwaite, MHSO, BLA-5122-CLA, 1 August 1978.

36 Clarke, interview, 2001.

37 Johnston, interview.

38 McLean and Cahill, interview.

39 Phillips, interview.

40 McLean and Cahill, interview.

41 Radforth, interview.

42 *Evening Telegram*, 29 January 1935, 30.

43 Canada, Dominion Bureau of Statistics, *Annual Survey of Education*, 1930, 127; *Annual Survey of Education*, 1933, 115. In 1937, seventeen different locations offered business courses in Toronto. The business school with the most schools around the city was Shaw's. *Annual Survey of Education, 1936*, 158–9.

44 Census, 1931, vol. XIII, 235–239.

45 *Evening Telegram*, 15 January 1932, 6.

46 *Evening Telegram,* January 12, 1932, 6.

47 Johnston, interview.

48 In both 1931 and 1941 men earned, on average, 16 to 20 per cent more per
   year than women. Lowe, *Women in the Administrative Revolution*, 145; Canada,
   Royal Commission on Price Spreads, *Minutes of Proceedings and Evidence*, 16
   January 1935, 4410.
49 *Toronto Daily Star*, 6 November 1935.
50 Her doctor told her she had better leave 'or they would be carrying her out
   of there.' Plunkett, interview. For more on the unhealthy conditions of
   women workers in Toronto see Catherine Macleod, 'Women in Production:
   The Toronto Dressmakers' Strike of 1931,' in Janice Acton, Penny
   Goldsmith, and Bonnie Shepard, eds, *Women at Work: Ontario, 1850–1930*
   (Toronto: Women's Press, 1974), 316–17.
51 Plunkett, interview.
52 A comptometer is similar to a calculator. Norma Vineham also reported that
   her company promoted her when she finished night schooling. Norma
   Vineham, interview, Toronto, Ontario, 28 October 1997.
53 In manufacturing, 8703 of 13,352 women worked in the textile industry.
   Census, 1931, vol. VII, 227–8.
54 Canada, Royal Commission on Price Spreads, *Report on Findings*, 119.
55 Mercedes Steedman, 'Skill and Gender in the Canadian Clothing Industry,
   1890–1940,' in Ian Radforth and Laurel Sefton MacDowell, eds, *Canadian
   Working Class History: Selected Readings* (Toronto: Canadian Scholars Press,
   2000), 453. See also Steedman, *Angels of the Workplace: Women and the
   Construction of Gender Relations in the Canadian Clothing Industry, 1890–1940*
   (Toronto: Oxford University Press, 1997).
56 Canada, Royal Commission on Price Spreads, *Evidence of Special Committee*, 28
   February 1934, 129–30.
57 Canada, Royal Commission on Price Spreads, *Evidence of Special Committee*,
   16, 17, 22 January 1935, pp. 4410, 4462, 4650; Royal Commission on Price
   Spreads, 'Garment Industry: The Speed-Up at Eaton's,' in Irving Abella and
   David Miller, eds, *The Canadian Worker in the Twentieth Century* (Toronto:
   Oxford University Press, 1978), 185–93. The Minister of Trade and Finance
   H.H. Stevens was forced to resign in October 1934 for exposing the
   exploitative practices of big business.
58 There were approximately 45,305 Jewish people in Toronto in 1931. Census,
   1931, vol. IV, 912. For more on Jewish women's experiences see Paula
   Draper and Janice B. Karlinsky, 'Abraham's Daughters: Women, Charity and
   Power in the Canadian Jewish Community,' in Iacovetta, Draper, and
   Ventresca, eds, *A Nation of Immigrants*, 186–202; Ruth Frager, *Sweatshop Strife:
   Class, Ethnicity, and Gender in the Jewish Labour Movement of Toronto, 1900–1939*
   (Toronto: University of Toronto Press, 1993).

59 Rose Edelist, interview, Toronto, Ontario, 23 January 2002; This point was
    echoed by Mrs R. Ducove when asked why she stopped working after her
    first child was born. Mrs R. Ducove, interview B. Swimmer (MHS, JEW-1754-
    DUC, 1977). Some women did not have a large family group to rely on for
    childcare, and this, rather than cost, affected their employment choices. For
    Rose Edelist, it was a matter of affordability.

60 There were several ways in which the immigrant working-class Jewish
    community was separated from the middle- and upper-class Jewish com-
    munity in Toronto. Middle- and upper-class Jews may have shopped in the
    Kensington Market area, but they did not live there. The longer-established
    Holy Blossom synagogue had both Saturday and Sunday services and was
    attended by the older Jewish community. Rabbi Eisendrath, who presided
    over Holy Blossom for part of the 1930s, had a radio spot on a Toronto
    station and was often invited to speak at city functions. The rabbis from
    synagogues around the Kensington Market did not seem to enjoy such
    acceptance or popularity. This separation may also have been related to
    country of origin and religious sect, such as the division between Hasidic
    Jews and other sects of Judaism. On the Jewish community in Toronto see
    Stephen A. Speisman, *The Jews of Toronto: A History to 1937* (Toronto:
    McClelland and Stewart, 1979).

61 Edelist, interview. For more on such strikes see MacLeod, 'Women in
    Production: The Toronto Dressmakers' Strike of 1931,' 309–29.

62 Edelist, interview.

63 Census, 1931, vol. IV, 912. The numbers reported on the Italian community
    varied widely depending on who was recording the numbers. This is in part
    a consequence of seasonal work patterns and migration. For further
    tabulation see Cumbo, 'As the twig is bent,' 461; John E. Zucchi, *Italians in
    Toronto: Development of a National Identity, 1875–1935* (Montreal and
    Kingston: McGill-Queen's University Press, 1988), 44.

64 On Canadian Italian settlement see Iacovetta and Gabbaccia, eds, *Women,
    Gender and Transnational Lives*; Robert F. Harney and Vincena Scarpaci, *Little
    Italies in North America* (Toronto: MHSO, 1981); Robert Harney, 'Men
    without Women: Italian Migrants in Canada, 1885–1930,' in Iacovetta,
    Draper, and Ventresca, eds, *A Nation of Immigrants*, 206–30. Zucchi, *Italians
    in Toronto*.

65 Census, 1941, vol. I, 338. In manufacturing in Canada 77 per cent of Italian
    women and 90 per cent of Jewish women were in the textile industry.
    Census, 1931, vol. VII, 418–27.

66 I am using the name 'Mrs Bassi' because this was the only way she was
    referred to in her daughter's interview.

67 Evelina Bassi, interview with F. Zucchi (MHSO, ITA-0661-BAS, 17 November 1977). For further discussion of this type of resistance see Angelo Principe, 'Glimpses of Lives in Canada's Shadow: Insiders, Outsiders, and Female Activism in the Fascist Era,' in Iacovetta and Gabaccia, eds, *Women, Gender and Transnational Lives*, 349–85.

68 As Franca Iacovetta and Donna Gabaccia establish in their important collection *Women, Gender, and Transnational Lives: Italian Workers of the World*, the persistent stereotype of passivity does not hold for Italian women workers and must be replaced with a greater awareness of the different forms that resistance took in women's lives.

69 Windeatt, interview.

70 For more information on women in management see G.L. Symons, 'Her View from the Executive Suite: Canadian Women in Management,' in Katerina Lundy and Barbara Warme, eds, *Work in the Canadian Context: Continuity Despite Change* (Toronto: Butterworths, 1981), 337–53. Also of interest here is the power Nora Windeatt had over the men in her department. As she recalls it, the men were from a similar ethnic and class background as Windeatt.

71 Marks, interview.

72 Duncan, interview.

73 Census, 1941, vol. VII, 218–19.

74 Erin Phillips and Paul Phillips, *Women's Work: Inequality in the Labour Market* (Toronto: James Lorimer, 1983), 28; Beth Light and Ruth Pierson, *No Easy Road: Women in Canada, 1920s to 1960s* (Toronto: New Hogtown Press, 1990), 209. Also see Alison Prentice, 'Themes in the Early History of the Women's Teachers' Association of Toronto,' in Paula Bourne, ed., *Women's Paid and Unpaid Work: Historical and Contemporary Perspectives* (Toronto: New Hogtown Press, 1985), 97–120; For the American experience see Lois Scharf, *To Work and to Wed: Female Employment, Feminism, and the Great Depression* (Westport, CT: Greenwood Press, 1980), 66–85.

75 For a poignant fictional account of this situation see Richard Wright, *Clara Callan* (Toronto: McClelland and Stewart, 2001).

76 Census, 1931, vol. VII, 236; Census, 1941, vol. VII, 222.

77 Of the 17,457 teachers in Ontario in 1931, 14,394 were of British origin, 1728 were French, 54 were Jewish, 46 were Italian, 14 were Indian [*sic*], and 12 were Asiatic. Census, 1941, vol. VII, 392–3.

78 Chenhall was enrolled at Victoria University, an affiliated college at the University of Toronto. Chenhall, *Memoirs*, 45; Chenhall and Mulligan, interview.

79 The University of Toronto *President's Report* for 1931 confirms this. In a city of
nearly 700,000 only 2190 men and 1680 women were enrolled in the Faculty
of Arts. There were 1,385 graduates receiving, like Mary, a Bachelor of Science;
959 of these graduates were men. In 1936–7, 4007 people were enrolled at the
University of Toronto. Toronto, *President's Report*, 1931, 99, 135, 161.

80 Canada, Dominion Bureau of Statistics, *Annual Survey of Education*, 1936,
xxvi. Enrolment at the University of Toronto generally hovered around
5000 for men and 2500 for women throughout the Depression years. See
Annual Survey of Education, 1929–39.

81 Paul Axelrod, 'Higher Education, Utilitarianism, and the Acquisitive
Society: Canada, 1930–1980,' in Michael Cross and Gregory Kealey, eds,
Modern Canada, 1930–1980 (Toronto: McClelland and Stewart, 1984), 180.

82 Mary Chenhall, *Memoirs: Forever in My Heart* (Toronto, 1998).

83 Wattie, interview.

84 'Sock Em Board,' *Evening Telegram*, 3 February 1932, 6.

85 Wattie, interview.

4: Where Is a Woman Safe? City Spaces, Workplaces, and Households

1 Joan Sangster, *Regulating Girls and Women: Sexuality, Family, and the Law in
Ontario, 1920–1960* (Toronto: Oxford University Press, 2001); Carolyn
Strange, *Toronto's Girl Problem: The Perils and Pleasures of the City, 1880–1930*
(Toronto: University of Toronto Press, 1995); Judith Walkowitz, *City of
Dreadful Delight: Narratives of Sexual Danger in Late-Victorian London* (Chicago:
University of Chicago Press, 1992).

2 Franca Iacovetta and Wendy Mitchinson, *On the Case: Explorations in Social
History* (Toronto: University of Toronto Press, 1998). See also Ruth
Alexander, *The 'Girl Problem': Female Sexual Delinquency in New York, 1900–
1930* (Ithaca, NY: Cornell University Press, 1995); Constance Backhouse,
Colour Coded: A Legal History of Racism in Canada, 1900–1950 (Toronto:
University of Toronto Press, 1999); Kerry Carrington, *Offending Girls: Sex,
Youth and Justice* (Sydney: Allen and Unwin Australia, 1993); Velma
Demerson, *Incorrigible* (Waterloo, ON: Wilfrid Laurier University Press,
2004); Karen Dubinsky, *Improper Advances: Rape and Heterosexual Conflict in
Ontario, 1880–1929* (Chicago: University of Chicago Press, 1993); Linda
Gordon, *Pitied but Not Entitled: Single Mothers and the History of Welfare,
1890–1935* (Cambridge, MA: Harvard University Press, 1995) Andrée
Lévesque, *Making and Breaking the Rules: Women in Quebec, 1919–1939*
(Toronto: University of Toronto Press, 1994); Margaret Hillyard-Little,

No Car, No Radio, No Liquor Permit: The Moral Regulation of Single Mothers in Ontario, 1920–1997 (Toronto: Oxford University Press, 1998); Tamara Myers, *Caught: Montreal's Modern Girls and the Law, 1869–1945* (Toronto: University of Toronto Press, 2006); Mary Odem, *Delinquent Daughters: Protecting and Policing Adolescent Female Sexuality in the United States, 1885–1920* (Chapel Hill: University of North Carolina Press, 1995).

3 Michiel Horn, *The Dirty Thirties: Canadians in the Great Depression* (Toronto: Copp Clark, 1972), 306–89.

4 Patterson presided at the Women's Court, which was created in 1918 in Toronto as a division of the Police Court to deal with cases associated with morality and domestic relations. For more on Patterson see Dorothy Chunn, *From Punishment to Doing Good: Family Courts and Socialized Justice in Ontario, 1880–1940* (Toronto: University of Toronto Press, 1992); Margaret Patterson, 'Bad Girl,' *Chatelaine*, October 1935, 8.

5 Patterson, 'Bad Girl,' 8.

6 Ibid., 8, 9. On such institutions see Sangster, *Regulating Girls and Women*; Strange, *Toronto's Girl Problem.*

7 Sangster, *Regulating Girls and Women*, 107.

8 Gabrielle Roy, *The Tin Flute* (Toronto: McClelland and Stewart, 1945); Hugh Garner, *Cabbagetown* (Toronto: McGraw-Hill Ryerson, 1968).

9 Margaret Hobbs, 'Gendering Work and Welfare: Women's Relationships to Wage-Work and Social Policy during the Great Depression' (PhD dissertation, University of Toronto, 1995), 135–9.

10 OA, YWCA series, RG 2, box 4, YWCA board of directors minutes, 19 November 1931.

11 *Evening Telegram*, 23 March 1935, 8; *Toronto Daily Star*, 12 October 1934; OA, 'Health of Jobless Girls Alarms Social Worker,' YWCA series, RG 2, box 16, scrapbooks, 1933–63.

12 OA, RG 22-517, box 50, file 3023.1

13 OA, RG 22-392, cont. 287, Rex v. Francis Wells.

14 Sangster, *Regulating Girls and Women*, 82.

15 Ibid., 93, 94–5.

16 Demerson, *Incorrigible*, 44.

17 Sangster, *Regulating Girls and Women*, 15, 114–21. Relationships between white women and Chinese men had always been a concern; however, in 1912 a white woman's labour law was put in place which stated that no Chinese person could 'employ in any capacity any white woman or girl, or permit any white woman or girl to reside or lodge in or to work in … [a] place of business or amusement owned, or kept, or managed by any Japanese, Chinamen or other Oriental person.' Backhouse, *Colour Coded*, 136.

18 Demerson, *Incorrigible*, 33–40.

19 Ibid., 33.

20 *Hush*, 12 October 1935, 1.

21 Ibid., 9.

22 Demerson, *Incorrigible*, 48.

23 Ibid., 45, 47.

24 On this issue see Franca Iacovetta, 'Gossip, Contest, and Power in the Making of Suburban Bad Girls: Toronto, 1945–1960,' *Canadian Historical Review* 80, 4 (1999): 585–623.

25 Erma Frank, interview, Toronto, Ontario, 15 March 2002.

26 Nell Moran, interview, Toronto, Ontario, 31 January 2002.

27 Sangster, *Regulating Girls and Women*, 1; Strange, *Toronto's Girl Problem*, 19.

28 Demerson, *Incorrigible*, 1–2, 14. Velma Demerson received a formal apology from the Ontario government in December 2002.

29 Connie Lancaster, interview, Toronto, Ontario, 11 March 2002; Sangster, *Regulating Girls and Women*, 102. See also Lévesque, *Making and Breaking the Rules*; Lévesque, 'Deviant Anonymous: Single Mothers at the Hôpital de la Miséricorde in Montreal, 1929–1939,' *Historical Papers* (1984): 168–84.

30 *Hush*, 6 July 1935, 7.

31 *Evening Telegram*, 6 November 1935, 1.

32 Forsythe, interview.

33 The papers made a point of the emphasizing the weather. As it turned out, the weather proved central to the prosecutions case, which was built on circumstantial evidence: O'Donnell's clothing was soiled and muddy, consistent with being in a ravine on a rainy evening. National Archives of Canada (NAC), RG 13, Capital Case Files, Harry O'Donnell.

34 Forsythe, interview.

35 Dubinsky, *Improper Advances*, 152, 145–6; Strange, *Toronto's Girl Problem*.

36 *Evening Telegram*, 30 November 1935, 4.

37 *Hush*, 9 November 1935, 3.

38 MacMillan, interview.

39 *Hush*, 13 June 1936, 1. On the white slave trade see Dubinsky, *Improper Advances*; Strange, *Toronto's Girl Problem*; Mariana Valverde, *The Age of Light, Soap, and Water: Moral Reform in English Canada, 1885–1925* (Toronto: McClelland and Stewart, 1991).

40 McLean and Cahill, interview.

41 Duncan, interview.

42 *Toronto Daily Star*, 7 November 1935, 1.

43 *Evening Telegram*, 20 November 1935, 2.

44 *Evening Telegram*, 30 November 1935, 4.

45 *Evening Telegram*, 19 November 1935, 2.
46 *Toronto Daily Star*, 9 November 1935, 2.
47 *Evening Telegram*, 7 November 1935, 38.
48 *Evening Telegram*, 30 November 1935, 4.
49 *Hush*, 11 April 1936, 14.
50 *Evening Telegram*, 6 November 1935, 3.
51 Ibid.
52 Carolyn Strange and Tina Loo, *True Crime, True North: The Golden Age of Canadian Pulp Magazines* (Vancouver: Raincoast Books, 2004), 87. See also Carolyn Strange and Tina Loo, 'The Moral of the Story: Gender and Murder in Canadian True Crime Magazines of the 1940s,' in Thornton, ed., *Romancing the Tomes*, 236–9.
53 *The Globe*, 6 November 1935, 1.
54 *Toronto Daily Star*, 6 November 1935, 3.
55 *Evening Telegram*, 8 November 1935, 3.
56 *Toronto Daily Star*, 6 November 1935, 3.
57 Strange and Loo, *True Crime, True North*, 83.
58 Jackson, interview.
59 Gammon, interview.
60 Johnston, interview.
61 Dubinsky, *Improper Advances*, 8.
62 Sangster, *Regulating Girls and Women*, 77, 78.
63 *Hush*, 27 July 1935, 6.
64 *Hush*, 23 October 1930, 10.
65 Sangster, *Regulating Girls and Women*, 10.
66 Ironically, men had the most to fear from strangers: 55 per cent of murders and attempted murders on males were perpetrated by strangers. CTA, Draper, *Annual Report*, 1929–39.
67 These numbers were compiled from the *Annual Reports* of the Chief Constable, 1929–39. There are inconsistencies in the police reports. For instance, while charts indicate that eleven women were murdered the chief constable only describes ten. Therefore, these numbers should be accepted as approximations.
68 CTA, Draper, *Annual Report*, 1930, 4.
69 CTA, Draper, *Annual Report*, 1931, 2; *Jack Canuck*, known for its racist epithets against Chinese men, raised concerns about 'white girls living with Chinese in Toronto.' *Jack Canuck*, 9 June 1932, 6; *Jack Canuck*, 23 June 1932, 6. See also Madge Pon, 'Like a Chinese Puzzle: The Construction of Chinese Masculinity in *Jack Canuck*,' in Joy Parr and Mark Rosenfeld, eds, *Gender and History in Canada* (Toronto: Copp Clark, 1996), 88–100.

70 McLean and Cahill, interview.
71 CTA, Draper, *Annual Report*, 1932, 2.
72 *Evening Telegram*, 10 May 1932, 1.
73 OA, RG 22-517, box 50, file 3026.
74 OA, RG 22-517, box 52, file, 3052; CTA, Draper, *Annual Report*, 1939.
75 *Hush*, 17 November 1934, 7.
76 *Hush*, 9 November 1935, 5.
77 Strange, *Toronto's Girl Problem*, 3.
78 Frederick Lewis Allen, *Only Yesterday: An Informal History of the Nineteen-Twenties* (New York: Harper Brothers, 1931), 97.
79 Dana L. Barron, 'Sex and Single Girls in the Twentieth-Century City,' *Journal of Urban History* 25, 6 (September 1999): 839; Strange, *Toronto's Girl Problem*, 39.
80 *Toronto Daily Star*, 9 November 1935, 7.
81 *Evening Telegram*, 21 November 1935, 8.
82 *Evening Telegram*, 7 November 1935, 38.
83 Duncan, interview.
84 McClintock, interview.
85 *Hush*, 13 July 1935, 1.
86 *Hush*, 5 June 1930, 11.
87 *Jack Canuck*, 20 April 1933, 3.
88 Demerson, *Incorrigible*, 33.
89 *Hush*, 9 April 1931, 7.
90 *Evening Telegram*, 30 April 1935, 6.
91 McLean and Cahill, interview.
92 Joanna Bornat, 'Oral History as a Social Movement: Reminiscences and Older People,' in Perks and Thomson, eds, *The Oral History Reader*.

5: The Rough 'n' Ready Spinsters' Club:
Working Women's Leisure and Respectability

1 Norma Vineham, interview, Toronto, Ontario, 15 April 2005.
2 Vineham, interview, 1997.
3 Michael Dawson, 'Taking the "D" Out of Depression': The Promise of Tourism in British Columbia, 1935–1939,' *BC Studies* 132 (Winter 2001–2): 31–56; Mariana Valverde, 'Families, Private Property, and the State: The Dionnes and the Toronto Stork Derby,' *Journal of Canadian Studies* 29, 4 (1994–5): 15–35.
4 Frederick Lewis Allen, *Only Yesterday: An Informal History of the Nineteen-Twenties* (New York: Harper Brothers, 1931), 98. See for instance: Ruth

Alexander, *The 'Girl Problem': Female Sexual Delinquency in New York, 1900–1930* (Ithaca, NY: Cornell University Press, 1995); Lizbeth Cohen, *Making a New Deal: Industrial Workers in Chicago, 1919–1939* (Cambridge: Cambridge University Press, 1990); Nan Enstad, *Ladies of Labor, Girls of Adventure: Working Women, Popular Culture, and Labor Politics at the Turn of the Twentieth Century* (New York: Columbia University Press, 1999); Joanne Meyerowitz, *Women Adrift: Independent Wage Earners in Chicago, 1880–1930* (Chicago: University of Chicago Press, 1988); Mary Odem, *Delinquent Daughters: Protecting and Policing Adolescent Female Sexuality in the United States, 1885–1920* (Chapel Hill: University of North Carolina Press, 1995); Kathy Peiss, *Cheap Amusements: Working Women and Leisure in Turn-of-the-Century New York* (Philadelphia: Temple University Press, 1986); Carolyn Strange, 'Sin or Salvation? Protecting Toronto's Working Girls,' *The Beaver* (June-July, 1997): 8–13; Carolyn Strange, *Toronto's Girl Problem: The Perils and Pleasures of the City, 1880–1930* (Toronto: University of Toronto Press, 1995); Valverde, 'Families, Private Property, and the State'; Judith Walkowitz, *City of Dreadful Delight: Narratives of Sexual Danger in Late-Victorian London* (Chicago: University of Chicago Press, 1992).

5 Strange, *Toronto's Girl Problem,* 18; Peiss, *Cheap Amusements.* For an earlier manifestation of this discourse in England see Walkowitz, *City of Dreadful Delight.*

6 Strange, *Toronto's Girl Problem,* 121.

7 Vineham, interview, 2005.

8 Michaels, interview.

9 Jackson, interview.

10 Wood, interview.

11 By 1941, fully 93 per cent of families in Toronto had a radio set. Census, 1941, vol. IX, 83.

12 Brigida Ely, interview with John Zucchi (MHS, ITA-0878-ELY, 12 July 1977).

13 Vineham, interview, 1997.

14 Jackson, interview.

15 McLean and Cahill, interview.

16 Mrs DeZori, interview J. Zucchi and F. Zucchi (MHSO, ITA-0651-DEZ, 18 November 1977, 10 December 1977).

17 Mrs Chiara Pillo, interview with Enrico Cumbo, Toronto, Ontario, 24 September 1990.

18 John. B. Lombardi, interview with Enrico Cumbo, Toronto, Ontario, 31 August 1989.

19 Mrs Antonietta Colapinto, interview with Enrico Cumbo, Toronto, Ontario, 20 June 1989. Pellegrino D'acierino, *The Italian American Heritage: A*

Companion to Literature and Arts (New York: Garland Publishing, 1999), 6. Cynthia Comacchio has similar findings for Montreal in the 1930s: 'Dancing to Perdition: Adolescence and Leisure in Interwar English Canada,' *Journal of Canadian Studies* 32, 3 (Autumn 1997): 11.

20 Franca Iacovetta and Donna Gabaccia, *Women, Gender, and Transnational Lives: Italian Workers of the World* (Toronto: University of Toronto Press, 2002).

21 Lynne Marks, *Revivals and Roller Rinks: Religion, Leisure and Identity in Late-Nineteenth-Century Small-Town Ontario* (Toronto: University of Toronto Press, 1996), 4. Religion has not been a central concept in labour history and has, for the most part, remained in the background of social history as well. Linda Kerber made this observation in 1989. Linda Kerber et al., 'Forum: Beyond Roles, beyond Spheres: Thinking about Gender in the Early Republic,' *William and Mary Quarterly* 46, 3 (July 1989): 582. In Canadian historiography there are some notable exceptions. See Ruth Compton Brouwer, *New Women for God* (Toronto: University of Toronto Press, 1990); Marta Danylewycz, *Taking the Veil* (Toronto: McClelland and Stewart, 1987); Rosemary Gagan, *A Sensitive Independence* (Montreal and Kingston: McGill-Queen's University Press, 1992); Cecilia Morgan, *Public Men and Virtuous Women: The Gendered Languages of Religion and Politics in Upper Canada, 1791–1850* (Toronto: University of Toronto Press, 1996).

22 Comacchio, 'Dancing to Perdition,' 20, 5–35. See also Nancy Christie, 'Introduction: Family, Community, and the Rise of Liberal Society,' in Christie, ed., *Households of Faith: Family, Gender, and Community in Canada, 1760–1969* (Montreal and Kingston: McGill-Queen's University Press, 2002), 14–15.

23 Patricia Dirks, 'Reinventing Christian Masculinity and Fatherhood: The Canadian Protestant Experience, 1900–1920,' in Christie, ed., *Households of Faith*, 297–8, 308.

24 Neil Semple, *The Lord's Dominion: The History of Canadian Methodism* (Montreal and Kingston: McGill-Queen's University Press, 1996), 215, 382–7.

25 Michaels, interview. Dirks, 'Reinventing Christian Masculinity and Fatherhood,' 310.

26 For a history of religion in Canada see Michael Gauvreau, *The Evangelical Century: College and Creed in English Canada from the Great Revival to the Great Depression* (Montreal and Kingston: McGill-Queen's University Press, 1991); Margaret Lindsay Holton, ed., *Spirit of Toronto: 1834–1984* (Toronto: Image Publishing, 1983); Hans Mol, *Faith and Fragility: Religion and Identity in Canada* (Burlington: Trinity Press, 1985); Marguerite van Die, *Religion and*

Public Life in Canada: Historical and Comparative Perspectives (Toronto: University of Toronto Press, 2001).

27   Census, 1931, vol. III, 430. By 1927 downtown Toronto had approximately thirty synagogues. Chris Cotter, *Toronto between the Wars: Life in the City, 1919–1939* (Toronto: Firefly, 2004), 130.

28   Census, 1931, vol. IV, 912–13.

29   *Evening Telegram*, 2 April 1935, 8. The relationship between religion and free time is well reflected in policing around the city's official day of rest, Sunday. The Lord's Day Act, one of Toronto's notorious blue laws, restricted activities or the sale of goods on the Christian Sabbath. Throughout most of the Depression years, roughly 600 people were charged with Lord's Day Act offences each year. Typically, the police only charged more citizens for city by-law, theft, liquor, traffic, and gambling offences. Draper, *Annual Report*, 1932–7.

30   Vineham, interview, 1997.

31   Vineham, interview, 2005.

32   Lois Wilson and June Pugseley, interview, Toronto, Ontario, 4 December 2001.

33   Johnston, interview.

34   Audrey Sewell, interview, Toronto, Ontario, 20 November 2001; On the nineteenth-century version of Dorcas societies see Morgan, *Public Men and Virtuous Women*, 180–2.

35   Vineham, interview, 1997.

36   Wilks, interview.

37   Plunkett, interview.

38   Clarke, interview.

39   Clarke, interview.

40   Daniel Braithwaite, interview with A. Holder (MHS, BLA-5124-BRA, 1978).

41   The salon, Clarke recalled, catered primarily to Jewish women, particularly those who were part of the Hadassah Jewish women's organization, a Zionist association founded in 1912 by New Yorker Henrietta Szold. C. Clarke, interview.

42   R. Braithwaite, interview, MHSO.

43   Clarke, interview.

44   Joe Soren with Gracie Soren, interview, Toronto, Ontario, 10 December 2001.

45   Edelist, interview.

46   Ruth Frager, *Sweatshop Strife: Class, Ethnicity, and Gender in the Jewish Labour Movement of Toronto, 1900–1939* (Toronto: University of Toronto Press, 1993), 40, 41.

47 Ibid., 109.

48 For example: Mike Filey, *Toronto Sketches: The Way We Were* (Toronto: Dundurn Press, 1992); Filey, *I Remember Sunnyside:The Rise and Fall of a Magical Era* (Toronto: The Dundurn Group, 1996); Filey, *Toronto Album 2: More Glimpses of the City That Was* (Toronto: The Dundurn Group, 2002).

49 Byers, interview; Filey, *A Toronto Album*, 96–100.

50 Duncan, interview.

51 MacMillan, interview.

52 Lawson and Lawson, interview.

53 Società Femminile Friulana, *La Nostra Storia, 1938–1988* (Toronto: MHSO, 1988), 21.

54 Jeanne Macdonald, Nadine Stoikoff, and Randall White, *Toronto Women: Changing Faces, 1900–2000* (Toronto: Eastendbooks, 1997), 62.

55 Johnston, interview.

56 MacMillan, interview.

57 Filey, *I Remember Sunnyside*, 100, 74, 75. Mike Filey, *A Toronto Album: Glimpses of the City That Was* (Toronto: The Dundurn Group, 2001), 82, 101.

58 Filey, *I Remember Sunnyside*, 82. The Easter parades were not formally organized; participants simply joined other Torontonians for a stroll on the boardwalk.

59 Mike Filey to Katrina Srigley, email correspondence, 3 April 2005. In 1934, workers involved in a city relief work project replaced the well-used and deteriorating boardwalk. The project cost $26,400 and involved 'a foreman, ten labourers, and eight carpenters.' Filey, *I Remember Sunnyside*, 82, 84–5; Mike Filey, *Toronto Sketches 8: The Way We Were* (Toronto: The Dundurn Group, 2004), 45–47.

60 For an excellent and detailed account of the development of motion pictures throughout the thirties see Robyn Karney ed., *Cinema Year by Year, 1894–2003* (London: DK Publishing, 2003), 211–305. See also Henry Forman, *Our Movie Made Children* (New York: MacMillan, 1935).

61 Canada, Dominion Bureau of Statistics, *Motion Picture Theatres and Film Distribution*, 1934. In Britain the trend was the same. Anthony Aldgate and Jeffrey Richards, *Best of British: Cinema and Society from 1930 to the Present* (London: I.B. Tauris, 1999), 1–2.

62 Filey, *A Toronto Album 2*, 58. Filey, *Toronto Sketches 5*, 156–8, 185–7; Filey, *Toronto Sketches 8*, 202–4.

63 John Thompson and Allen Seager, *Canada 1922–1939: Decades of Discord* (Toronto: McClelland and Stewart, 1985), 175.

64 Johnston, interview.

65 Thompson and Seager, *Canada 1922–1939*, 175–6.

66 Lawson and Lawson, interview. I am spelling Val Kee Man Shu phonetically
    because I was unable to find a reference to it anywhere else. She is likely
    referring to *The Mask of Fu Manchu* (1932).
67 Gina Marchetti, *Romance and the 'Yellow Peril': Race, Sex, and Discursive
    Strategies in Hollywood Fiction* (Los Angeles: University of California Press,
    1993). See also Pon, 'Like a Chinese Puzzle.'
68 Demerson, *Incorrigible*, 55–6.
69 McLean and Cahill, interview.
70 Lary May, *Screening Out the Past: The Birth of Mass Culture and the Motion
    Picture Industry* (New York: Oxford University Press, 1980).
71 Forman, *Our Movie Made Children*, 46.
72 Ibid., 50.
73 *Divorcée*, MGM, 1930. Shearer won the Academy Award for Best Actress for
    her role in this film. Apparently, Greta Garbo did not accept the initial offer
    to play this role 'because she was offended by the story of a liberated woman
    who seeks vengeance on her philandering husband by taking two lovers.'
    Karney, *Cinema Year by Year*, 220, 214.
74 Forman, *Our Movie Made Children*, 50–1.
75 Patricia Medeiros, 'Images of Women during the Great Depression and the
    Golden Age of American Film' (PhD dissertation, University of California,
    San Diego, 1988), 268–9, 105.
76 Ibid., 408; Mick Lasalle, *Complicated Women: Sex and Power in Pre-Code
    Hollywood* (New York: Thomas Dunn, 2000), 4.
77 Windeatt, interview; Gammon, interview.
78 Herbert Blumer, *Movies and Conduct* (New York: MacMillan, 1933), 31.
79 Ibid., 32.
80 Lasalle, *Complicated Women*, 3.
81 Sarah Berry, *Screen Style: Fashion and Femininity in 1930s Hollywood*
    (Minneapolis: University of Minnesota Press, 2000), xi.
82 Enstad, *Ladies of Labor*, 182.
83 Lasalle, *Complicated Women*, 2.
84 C.J. Pennethorne Hughes, 'Dreams: Films,' in James Donely, Anne
    Freedberg and Laura Marcus, eds, *Close-Up, 1927–1933: Cinema and
    Modernism* (Princeton: Princeton University Press, 1998), 260–2.
85 Blumer, *Movies and Conduct*, 1–2.
86 *Evening Telegram*, 25 November 1929, 1.
87 Thompson and Seager, *Canada 1922–1939*, 178–9. For more on Canadian
    film and film policy see Douglas Fetherling, *Documents in Canadian Film*
    (Peterborough: Broadview Press, 1988); Michael Dorland, *So Close to the*

States: The Emergence of Canadian Feature Film Policy (Toronto: University of Toronto Press, 1998).

88 *Labour Gazette* (1933), 1901.
89 Ibid.
90 Ibid.
91 Karney, *Cinema Year by Year*, 216. See also Medieros, 'Images of Women during the Great Depression,' 421. Pope Pius XI became involved in 1936 when he recommended that indecent films be boycotted and claimed that 'above all else, the portrayal of women' had to be altered. 'A heroine in a melodrama has to be a virgin, a faithful wife and mother.' Karney, *Cinema Year by Year*, 270. For more on the code see John Belton, ed., *Movies and Mass Culture* (New Jersey: Rutgers University Press, 1996), 135–49.
92 William Manchester, *The Glory and the Dream: A Narrative History of America, 1932–1972* (New York: Bantam, 1974), 120.
93 Campbell, interview.
94 Allen, *Only Yesterday*, 92.
95 Watson, interview.
96 Peiss, *Cheap Amusements*, 88.
97 CTA, Draper, *Annual Report*, 1930, 19.
98 Coles, interview. See also Mike Filey, *Toronto Sketches 5: The Way We Were* (Toronto: Dundurn Press, 1997), 126–7; Filey, *Toronto Sketches 6: The Way We Were* (Toronto: Dundurn Press, 2000), 291–4; Filey, *Toronto Sketches 7: The Way We Were* (Toronto: Dundurn Press, 2003), 61–3; Peter Young, *Let's Dance: A Celebration of Ontario's Dance Halls and Summer Pavilions* (Toronto: Natural Heritage Books, 2002), 3, 16.
99 Wood, interview.
100 *Evening Telegram*, 15 October 1932, 2.
101 Filey, *I Remember Sunnyside*, 103; Filey, *Toronto Sketches 6*, 262–4; Filey, *Toronto Sketches 8*, 180–3.
102 Sydney Palmer, interview, Toronto, Ontario, 4 December 2001.
103 Young, *Let's Dance*, 6.
104 Soren, interview.
105 Randel White, *Too Good to Be True: Toronto in the 1920s* (Toronto: Dundurn Press, 1993), 169.
106 Rand Sparling, interview, Toronto, Ontario, 2002.
107 *Evening Telegram*, 7 November 1929, 8.
108 Byers, interview.
109 Peiss, *Cheap Amusements*, 100; Young, *Let's Dance*, 15.
110 Comacchio,'Dancing to Perdition,' 13.

111 Moran, interview. On 'Booze and Brown Bags,' see Young, *Let's Dance*, 5–6.
112 Wilks, interview. On the use of this term, see Young, *Let's Dance.*
113 Ruth Fowler, interview, Aurora, Ontario, 7 December 2001.
114 Edelist, interview.
115 J. Clarke, interview, MHSO.
116 The UNIA, founded in 1914 by Marcus Garvey, was first established in Toronto in 1920. Garvey envisioned an organization that instilled pride and inspired purpose among blacks. See also Harry Gairey, *A Black Man's Toronto, 1914–1980*, ed. Donna Hill (Toronto: MHSO, 1981), 12.
117 R. Braithwaite, interview, MHS.
118 For more on female leadership in black churches see Evelyn Brooks Higginbotham, *Righteous Discontent: The Women's Movement in the Black Baptist Church, 1880–1920* (Cambridge, MA: Harvard University Press, 1993).
119 Clarke, interview.
120 Daniel Braithwaite, interview with Diana Braithwaite (MHSO, BLA-7986-BRA, 1981).
121 Clarke, interview.
122 Ibid.

Conclusion

1 Claire Clarke, interview, Toronto, Ontario, 28 April 2005.

Bibliography

Primary Sources

Archival Records

CITY OF TORONTO ARCHIVES, TORONTO
Draper, Dennis. *Chief Constable's Annual Reports.* Toronto: Carswell, 1929–39,
   Reports Collection, RG 9, Box 218.
Larry Becker Collection, Font 70, series 547, 600, 640, 756.

GOVERNMENT DOCUMENTS, UNIVERSITY OF TORONTO
Toronto, *President's Report,* University of Toronto, 1929–39.
Ontario, *Sessional Papers,* 1929–39.
Canada, Statistics Canada, *Selected Marriage Statistics,* 1992.
Canada, Dominion Bureau of Statistics, *Census,* 1921–41.
– *Annual Survey of Education,* 1929–39.
– *Motion Picture Theatres and Film Distribution,* 1934.
Canada, Department of Labour, *Labour Gazette,* 1929–39.
Canada, Royal Commission on Price Spreads, *Minutes of Proceedings and Evidence,*
   1935.
Canada, Royal Commission on Price Spreads, *Evidence of Special Committee,* 1934–35.
Canada, Royal Commission on Price Spreads, *Report,* 1935.
Canada, *Yearbooks,* 1929–39.

ARCHIVES OF ONTARIO, TORONTO
YWCA Series, RG 2.
Supreme Court of Ontario, RG22.

NATIONAL ARCHIVES OF CANADA, OTTAWA
Capital Case Files, RG13.

Newspapers

Evening Telegram
Globe
Globe and Mail
Hush
Jack Canuck
Mail and Empire
Toronto Daily Star

Interviews

INTERVIEWS CONDUCTED BY AUTHOR
Betty Adams, Toronto, Ontario, 29 January 2002.
Thomas Allan, Toronto, Ontario, 29 January 2002.
Elsie Andrews, Toronto, Ontario, 29 November 2001.
Ernie Atkinson, written correspondence, 20 May 2002.
Arthur Ballantine, Toronto, Ontario, 24 March 2002.
Ethel Bird, Toronto, Ontario, 26 February 2002.
Audrey Byers, Toronto, Ontario, 6 December 2001.
Helen Campbell, Toronto, Ontario, 4 July 1997.
Frances Campbell Douglas, Toronto, Ontario, 24 December 2000.
Mary Chenhall and Pat Mulligan, Toronto, Ontario, 12 December 2001.
Mary Chenhall, Toronto, Ontario, 17 January 2002.
Alice Chrysler, Toronto, Ontario, 26 February 2002.
Claire Clarke, Toronto, Ontario, 15 May 2001; 3 December 2001; 16 April 2002;
    10 October 2003; 8 March 2004; 3 February 2005; 28 April 2005.
Dorothy Coles, Toronto, Ontario, 15 March 2001.
Audrey DeFoe, Toronto, Ontario, 28 March 2002.
Doreen Doan, Toronto, Ontario, 6 December 2001.
Mabel Duncan, Toronto, Ontario, 23 November 2001.
Marion Dunlop, Toronto, Ontario, 5 June 2000.
Rose Edelist, Toronto, Ontario, 23 January 2002.
George Fass, Thornhill, Ontario, 10 December 2001.
Marion Forsythe, Toronto, Ontario, 13 March 2002.
Ruth Fowler, Aurora, Ontario, 7 December 2001.
Erma Frank, Toronto, Ontario, 15 March 2002.

William Frost, Toronto, Ontario, 15 January 2002.
Florence Fry, Toronto, Ontario, 19 March 2002.
Margaret Gairns, Toronto, Ontario, 12 November 2002.
Barbara Gallivan, Toronto, Ontario, 11 March 2002.
Elizabeth Gammon, Toronto, Ontario, 11 December 2001.
Joseph Gorenkoff, Toronto, Ontario, 14 March 2002.
Norma Hall, Toronto, Ontario, 3 December 1998.
Jean Jackson, Toronto, Ontario, 15 May 2002.
Ada Johnson, Aurora, Ontario, 7 December 2001.
Mildred Johnston, Toronto, Ontario, 28 February 2002.
Phyllis Kayler, Toronto, Ontario, 28 March 2002.
Connie Lancaster, Toronto, Ontario, 11 March 2002.
Margaret and William Lawson, Toronto, Ontario, 18 November 1999.
Rocco Longo, Toronto, Ontario, 15 February 2002.
Luella Luno, Stroud, Ontario, 23 February 2001.
Ron and Diana MacFeeters, Toronto, Ontario, 14 March 2002
Audrey Macmillan, Barrie, Ontario, 7 February 2002.
Mary Macnamara, Maple, Ontario, 15 December 2001.
Edward Mann, Richmond Hill, Ontario, 21 March 2002.
Agnes Marks, Toronto, Ontario, 11 December 2001.
Mary Marshall, Toronto, Ontario, 14 March 2002.
Margaret McLean and Joyce Cahill, Ajax, Ontario, 23 February 2002.
William McLean, Toronto, Ontario, 7 March 2002.
James McClintock, Toronto, Ontario, 20 November 2001.
Leonie McQuarrie, Toronto, Ontario, 16 November 2001.
Grace Michaels, Toronto, Ontario, 29 November 2001.
Nell Moran, Toronto, Ontario, 31 January 2002.
Sydney Palmer, Toronto, Ontario, 4 December 2001.
Sam O'Reilly, Toronto, Ontario, 27 November 2002.
William and Margie Pearson, Toronto, Ontario, 14 March 2002.
Ivy Phillips, Toronto, Ontario, 22 March 2002.
Thelma Plunkett, Toronto, Ontario, 3 November 1997.
Ian Radforth, Toronto, Ontario, 22 December 2003.
Joan Rankan, Toronto, Ontario, 22 May 2002.
Donald Ritchie, Toronto, Ontario, 22 January 2002.
Audrey Sewell, Toronto, Ontario, 20 November 2001.
Hazel Sharpe, Toronto, Ontario, 17 May 2001.
Evelyn Smith, Toronto, Ontario, 11 March 2002.
Howard Smith, Toronto, Ontario, 22 May 2002.
Margaret Snowball, Toronto, Ontario, 26 February 2002.

Joe Soren, with Gracie Soren, Toronto, Ontario, 10 December 2001.
Rand Sparling, Toronto, Ontario, 13 January 2002.
Gladys Stiff, Toronto, Ontario, 26 February 2002.
Robert Tomalin, written correspondence, 27 February 2002.
Anne Thompson, Toronto, Ontario, 28 March 2002.
Norma Vineham, Toronto, Ontario, 27 October 1997; 15 April 2005.
Ethel Watson, Toronto, Ontario, 19 March 2002.
Dora Wattie, Toronto, Ontario, 23 November 1997.
Joan Wilcox, Toronto, Ontario, 22 May 2002.
Helen Wilks, Toronto, Ontario, 31 May 2000.
Lois Wilson and June Pugsley, Toronto, Ontario, 4 December 2001.
Nora Windeatt, Reading, Pennsylvannia, 3 June 1997.
Wilfred Wood, Toronto, Ontario, 27 November 2001.

INTERVIEWS – MULTICULTURAL HISTORY SOCIETY OF ONTARIO (MHSO), TORONTO
Isobel Bailey, interview by D. Bailey, MHSO, BLA-09686-BAI, 6 August 1982.
Evelina Bassi, interview by F. Zucchi, MHSO, ITA-0661-BAS, 17 November 1977.
Constance Belfon, interview by Roy Thompson, MHSO, BLA-9718-BEL, date unrecorded.
Violet Blackman, interview by H. Casimir, MHSO, BLA-6894-BLA, 15 January 1979.
Daniel Braithwaite, interview by A. Holder, MHSO, BLA-5124-BRA, 17 August 1978.
Daniel Braithwaite, interview by Diana Braithwaite, MHSO, BLA-7986-BRA, 23 September 1981.
June Braithwaite, interview by D. Braithwaite, MHSO, BLA-7985-BRA, 20 October 1981.
Rella Braithwaite, interview by Diana Braithwaite, MHSO, BLA-7987-BRA, 26 July 1981.
J.E. Clarke, interview by Diana Braithwaite, MHSO, BLA-5122-CLA, 1 August 1978.
Verda B. Cook, interview by L. Hubbard, MHSO, BLA-7806-COO, 20 August 1980.
Mrs M. Cordone, interviewee unknown, MHSO, ITA-0775-COR, date unrecorded.
Mrs DeZori, interview by J. Zucchi, and F. Zucchi, 18 November 1977.
Mrs DiValentin, interview by J. Zucchi, MHSO, ITA-0648-DIV, 18 October 1977.
Mrs R. Ducove, interview by B. Swimmer, MHSO, JEW-1754-DUC, 1977.
Brigida Ely, interview by John Zucchi, MHSO, ITA-0878-ELY, 12 July 1977.
Mrs R. Freed, interview by S. Levitt, MHSO, JEW-2666-FRE, 16 October 1977.
Mrs Audrey Geniole, interview by A. McPeek, MHSO, ITA-3404-GEN, 20 September 1977.
Mrs Herta Frolic, interview by G. Wallen, MHSO, JEW-0796-FRO, 14 June 1977.
Mrs Carola Kahn, interview by G. Wallen, MHSO, JEW-1300-KAH, 27 July 1977.

Mrs Fanny Levine, interview by K. Levine, MHSO, JEW-0845-LEV, 17 May 1977.
Rose Orlando, interview by G. DiNardo, MHSO, ITA-6574-ORLAND, 1 May 1980.
Mrs Helen Perlmutter, interview by G. Wallen, MHSO, JEW-O798-PER, 26 June
    1977.
Rita Santagapita, interview by J. Zucchi, MHSO, ITA-664-SAN, 28 January,
    22 April 1978.
Mrs K. Shelley, interview by G. Wallen, MHSO, JEW-1173-SHE, 13 July 1977.
Geraldine Williams, interview by Donna Bailey, MHSO, BLA-8998-WIL,
    15 December 1981.

INTERVIEWS – OTHER COLLECTIONS
Mrs Antonietta Colapinto, interview by Enrico Cumbo, Toronto, Ontario,
    20 June 1989.
Anne Hinsta, Wayne Robert's Collection, Ontario Archives Sound Room, 1972.
Mr John B. Lombardi, interview by Enrico Cumbo, Toronto, Ontario,
    31 August 1989.
Mrs Chiara Pillo, interview by Enrico Cumbo, Toronto, Ontario, 24 September
    1990.

Articles

Bride, W.W. 'Trailing Toronto's Love Slayer.' *Daring Crime Cases* (April 1946):
    14–17.
Deacon, William Arthur. 'Toronto.' *Canadian Geographical Journal* 2, 5 (May
    1931): 340.
Dingman, Isabell Tumball. 'Can She Manage Alone.' *Chatelaine*, April 1932, 12,
    50, 53.
Lendrum, Arthur. 'On Relief.' *Maclean's*, April 1933, 9, 41.
MacGill, Helen Gregory. 'What of the Wage-Earning Wife?' *Chatelaine*, March
    1930, 8–9, 64–6.
– 'The Jobless Women.' *Chatelaine*, September 1930, 5, 47–8.
MacPhail, Agnes. 'Go Home Young Women, Ha, Ha.' *Chatelaine*, October 1933,
    13, 53.
Martin, Merderic. 'Go Home Young Women.' *Chatelaine*, September 1933, 10, 37.
Parson, Alice H. 'Careers or Marriage?' *Canadian Home Journal*, June 1938, 26,
    63–4.
Robins, Nan. 'I Would Rather Have Beauty Than Brains.' *Chatelaine*, February
    1931, 3, 56–7.
Royal Commission on Price Spreads. 'Garment Industry: The Speed-up at
    Eaton's.' In Irving Abella and David Miller, eds, *The Canadian Worker in the
    Twentieth Century*, 184–94 Toronto: Oxford University Press, 1978.

Sanders, Byrne Hope. 'Is Family Life on the Wane?' *Chatelaine,* June 1930, 16.
– 'The Editor's Own Page for February.' *Chatelaine,* February 1932, 4.
Templeton, Constance. 'Can Domestic Service Be Run on a Business Basis?'
   Chatelaine, December 1932, 17, 54.

Books

Allen, Frederick Lewis. *Only Yesterday: An Informal History of the Nineteen-Twenties.*
   New York: Harper Brothers, 1931.
Blumer, Herbert. *Movies and Conduct.* New York: MacMillan, 1933.
Bowden-Smart, Rodney, and Frank J. Beech, eds. *Toronto: An Illustrated Tour
   through Its Highways and Byways.* Toronto: Canadian Gravure Company, 1930.
Cassidy, Harry. *Unemployment and Relief in Ontario, 1929–1932.* Toronto: J.M.
   Dent, 1933.
Chenhall, Mary. *Memoirs: Forever in My Heart.* Toronto: unpublished, 1998.
Forman, Henry. *Our Movie Made Children.* New York: MacMillan, 1935.
Steiner, Jesse Frederic. *Americans at Play.* New York: Arno Press and New York
   Times, 1933.

Secondary Sources

Abel, Kerry. *Changing Places: History, Community, and Identity in Northeastern
   Ontario.* Montreal and Kingston: McGill-Queen's University Press, 2006.
Abella, Irving. *A Coat of Many Colours: Two Centuries of Jewish Life in Canada.*
   Toronto: Key Porter Books, 1999.
Abella, Irving, and David Miller, eds. *The Canadian Worker in the Twentieth
   Century.* Toronto: Oxford University Press, 1978.
Abella, Irving, and Harold Troper. *None Is Too Many: Canada and the Jews of
   Europe,1933–1948,* 3rd ed. Toronto: Key Porter Books, 2000.
Acton, Janice, Penny Goldsmith, and Bonnie Shepard, eds. *Women at Work:
   Ontario, 1850–1930.* Toronto: Women's Press, 1974.
Adamoski, Robert, Dorothy E. Chunn, and Robert Menzies, eds. *Contesting
   Canadian Citizenship: Historical Readings.* Peterborough, ON: Broadview Press,
   2002.
Aldgate, Anthony, and Jeffrey Richards. *Best of British: Cinema and Society from
   1930 to the Present.* London: I.B. Tauris, 1999.
Alexander, Ruth M. *The 'Girl Problem': Female Delinquency in New York: 1900–1930.*
   Ithaca, NY: Cornell University Press, 1995.
Allison, Fred. 'Remembering a Vietnam War Firefight: Changing Perspectives
   Over Time.' *Oral History Review* 31, 2 (2004): 69–83.

Archibald, Peter. 'Distress, Dissent and Alienation: Hamilton Workers in the
    Great Depression.' *Urban History Review* 21, 1 (October 1992): 2–32.
Armatage, Kay. *Gendering the Nation: Canadian Women's Cinema.* Toronto:
    University of Toronto Press, 1999.
Armstrong, Pat, and Hugh Armstrong. *The Double Ghetto: The Segregation of
    Women's Work in Canada.* Toronto: McClelland and Stewart, 1978.
Arnup, Katherine. 'Raising the Dionne Quintuplets: Lessons for Modern
    Mothers.' *The Journal of Canadian Studies* 29 (1994–5): 65–85.
– *Education for Motherhood: Advice for Mothers in Twentieth-Century Canada.*
    Toronto: University of Toronto Press, 1994.
Avery, Donald. *Reluctant Host: Canada's Response to Immigrant Workers, 1896–1894.*
    McClelland and Stewart, 1985.
Axelrod, Paul. 'Higher Education, Utilitarianism, and the Acquisitive Society:
    Canada, 1930–1980.' In Michael Cross and Gregory Kealey, eds, *Modern
    Canada*, 179–205.
Backhouse, Constance. *Colour Coded: A Legal History of Racism in Canada,
    1900–1950.* Toronto: University of Toronto Press, 1999.
Baillargeon, Denise. 'Beyond Romance: Courtship and Marriage in Montreal
    between the Wars.' In Veronica Strong-Boag, Adele Perry, and Mona
    Gleason, eds, *Rethinking Canada: The Promise of Women's History*, 203–220.
– *Making Do: Women, Family and Home in Montreal during the Great Depression.*
    Trans. Yvonne Klein. Waterloo: Wilfred Laurier University Press, 1999.
– 'If You Had No Money, You Had No Trouble. Did You? Montreal Working-
    Class Housewives during the Great Depression.' In Wendy Mitchinson et al.,
    eds, *Canadian Women: A Reader*, 251–68.
– *Ménagères au temps de la crise.* Montreal: Éditions de Remue-Ménage, 1991.
Barber, Marilyn. *Immigrant Domestic Servants in Canada.* Canadian Historical
    Association pamphlet. Ottawa: CHA, 1991.
Barron, Dana L. 'Sex and Single Girls in the Twentieth-Century City.' *Journal of
    Urban History* 25, 6 (September 1999): 839.
Belton, John, ed. *Movies and Mass Culture.* New Jersey: Rutgers University Press,
    1996.
Berry, Sarah. *Screen Style: Fashion and Femininity in 1930s Hollywood.* Minneapolis:
    University of Minnesota Press, 2000.
Berton, Pierre. *The Great Depression, 1929–1939.* Toronto: McClelland and
    Stewart, 1990.
Betcherman, Lita-Rose. *The Swastika and the Maple Leaf: Fascist Movements in
    Canada in the Thirties.* Toronto: Fitzhenry and Whiteside, 1975.
Bhavnani, Kum-Kum. *Feminism and 'Race'.* Oxford: Oxford University Press,
    2001.

Bird, Pat. 'Hamilton Working Women in the Period of the Great Depression.' *Atlantis* 8, 2 (1982): 125–36.

Borland, Katherine. '"That's not what I said": Interpretive Conflict in Oral Narrative Research.' In Robert Perks and Alistair Thomson, eds, *The Oral History Reader*, 320–32.

Bornat, Joanna. 'A Second Take: Revisiting Interviews with a Different Purpose.' *The Journal of Oral History* 31, 1 (2003): 47–54.

– 'Oral History as a Social Movement: Reminiscences and Older People.' In Robert Perks and Alistair Thomson, eds, *The Oral History Reader*, 189–205.

Bourne, Paula, ed. *Women's Paid: Unpaid Work: History and Contemporary Perspectives*. Toronto: New Hogtown Press, 1985.

Bradbury, Bettina, ed. *Canadian Family History*, 2nd ed. Toronto: Irwin, 2000.

– 'Gender at Work at Home: Family Decisions, the Labour Market and Girls' Contributions to the Family Income.' In Bettina Bradbury, ed., *Canadian Family History*, 177–98.

– 'Introduction.' In Bettina Bradbury, ed., *Canadian Family History*, 2nd ed., 1–12.

– *Working Families: Age, Gender, and Daily Survival in Industrializing Montreal*. Oxford: Oxford University Press, 1993.

– 'Women's History and Working-Class History.' *Labour/Le Travail* 19 (Spring 1987): 23–44.

Brah, Avtar. 'Difference, Diversity, Differentiation.' In Kum-Kum Bhavnani, ed., *Feminism and Race*, 456–78.

Braithwaite, Rella. *The Black Women in Canada*. Toronto: Ontario Institute for Studies in Education, 1975.

Brand, Dionne. *No Burden to Carry: Narratives of Black Working Women in Ontario, 1920s–1950s*. Toronto: Women's Press, 1991.

Briskin, L., and L. Yanz, eds. *Union Sisters: Women in the Labour Movement*. Toronto: Women's Press, 1983.

Broadfoot, Barry. *Ten Lost Years: Memories of Canadians Who Survived the Depression*. Toronto: Doubleday, 1973.

Brouwer, Ruth Compton. *New Women for God*. Toronto: University of Toronto Press, 1990.

Brown, Jennifer. *Strangers in Blood: Fur Trade Company Families in Indian Country*. Vancouver: University of British Columbia Press, 1980.

Brown, Jennifer, and Elizabeth Vibert, eds. *Reading beyond Words: Context for Native History*. Peterborough, ON: Broadview Press, 1995.

Brown, Lorne. *When Freedom Was Lost: The Unemployed, the Agitator and the State*. Montreal-Buffalo: Black Rose Books, 1987.

Bullen, John. 'Hidden Workers: Child Labour and the Family Economy in Late Nineteenth-Century Urban Ontario.' In Bettina Bradbury, ed., *Canadian Family History*, 2nd ed., 199–219.

Burman, Barbara, and Carole Turbin, eds. *Material Strategies: Dress and Gender in Historical Perspective*. Oxford: Blackwell, 2003.

Burton, Antoinette. *Burdens of History: British Feminists, Indian Women, and Imperial Culture, 1865–1915*. Chapel Hill: University of North Carolina Press, 1994.

Bye, Christina. 'I Like to Hoe My Own Row: A Saskatchewan Farm Woman's Notions about Work and Womanhood during the Great Depression.' *Frontiers* 26, 3 (2005): 135–67.

Cameron, Ardis. *Radicals of the Worst Sort: Laboring Women in Lawrence Massachusetts, 1860–1912*. Urbana: University of Illinois Press, 1993.

Campbell, Lara. 'Respectable Citizens of Canada: Gender, Family, and Unemployment in the Great Depression, Ontario.' PhD dissertation, Queen's University, 2002.

Canning, Kathleen. *Gender History and Practice: Historical Perspectives on Bodies, Class, and Citizenship*. Ithaca and London: Cornell University Press, 2006.

Carrington, Kerry. *Offending Girls: Sex, Youth and Justice*. Sydney, Australia: Allen and Unwin, 1993.

Chauncey, George. *Gay New York: Gender, Urban Culture, and the Making of the Gay World, 1890–1940*. New York: Basic Books, 1994.

Christie, Nancy, ed. *Households of Faith: Family, Gender, and Community in Canada, 1760–1969*. Montreal and Kingston: McGill-Queen's University Press, 2002.

– *Engendering the State: Family, Work, and Welfare in Canada*. Toronto: University of Toronto Press, 2000.

Christie, Nancy, and Michael Gauvreau, eds. *Mapping the Margins: The Family and Social Discipline in Canada, 1700–1975*. Montreal and Kingston: McGill-Queen's University Press, 2004.

Chunn, Dorothy. *From Punishment to Doing Good: Family Courts and Socialized Justice in Ontario, 1880–1940*. Toronto: University of Toronto Press, 1992.

Clegg, Brenda. 'Black Female Domestics during the Great Depression in New York City, 1930–1940.' PhD dissertation, University of Michigan, 1983.

Clio Collective. *Quebec Women: A History*. Trans. Roger Gannon, and Rosalind Gill. Toronto: The Women's Press, 1987.

Cohen, Lizbeth. *Making a New Deal: Industrial Workers in Chicago, 1919–1939*. Cambridge: Cambridge University Press, 1990.

Collins, Robert. *You Had to Be There: An Intimate Portrait of the Generation That Survived the Depression, Won the War, and Re-Invented Canada*. Toronto: McClelland and Stewart, 1997.

Comacchio, Cynthia R. 'History of Us: Social Science, History, and the Relations of Family in Canada.' *Labour/Le Travail* 46 (Fall 2000): 167.

– *Infinite Bonds of Family: Domesticity in Canada, 1890–1940*. Toronto: University of Toronto Press, 1999.

– 'A Postscript for Father: Defining a New Fatherhood in Interwar Canada.' *Canadian Historical Review* 78, 3 (1997): 385–408.

- 'Dancing to Perdition: Adolescence and Leisure in Interwar English Canada.'
  Journal of Canadian Studies 32, 3 (Autumn 1997): 5–35.
- 'Beneath the Sentimental Veil: Families and Family History in Canada.'
  Labour/Le Travail 33 (Spring 1994): 279–302.
- *Nations Are Built of Babies: Saving Ontario's Mothers and Children, 1900–1940.*
  Montreal and Kingston: McGill-Queen's University Press, 1993.
- 'Another Brick in the Wall: Toward a History of the Welfare State in Canada.'
  left history 1, 1 (Spring 1993): 103–8.
Cooper, Afua. 'Constructing Black Women's Historical Knowledge.' *Atlantis* 25,
  1 (2000): 39.
Cott, Nancy F. 'Passionlessness: An Interpretation of Victorian Sexual Ideology,
  1790–1850.' *Signs* 4 (1978): 219–36.
Cotter, Chris. *Toronto between the Wars: Life in the City, 1919–1939.* Toronto:
  Firefly, 2004.
Crane, Susan. 'Writing the Individual Back into Collective Memory.' *American
  Historical Review* 102, 5 (December 1997): 1372–85.
Creese, Gillian. 'The Politics of Dependence: Women, Work, and
  Unemployment in the Vancouver Labour Movement.' In Gillian Creese, and
  Veronica Strong-Boag, eds, *British Columbia Reconsidered: Essays on Women*,
  364–90.
Creese, Gillian, and Veronica Strong-Boag. *British Columbia Reconsidered: Essays
  in Women's History.* Vancouver: Press Gang, 1992.
Cross, Michael, and Gregory Kealey. *Modern Canada, 1930–1980s.* Toronto:
  McClelland and Stewart, 1984.
Crowley, Terry. 'Agnes MacPhail and the Politics of Equality.' *Labour/Le Travail*
  28 (1991): 129–48.
Cruikshank, Julie. *The Social Life of Stories: Narrative and Knowledge in Yukon
  Territory.* Lincoln: University of Nebraska Press, 1998.
- 'Discovery of Gold on the Klondike: Perspectives from Oral Tradition.' In
  Jennifer Brown and Elizabeth Vibert, eds, *Reading beyond Words: Context for
  Native History*, 433–59.
- *Life Lived Like a Story: Life Stories of Three Yukon Native Elders.* Lincoln:
  University of Nebraska Press, 1990.
Cumbo, Eric. 'As the Twig Is Bent, the Tree's Inclined: Growing Up Italian in
  Toronto, 1905–1940.' PhD dissertation, University of Toronto 1996.
D'acierino, Pellegrino. *The Italian American Heritage: A Companion to Literature
  and Arts.* New York: Garland, 1999.
Danylewycz, Marta. *Taking the Veil.* Toronto: McClelland and Stewart, 1987.
Das Gupta, Tania. 'Families of Native People, Immigrants, and People of
  Colour.' In Nancy Mandell and Ann Duffy, eds, *Canadian Families: Diversity,
  Conflict and Change*, 141–74.

Das Gupta, Tania, and Franca Iacovetta. 'Whose Canada Is It? Immigrant
  Women, Women of Colour and Feminist Critiques of 'Multiculturalism.'
  Atlantis 24, 2 (Spring 2000): 1–4.
Davidoff, Leonore, and Catherine Hall. *Family Fortunes: Men and Women of the
  English Middle Class, 1780–1850.* London: Hutchinson, 1987.
Davies, Margery. *Women's Place Is at the Typewriter: Office Work and Office Workers,
  1870–1882.* Philadelphia: Temple University Press, 1982.
Davis, Lauren B. *The Stubborn Season.* Toronto: Harper Flamingo, 2002.
Dawson, Michael. 'Taking the "D" out of "Depression": The Promise of Tourism
  in British Columbia, 1935–1939.' *BC Studies* 132 (Winter 2001–2): 31–56.
Demerson, Velma. *Incorrigible.* Waterloo: Wilfred Laurier University Press, 2004.
Dennis, Richard. 'Territorial Maneuvers: Space and Place in Canadian Cities.'
  International Journal of Canadian Studies 24 (2001): 217–26.
– '"Zoning" before Zoning: The Regulation of Apartment Housing in Early
  Twentieth-Century Winnipeg and Toronto.' *Planning Perspectives* 15 (2000):
  268.
– 'Morley Callaghan and the Moral Geography of Toronto.' *British Journal of
  Canadian Studies* 14, 1 (1999): 35–51.
– 'Apartment Housing in Canada, 1900–1940.' *Urban History Review* 26, 2
  (March 1998): 17.
Dirks, Patricia. 'Reinventing Christian Masculinity and Fatherhood: The
  Canadian Protestant Experience, 1900–1920.' In Nancy Christie, ed.,
  Households of Faith: Family, Gender, and Community in Canada, 1760–1969,
  290–318.
Donely, James, Anne Freedberg, and Laura Marcus, eds. *Close Up, 1927–1933:
  Cinema and Modernism.* Princeton: Princeton University Press, 1998.
Dorland, Michael. *So Close to the States: The Emergence of Canadian Feature Film
  Policy.* Toronto: University of Toronto Press, 1998.
Draper, Paula. 'Surviving Their Survival: Women, Memory and the Holocaust.'
  In Marlene Epp, Franca Iacovetta, and Frances Swyripa, eds, *Sisters or
  Strangers? Immigrant, Ethnic and Racialized Women in Canadian History,*
  399–414.
Draper, Paula, and Janice B. Karlinsky. 'Abraham's Daughters: Women, Charity
  and Power in the Canadian Jewish Community.' In Franca Iacovetta, Paula
  Draper, and Robert Ventresca, eds, *A Nation of Immigrants: Women, Workers, and
  Communities in Canadian History, 1840s–1960s,* 186–202.
Dua, Enaskhi. *Scratching the Surface, Canadian Anti-Racist Feminist Thought.*
  Toronto: Women's Press, 1999.
– 'Beyond Diversity: Exploring the Ways in which the Discourse of Race Has
  Shaped the Institution of the Nuclear Family.' In Enaskhi Dua, ed., *Scratching
  the Surface, Canadian Anti-Racist Feminist Thought,* 237–60.

Dubinsky, Karen. *The Second Greatest Disappointment: Honeymooning and Tourism at Niagara Falls*. Toronto: Between the Lines, 1999.
– *Improper Advances: Rape and Heterosexual Conflict in Ontario, 1880–1929*. Chicago: University of Chicago Press, 1993.
Eicher, Joanne E., ed. *Dress and Ethnicity*. Oxford: Berg, 1995.
Ely, Melvin Patrick. *The Adventures of Amos 'n' Andy: A Social History of an American Phenomenon*. New York: Free Press, 1991.
Enstad, Nan. *Ladies of Labor, Girls of Adventure: Working Women, Popular Culture, and Labor Politics at the Turn of the Twentieth Century*. New York: Columbia University Press, 1999.
Epp, Marlene, Franca Iacovetta, and Frances Swyripa, eds. *Sisters or Strangers? Immigrant, Ethnic, and Racialized Women in Canadian History*. Toronto: University of Toronto Press, 2004.
– *Women without Men: Mennonite Refugees of the Second World War*. Toronto: University of Toronto Press, 2000.
– 'The Memory of Violence: Soviet and East European Mennonite Refugees and Rape in the Second World War.' *Journal of Women's History* 9, 1 (1997): 58–87.
Etter-Lewis, Gwendolyn. 'Black Women's Life Stories: Reclaiming Self in Narrative Texts.' In Sherna Berger Gluck and Daphne Patai, eds, *Women's Words: The Feminist Practice of Oral History*, 43–58.
Ewen, Elizabeth. *Immigrant Women in the Land of Dollars: Life and Culture on the Lower East Side, 1890–1925*. New York: Monthly Review Press, 1985.
Faderman, Lillian. *Odd Girls and Twilight Lovers: A History of Lesbian Life in Twentieth-Century America*. New York: Penguin, 1991.
Fahrni, Magda. '"Ruffled" Mistresses and "Discontented" Maids: Respectability and the Case of Domestic Service, 1880–1914.' *Labour/Le Travail* 39 (1997): 69–97.
Fetherling, Douglas. *Documents in Canadian Film*. Peterborough: Broadview Press, 1988.
Filey, Mike. *Toronto Sketches 8: The Way We Were*. Toronto: Dundurn Press, 2004.
– *Toronto Sketches 7: The Way We Were*. Toronto: Dundurn Press, 2003.
– *A Toronto Album 2: More Glimpses of the City That Was*. Toronto: The Dundurn Group, 2002.
– *A Toronto Album: Glimpses of the City That Was*. Toronto: The Dundurn Group, 2001.
– *Toronto Sketches 6: The Way We Were*. Toronto: Dundurn Press, 2000.
– *Toronto Sketches 5: The Way We Were*. Toronto: Dundurn Press, 1997.
– *I Remember Sunnyside: The Rise and Fall of a Magical Era*. Toronto: The Dundurn Group, 1996.

– *Toronto Sketches: The Way We Were*. Toronto: Dundurn Press, 1992.

Finkel, Alvin. *Business and Social Reform in the Thirties*. Toronto: James Lorimer, 1970.

Flynn, Karen. 'Experience and Identity: Black Immigrant Nurses to Canada, 1950–1980.' In Marlene Epp, Franca Iacovetta, and Frances Swyripa, eds, *Sisters or Strangers? Immigrant, Ethnic and Racialized Women in Canadian History*, 381–98.

Frager, Ruth. *Sweatshop Strife: Class, Ethnicity, and Gender in the Jewish Labour Movement of Toronto, 1900–1939*. Toronto: University of Toronto Press, 1993.

– 'Class, Ethnicity and Gender in the Eaton Strikes of 1912 and 1934.' In Franca Iacovetta and Mariana Valverde, eds, *Gender Conflicts: New Essays in Women's History*, 189–228.

– 'No Proper Deal: Women Workers and the Canadian Labour Movement, 1870–1940.' In L. Briskin and L. Yanz, eds, *Union Sisters: Women in the Labour Movement*, 44–66.

Frankenberg, Ruth. *The Social Construction of White Women: Whiteness Race Matters*.Minneapolis: University of Minnesota Press, 1993.

Gabaccia, Donna, and Franca Iacovetta, eds. *Women, Gender and Transnational Lives:Italian Workers of the World*. Toronto: University of Toronto Press, 2002.

Gabaccia, Donna, Franca Iacovetta, and Fraser Ottanelli. 'Labouring across National Borders: Class, Gender and Militancy in the Proletarian Mass Migration.' *International Labor and Working Class History* 66 (2004): 57–77.

Gagan, Rosemary. *A Sensitive Independence*. Montreal and Kingston: McGill-Queen's University Press, 1992.

Gairey, Harry. *A Black Man's Toronto, 1914–1980*. Ed. Donna Hill. Toronto: MHSO, 1981.

Garner, Hugh. *Cabbagetown*. Toronto: McGraw-Hill Ryerson, 1968.

Gaskell, Jane. 'Education and Job Opportunities for Women: Patterns of Enrolment and Economic Returns.' In Naomi Hersom and Dorothy Smith, eds, *Women and the Canadian Labour Force*, 257–306.

Gauvreau, Michael. *The Evangelical Century: College and Creed in English Canada from the Great Revival to the Great Depression*. Montreal and Kingston: McGill-Queen's University Press, 1991.

Georges, Robert, and Michael Owen Jones. *People Studying People: The Human Element in Fieldwork*. Berkeley and Los Angeles: University of California Press, 1980.

Gluck, Sherna Berger, and Daphne Patai. *Women's Words: The Feminist Practice of Oral History*. New York: Routledge, 1991.

Gordon, Linda. *Pitied But Not Entitled: Single Mothers and the History of Welfare, 1890–1935*. Cambridge, MA: Harvard University Press, 1995.

– 'Black and White Visions of Welfare: Women's Welfare Activism, 1890–1945.'
In Vicki L. Ruiz and Ellen Carol Dubois, eds, *Unequal Sisters: A Multicultural
Reader in U. S. Women's History*, 157–85.
– *Heroes of Their Own Lives: The Politics and History of Family Violence, Boston,
1880–1960.* New York: Penguin, 1988.
Gorham, Deborah. *Caring and Curing: Historical Perspectives on Women and
Healing in Canada.* Ottawa: Ottawa University Press, 1994.
Graves, Pamela. *Labour Women: Women in British Working-Class Politics, 1918–
1939.* Cambridge: Cambridge University Press, 1994.
Grayson, L.M., and Michael Bliss. *The Wretched of Canada: Letters to R.B. Bennett,
1930–1935.* Toronto: University of Toronto Press, 1971.
Gross, Jan. *Neighbours: The Destruction of the Jewish Community in Jedwabne, Poland.*
Princeton: Princeton University Press, 2001.
Guard, Julie. 'Authenticity on the Line: Women Workers, Native "Scabs," and
the Multi-ethnic Politics of Identity in a Left-Led Strike in Cold War Canada.'
Journal of Women's History 15, 4 (Winter 2004): 117–40.
Guglielmo, Jennifer. 'Italian Women's Proletarian Feminism in New York City
Garment Trades, 1890s–1940s.' In Donna Gabaccia and Franca Iacovetta,
eds, *Women, Gender, and Transnational Lives: Italian Workers of the World*,
247–98.
Hagemann, Karen. *Frauenalltag und Männerpolitik: Alltagsleben und gesellschaft-
liches Handeln von Arbeiterfrauen in der Weimarer Republik.* Bonn: Verlag J.H.W.
Dietz Nachf., 1990.
Halbwachs, Maurice. *The Collective Memory.* Trans. Francis J. Ditter, Jr, and Vida
Yazdi Ditter. New York: Harper and Row, 1980.
– *On Collective Memory.* Trans. Lewis A. Coser. Chicago: University of Chicago
Press, 1992.
Hall, Catherine. *White, Male and Middle-Class: Explorations in Feminism and
History.* New York: Routledge, 1992.
Hall, Catherine, and Sonya Rose, eds. *At Home with the Empire: Metropolitan
Culture and the Imperial World.* Cambridge: Cambridge University Press, 2006.
Harney, Robert. 'Men without Women: Italian Migrants in Canada, 1885–1930.'
In Franca Iacovetta, Paula Draper, and Robert Ventresca, eds, *A Nation of
Immigrants: Women, Workers, and Communities in Canadian History, 1840s–1960s*,
206–30.
Harney, Robert F., and Vincena Scarpaci. *Little Italies in North America.* Toronto:
MHSO, 1981.
Healey, Theresa M. 'Trouble Enough: Gender, Social Policy and the Politics of
Place in Vancouver and Saskatoon, 1929–1939.' PhD dissertation, Simon
Fraser University, 1998.

Heap, Ruby, and Alison Prentice. *Gender and Education in Ontario: An Historical Reader.* Toronto: Canadian Scholars' Press, 1991.

Henry, Keith S. *Black Politics in Toronto since WWI.* Toronto: Multicultural History Society of Ontario, 1981.

Heron, Craig. *The Canadian Labour Movement: A Short History*, 2nd ed. Toronto: James Lorimer, 1996.

– 'The High School and the Household Economy in Working-Class Hamilton, 1890–1940.' *Historical Studies in Education* 7, 2 (1995): 217–59.

– *Working in Steel: The Early Years in Canada, 1883–1935.* Toronto: McClelland and Stewart, 1988.

Hersom, Naomi, and Dorothy Smith, eds. *Women and the Canadian Labour Force.* Ottawa: Social Science and Humanities Research Council, 1982.

Hewitt, Nancy A. *Southern Discomfort: Women's Activism in Tampa Florida, 1880–1920s.* Urbana: University of Illinois Press, 2001.

– 'Beyond the Search for Sisterhood: American Women's History in the 1980s.' *Social History* 10 (October 1985): 299–322.

Higginbotham, Evelyn Brooks. *Righteous Discontent: The Women's Movement in the Black Baptist Church, 1880–1920.* Cambridge: Harvard University Press, 1993.

– 'African American Women's History and the Meta-language of Race.' *Signs* (1992): 251–74.

Hill-Collins, Patricia. *Black Feminist Thought, Knowledge, Consciousness, and the Politics of Empowerment.* Boston: Unwin Hyman, 1990.

Hillyard-Little, Margaret. *No Car, No Radio, No Liquor Permit: The Moral Regulation of Single Mothers in Ontario, 1920–1997.* Toronto: Oxford University Press, 1998.

– 'The Blurring of Boundaries: Private and Public Welfare for Single Mothers in Ontario.' *Studies in Political Economy* 47 (Summer 1995): 89–109.

Hobbs, Margaret. 'Gendering Work and Welfare: Women's Relationships to Wage-Work and Social Policy during the Great Depression.' PhD dissertation, University of Toronto 1995.

– 'Equality and Difference: Feminism and the Defence of Women Workers during the Depression.' *Labour/Le Travail* 32 (Fall 1993): 201–223.

– 'Rethinking Antifeminism in the 1930s: Gender Crisis or Workplace Justice? A Response to Alice Kessler-Harris.' *Gender and History* 5, 1 (Spring 1993): 4–15.

Hobbs, Margaret, and Ruth Roach Pierson. 'A Kitchen That Wastes No Steps: Gender, Class and the Home Improvement Plan, 1936–1940.' *Histoire Sociale/Social History* 31 (May 1988): 9–37.

Hogarth, David. 'The Other Documentary Tradition: Early Radio Documentaries in Canada.' *Historical Journal of Film, Radio and Television* 21, 2 (2001): 123–35.

Holton, Margaret Lindsay, ed. *Spirit of Toronto: 1834–1984*. Toronto: Image Publishing, 1983.

Horn, Michiel. *The Dirty Thirties: Canadians in the Great Depression*. Toronto: Copp Clark, 1972.

– *The Great Depression of the 1930s in Canada*. Ottawa: Canadian Historical Assocation Booklet #39, 1984.

Houston, Susan E. '"A little steam, a little sizzle and a little sleaze": English Language Tabloids in the Interwar Period.' *Papers of the Bibliographical Society of Canada* 40, 1 (2002): 37–59.

Howard, Irene. 'The Mothers' Council of Vancouver: Holding the Fort for the Unemployed, 1935–38.' *BC Studies* 69–70 (Spring 1988): 249–87.

Hughes, Pennethorne C.J. 'Dreams: Films.' In James Donely, Anne Freedberg, and Laura Marcus, eds, *Close-Up, 1927–1933: Cinema and Modernism*, 260–2.

Hunter, Tera W. *To 'joy my freedom: Southern Black Women's Lives and Labors after the Civil War*. Cambridge, MA: Harvard University Press, 1997.

Iacovetta, Franca. 'Gendering Trans/National Historiographies: Feminists Rewriting Canadian History.' *Journal of Women's History* 19, 1 (Spring 2007): 206–13.

– 'Post Modern Ethnography, Historical Materialism and Decenteringthe (Male) Authorial Voice: A Feminist Conversation.' *Histoire Sociale / Social History* 64, 132 (November 1999): 275–93.

– 'Gossip, Contest, and Power in the Making of Suburban Bad Girls: Toronto, 1945–1960.' *Canadian Historical Review* 80, 4 (1999): 585–623.

– 'Manly Militants, Cohesive Communities and Defiant Domestics: Writing about Immigrants in Canadian Historical Scholarship.' *Labour / Le Travail* 36 (1995): 217–52.

– *Such Hardworking People: Italian Immigrants in Postwar Toronto*. Montreal and Kingston: McGill-Queen's University Press, 1992.

Iacovetta, Franca, and Donna Gabaccia. *Women, Gender and Transnational Lives: Italian Workers of the World*. Toronto: University of Toronto Press, 2002.

Iacovetta, Franca, and Wendy Mitchinson, eds. *On the Case: Explorations in Social History*. Toronto: University of Toronto Press, 1998.

Iacovetta, Franca, and Mariana Valverde, eds. *Gender Conflicts: New Essays in Women's History*. Toronto: University of Toronto Press, 1992.

Iacovetta, Franca, Paula Draper, and Robert Ventresca, eds. *A Nation of Immigrants: Women, Workers, and Communities in Canadian History, 1840s–1960s*. Toronto: University of Toronto Press, 1998.

Iacovetta, Franca, Roberto Perin, and Angelo Principe. *Enemies Within: Italian and Other Internees in Canada and Abroad*. Toronto: University of Toronto Press, 2000.

James, Carl E. *Seeing Ourselves: Exploring Ethnicity, Race and Culture,* 3rd ed. Toronto: Thomson Educational, 2003.

– *Experiencing Difference.* Halifax: Fernwood, 2000.

James, Carl E., and Adrienne Shadd, eds. *Talking about Identity: Encounters in Race, Ethnicity, and Language.* Toronto: Between the Lines, 2001.

Jones, Jacqueline. 'Race and Gender in Modern America.' *Reviews in American History* (March 1998): 220–38.

Karney, Robyn, ed. *Cinema Year by Year, 1894–2003.* London: DK Publishing, 2003.

Katz, Jonathan. *The Invention of Heterosexuality.* New York: Penguin Books, 1995.

Kealey, Linda. *Enlisting Women for the Cause: Women, Labour, and the Left in Canada, 1890–1920.* Toronto: University of Toronto Press, 1998.

– 'Canadian Socialism and the Woman Question, 1900–1914.' *Labour/Le Travail* 13 (Spring 1984): 77–100.

– ed. *A Not Unreasonable Claim: Women and Reform in Canada, 1890–1920.* Toronto: Canadian Women's Educational Press, 1979.

Kealey, Linda, and Joan Sangster. *Beyond the Vote: Canadian Women and Politics.* Toronto: University of Toronto Press, 1989.

Kerber, Linda, et al. 'Forum: Beyond Rules, beyond Spheres: Thinking about Gender in the Early Republic.' *William and Mary Quarterly* 46, 3 (July 1989): 565–85.

– 'Separate Spheres, Female Worlds, Woman's Place: The Rhetoric of Women's History.' *The Journal of American History* 75, 1 (June 1988): 9–39.

Kessler-Harris, Alice. *Out to Work: A History of Wage-Earning Women in the United States,* 20th anniversary edition. New York: Oxford University Press, 2003.

– 'Reply to Hobbs.' *Gender and History* 5, 1 (Spring 1993): 16–19.

– 'Gender Ideology in Historical Reconstruction: A Case Study from the 1930s.' *Gender and History* 1, 1 (Spring 1989): 31–49.

Klee, Marcus. 'Fighting the Sweatshop in Depression Ontario: Capital, Labour and the Industrial Standards Act.' *Labour/Le Travail* 45 (Spring 2000): 13–51.

– 'Between the Scylla and Charybdis of Anarchy and Despotism: The State, Capital, and the Working Class in the Great Depression Toronto, 1929–1940.' PhD dissertation, Queen's University 1998.

Klubock, Thomas. 'History and Memory in Neoliberal Chile: Patricio Guzman's Obstinate Memory and the Battle of Chile.' *Radical History Review* 85 (2003): 272–82.

Koven, Seth, and Sonya Michel, eds. *Mothers of the New World: Maternalist Politics and the Origins of Welfare States.* New York: Routledge, 1993.

Lasalle, Mick. *Complicated Women: Sex and Power in Pre-Code Hollywood.* New York: Thomas Dunn, 2000.

Latham, Barbara, and Roberta J. Pazdro, eds. *Not Just Pin Money: Selected Essays on the History of Women's Work in British Columbia.* Victoria: Canadian Catalogue Publications, 1984.

Lemon, James. *Toronto since 1918: An Illustrated History.* Toronto: James Lorimer, 1985.

Lerner, Gerda. 'Reconceptualizing Difference among Women.' *Journal of Women's History* 1 (Winter 1990): 106–22.

– *The Creation of Patriarchy.* Oxford: Oxford University Press, 1986.

Lévesque, Andrée. *Making and Breaking the Rules: Women in Quebec, 1919–1939.* Trans. Yvonne M. Klein. Toronto: McClelland and Stewart, 1994.

– 'Deviant Anonymous: Single Mothers at the Hôpital de la Miséricorde in Montreal, 1929–1939.' *Historical Papers* (1984): 168–84.

Light, Beth, and Ruth Roach Pierson. *No Easy Road: Women in Canada, 1920s to 1960s.* Toronto: New Hogtown Press, 1990.

Lindstrom, Varpu. '"I Won't Be A Slave!": Finnish Domestics in Canada, 1911–1930.' In Franca Iacovetta, Paula Draper, and Robert Ventresca, eds, *A Nation of Immigrants: Women, Workers, and Communities in Canadian History, 1840s–1960s,* 166–85.

– *Defiant Sisters: A Social History of Finnish Women in Canada, 1890–1930.* Toronto: Multicultural History Society of Ontario, 1988.

Liversedge, Ronald. *Recollections of the On to Ottawa Trek.* Ed. Victor Hoar. Toronto: McClelland and Stewart, 1973.

Livesay, Dorothy. *Right Hand Life Hand: A True Life of the Thirties: Paris, Toronto, Montreal, the West and Vancouver. Love Politics, the Depression and Feminism.* Toronto: Porcepic, 1977.

Llewellyn, Kristina. 'Productive Tensions: Feminist Readings for Women Teachers' Oral Histories.' *Oral History Forum / Forum d'histoire orale* 23(2003): 89–112.

Lowe, Graham. *Women in the Administrative Revolution: The Feminization of Clerical Work.* Toronto: University of Toronto Press, 1987.

Lummis, Trevor. 'Structure and Validity in Oral Evidence.' In Robert Perks and Alistair Thomson, eds, *The Oral History Reader,* 273–83.

– *Listening to History: The Authenticity of Oral Evidence.* London: Hutchinson Education Press, 1987.

Lundy, Katerina, and Barbara Warme, eds. *Work in the Canadian Context: Continuity despite Change.* Toronto: Butterworths, 1981.

Lurie, Alison. *The Language of Clothes.* Toronto: Random House, 1981.

Luxton, Meg. *More Than a Labour of Love.* Toronto: Women's Press, 1980.

Macdonald, Jeanne, Nadine Stoikoff, and Randall White. *Toronto Women: Changing Faces, 1900–2000. A Photographic Journey.* Toronto: Eastendbooks, 1997.

Macleod, Catherine. 'Women in Production: The Toronto Dressmakers' Strike of 1931.' In Janice Acton, Penny Goldsmith, and Bonnie Shepherd, eds, *Women at Work: Ontario, 1850–1930*, 309–29.

Manchester, William. *The Glory and the Dream: A Narrative History of America, 1932–1972*. New York: Bantam Books, 1974.

Mandell, Nancy, and Ann Duffy. *Canadian Families: Diversity, Conflict and Change*. Toronto: Harcourt Brace, 1995.

Manley, John. '"Starve, Be Damned!": Communists and Canada's Urban Unemployed, 1929–1939.' *Canadian Historical Review* 79, 3 (September 1998): 466–91.

– 'Communism and the Canadian Working Class during the Great Depression: The Workers' Unity League, 1930–36.' PhD dissertation, Dalhousie University, 1984.

Mann, Edward. *A Mann for All Seasons: A Memoir*. Toronto: Lugus, 1996.

Mansell, Diana. *Forging the Future: a History of Nursing in Canada*. Ann Arbor, MI: Thomas Press, 2004.

Marchetti, Gina. *Romance and the 'Yellow Peril': Race, Sex, and Discursive Strategies in Hollywood Fiction*. Los Angeles: University of California Press, 1993.

Marks, Lynne. *Revivals and Roller Rinks: Religion, Leisure and Identity in Late-Nineteenth-Century Small-Town Ontario*. Toronto: University of Toronto Press, 1996.

May, Lary. *Screening Out the Past: The Birth of Mass Culture and the Motion Picture Industry*. Chicago: University of Chicago Press, 1980.

McCallum, Margaret E. 'Keeping Women in Their Place: The Minimum Wage in Canada, 1910–1925.' *Labour/Le Travail* 17 (1986): 29–56.

McClelland, Susan. 'Nanny Abuse: Why Ottawa Played Along.' *The Walrus* (March 2005): 42–9

McLaren, Angus. *Our Own Master Race: Eugenics in Canada, 1885–1945*. Toronto: McClelland and Stewart, 1990.

McLean, Lorna R., and Marilyn Barber. 'In Search of Comfort and Independence: Irish Immigrant Domestic Servants Encounter the Courts, Jails and Asylums in 19th Century Ontario.' In Marlene Epp, Franca Iacovetta, and Frances Swyripa, eds, *Sisters or Strangers? Immigrant, Ethnic, and Racialized Women in Canadian History*, 133–60.

McLintock, Anne. *Imperial Leather: Race, Gender and Sexuality in the Colonial Contest*. New York: Routledge, 1995.

McPherson, Kathryn. *Bedside Matters: The Transformation of Canadian Nursing, 1900–1990*. Toronto: Oxford University Press, 1996.

Medeiros, Patricia. 'Images of Women during the Great Depression and the Golden Age of American Film.' PhD dissertation, University of California, San Diego, 1988.

Meyerowitz, Joanne. *Women Adrift: Independent Wage Earners in Chicago, 1880–1930*. Chicago: University of Chicago Press, 1988.

Michel, Sonya, and Seth Koven, eds. *Mothers of a New World: Maternalist Politics and the Origins of Welfare States*. New York: Routledge, 1993.

Milkman, Ruth. *Gender at Work: The Dynamics of Job Segregation during World War Two*. Chicago: University of Illinois Press, 1987.

– ed. *Women, Work and Protest: A Century of Women's Labor History*. Boston: Routledge and Kegan Paul, 1985.

– 'Women's Work and the Economic Crisis: Some Lessons of the Great Depression.' *Radical Review of Political Economics* 8, 71 (1976): 71–97.

Mitchinson, Wendy, et al., eds. *Canadian Women: A Reader*. Toronto: Harcourt Brace, 1996.

Mol, Hans. *Faith and Fragility: Religion and Identity in Canada*. Burlington: Trinity Press, 1985.

Moore, Dawn. *Who's Who in Black Canada*. Toronto: D. Williams, 2002.

– *An Autobiography*. Toronto: Williams Wallace, 1985.

Morgan, Cecilia. *Public Men and Virtuous Women: The Gendered Languages of Religion and Politics in Upper Canada, 1791–1850*. Toronto: University of Toronto Press, 1996.

Morton, Suzanne. *At Odds: Gambling and Canadians, 1919–1969*. Toronto: University of Toronto Press, 2003.

– 'The June Bride as the Working-Class Bride: Getting Married in a Halifax Working-Class Neighbourhood in the 1920s.' In Bettina Bradbury, ed., *Canadian Family History*, 360–79.

– *Ideal Surroundings: Domestic Life in a Working-Class Suburb in the 1920s*. Toronto: University of Toronto Press, 1992.

Moscovitch, Allan, and Jim Albert, eds. *The Benevolent State: The Growth of Welfare in Canada*. Toronto: Garamond Press, 1987.

Myers, Tamara. *Caught: Montreal's Modern Girls and the Law, 1869–1945*. Toronto: University of Toronto Press, 2006.

Neatby, Blair. *The Politics of Chaos: Canada in the Thirties*. Toronto: MacMillan, 1972.

Nora, Pierre. 'Between Memory and History: Les Lieux de Mémoire.' *Representations* 26 (Spring 1989): 7–24.

Odem, Mary E. *Delinquent Daughters: Protecting and Policing Adolescent Female Sexuality in the United States, 1885–1920*. Chapel Hill: University of North Carolina Press, 1995.

Palmer, Bryan. *Working-Class Experience: Rethinking the History of Canadian Labour, 1800–1991*. Toronto: McClelland and Stewart, 1997.

Palmer, Phyllis. 'Black Domestics during the Depression: Workers, Organizers, Social Commentators.' *Prologue* 29, 2 (1997): 127–31.

Parr, Joy. *The Gender of Breadwinners: Women, Men, and Change in Two Industrial Towns, 1880–1950.* Toronto: University of Toronto Press, 1990.

Parr, Joy, and Mark Rosenfeld, eds. *Gender and History in Canada.* Toronto: Copp Clark Pitman, 1996.

Passerini, Luisa. 'Work Ideology and Consensus under Italian Fascism.' In Robert Perks and Alistair Thomson, eds, *The Oral History Reader,* 53–62.

– 'Mythbiography in Oral History.' In Raphael Samuel and Paul Thompson, eds, *The Myths We Live By,* 49–60.

– 'Women's Personal Narratives: Myths, Experiences, and Emotions.' In Personal Narratives Group, eds, *Interpreting Women's Lives: Feminist Theory and Personal Narratives,* 189–97.

– *Fascism in Popular Memory: The Cultural Experience of the Turin Working Class.* Cambridge: Cambridge University Press, 1988.

Patrias, Carmela. *Patriots and Proletarians: Politicizing Hungarian Immigrants in Interwar Canada.* Montreal: McGill-Queen's University Press, 1994.

– *Relief Strike: Immigrant Workers and the Great Depression in Crowland Ontario, 1930–1935.* Toronto: New Hogtown Press, 1990.

Peiss, Kathy. *Cheap Amusements: Working Women and Leisure in Turn-of-the-Century New York.* Philadelphia: Temple University Press, 1986.

Perks, Robert, and Alistair Thomson, eds. *The Oral History Reader.* New York: Routledge, 1998.

Perry, Adele. *On the Edge of Empire: Gender, Race, and the Making of British Columbia, 1849–1871.* Toronto: University of Toronto Press, 2001.

Personal Narratives Group, ed. *Interpreting Women's Lives: Feminist Theory and Personal Narratives.* Bloomington: Indiana University Press, 1989.

Phillips, Erin, and Paul Phillips. *Women's Work: Inequality in the Labour Market.* Toronto: James Lorimer, 1983.

Pierson, Ruth Roach. 'Gender and the Unemployment Insurance Debates in Canada.' *Labour/Le Travail* 25 (Spring 1990): 77–103.

– *'They're still women after all': The Second World War and Canadian Womanhood.* Toronto: McClelland and Stewart, 1986.

Pon, Madge. 'Like a Chinese Puzzle: The Construction of Chinese Masculinity in *Jack Canuck.*' In Joy Parr and Mark Rosenfeld, eds, *Gender and History in Canada,* 88–100.

Portelli, Alessandro. *The Death of Luigi Trastulli, and Others Stories: Form and Meaning in Oral History.* New York: State University of New York Press, 1991.

– *The Battle of Valle Giulia: Oral History and the Art of Dialogue.* Madison: University of Wisconsin Press, 1997.

– *The Order Has Been Carried Out: History, Memory, and Meaning of a Nazi Massacre in Rome.* New York: Palgrave Macmillan, 2003.

Porter-Benson, Susan. *Household Accounts: Working-Class Family Economies in the United States*. New York: Cornell University Press, 2007.

Prentice, Alison. *The History of Women and Education in Canada*. Toronto: Canadian Scholars' Press, 1992.

– 'Themes in the Early History of the Women's Teachers' Association of Toronto.' In Paula Bourne, ed., *Women's Paid and Unpaid Work: Historical and Contemporary Perspectives*, 97–120.

Prentice, Alison, Paula Bourne, Gail Cuthbert Brandt, Beth Light, Wendy Mitchinson, and Naomi Black. *Canadian Women: A History*. Toronto: Harcourt and Brace, 1996.

Principe, Angelo. 'Glimpses of Lives in Canada's Shadow: Insiders, Outsiders, and Female Activism in the Fascist Era.' In Franca Iacovetta and Donna Gabaccia, eds, *Women, Gender and Transnational Lives*, 349–385.

Radforth, Ian. *Bushworkers and Bosses: Logging in Northern Ontario, 1900–1980*. Toronto: University of Toronto Press, 1987.

Radforth, Ian, and Laurel Sefton MacDowell, eds. *Canadian Working Class History: Selected Readings*. Toronto: Canadian Scholars' Press, 2000.

Rasky, Frank. 'Canada's Scandalous Scandal Sheets.' *Liberty* 31, 9 (1954): 17–80.

Rasky, Harry. *Nobody Swings on Sundays: The Many Lives and Films of Harry Rasky*. Toronto: Collier MacMillan, 1980.

Razack, Sherene. *Looking White People in the Eye: Gender, Race and Culture in Courtrooms and Classrooms*. Toronto: University of Toronto Press, 1998.

Reverby, Susan. *Ordered to Care: The Dilemma of American Nursing, 1850–1945*. New York: Cambridge University Press, 1987.

Ritchie, Donald. *Doing Oral History: A Practical Guide*, 2nd ed. New York: Oxford University Press, 2003.

Roberts, Barbara. *Whence They Came: Deportation from Canada, 1900–1935*. Ottawa: University of Ottawa, 1988.

Roberts, Elizabeth. *A Woman's Place: An Oral History of Working Class Women, 1890–1940*. Oxford: Oxford University Press, 1984.

Roberts, Wayne. 'Hobos and Songsters: Working-Class Culture.' *Oral History Forum / Forum d'histoire orale* 7 (1984): 24–7.

Robin, Martin. *Shades of Right: Nativist and Fascist Politics in Canada, 1920–1940*. Toronto: University of Toronto Press, 1991.

Rosenzweig, Roy, and David Thelen. *The Presence of the Past: Popular Uses of History in American Life*. New York: Columbia University Press, 1998.

Ross, Ellen. *Love and Toil: Motherhood in Outcast London, 1870–1918*. Oxford: Oxford University Press, 1993.

Roy, Gabrielle. *The Tin Flute*. Toronto: McClelland and Stewart, 1945.

Ruiz, Vicki L., and Ellen Carol Dubois, eds. *Unequal Sisters: A Multicultural Reader in U.S. Women's History.* New York: Routledge, 1994.

Safarian, A.F. *The Canadian Economy in the Great Depression.* Toronto: McClelland and Stewart, 1972.

Samuel, Raphael. *Theatres of Memory: the Past and Present in Contemporary Culture.* Vol. 1. London: Verso, 1994.

Samuel, Raphael, and Paul Thompson, eds. *The Myths We Live By.* London: Routledge, 1990.

Sangster, Joan. *Regulating Girls and Women: Sexuality, Family, and the Law in Ontario, 1920–1960.* Toronto: Oxford University Press, 2001.

– 'Telling Our Stories: Feminist Debates and the Use of Oral History.' In Robert Perks and Alistair Thomson, eds, *The Oral History Reader,* 87–100.

– *Earning Respect: The Lives of Working Women in Small Town Ontario, 1920–1960.* Toronto: University of Toronto Press, 1995.

– *Dreams of Equality: Women on the Canadian Left, 1920–1950.* Toronto: McClelland and Stewart, 1989.

– 'The 1907 Bell Telephone Strike: Organizing Women Workers.' *Labour/Le Travail* 3 (1978): 109–30.

Scharf, Lois. *To Work and to Wed: Female Employment, Feminism, and the Great Depression.* Westport, CT: Greenwood Press, 1980.

Semple, Neil. *The Lord's Dominion: The History of Canadian Methodism.* Montreal and Kingston: McGill-Queen's University Press, 1996.

Silvera, Makeda. *Silenced,* 2nd ed.. Toronto: Sister Vision Press, 1989.

Sinha, Mrinalina. 'Mapping the Imperial Social Formation: A Modest Proposal for Feminist History.' *Signs* 25, 4 (Summer 2000): 1077–82.

Smith-Rosenberg, Carol. *Disorderly Conduct: Visions of Gender in Victorian America.* New York: Oxford University Press, 1985.

Società Femminile Friulana. *La Nostra Storia, 1938–1988.* Toronto: MHSO, 1988.

Speisman, Stephen A. *The Jews of Toronto: A History to 1937.* Toronto: McClelland and Stewart, 1979.

Spelman, Elizabeth V. *Inessential Woman: Problems of Exclusion in Feminist Thought.* Boston: Beacon Press, 1988.

Srigley, Katrina. 'Stories of Strife? Memories of the Great Depression.' *Oral History Forum/Forum d'histoire orale,* forthcoming.

– 'Clothing Stories: Consumption, Identity, and Desire in Depression-Era Toronto.' *Journal of Women's History* 19, 1 (2007): 82–104.

– 'In Case You Hadn't Noticed!? Race, Ethnicity and Women's Wage-Earning in a Depression-Era City.' *Labour/Le Travail* 55 (Spring 2005): 69–105.

Steedman, Mercedes. 'Skill and Gender in the Canadian Clothing Industry, 1890–1940.' In Ian Radforth and Laurel Sefton MacDowell, eds, *Canadian Working Class History: Selected Readings*, 450–470.
– *Angels of the Workplace: Women and the Construction of Gender Relations in the Canadian Clothing Industry, 1890–1940*. Toronto: Oxford University Press, 1997.
Stephen, Jennifer. *Pick One Intelligent Girl: Employability, Domesticity, and the Gendering of Canada's Welfare State, 1939–1947*. (Toronto: University of Toronto Press, 2007).
– 'Deploying Discourses of Employability and Domesticity: Women's Employment and Training Policies and the Formation of the Canadian Welfare State, 1935–1947.' PhD dissertation, University of Toronto, 2000.
Strange, Carolyn. 'Sin or Salvation? Protecting Toronto's Working Girls.' *The Beaver* (June-July 1997): 8–13.
– *Toronto's Girl Problem: The Perils and Pleasures of the City, 1880–1930*. Toronto: University of Toronto Press, 1995.
– 'Wounded Womanhood and Dead Men: Chivalry and the Trials of Clara Ford and Carrie Davies.' In Franca Iacovetta, and Marianna Valverde, eds, *Gender Conflicts: New Essays in Women's History*, 149–88.
Strange, Carolyn, and Tina Loo. *True Crime, True North: The Golden Age of Canadian Pulp Magazines*. Vancouver: Raincoast Books, 2004.
– 'The Moral of the Story: Gender and Murder in Canadian True Crime Magazines of the 1940s.' In Margaret Thornton, ed., *Romancing the Tomes: Popular Culture, Law and Feminism*, 221–39.
– 'From Hewers of Wood to Producers of Pulp: True Crime in Canadian Pulp Magazines of the 1940s.' *Journal of Canadian Studies* 37, 2 (Summer 2002): 11–32.
Strong-Boag, Veronica. *Janey Canuck: Women in Canada, 1919–1939*. Ottawa: Canadian Historical Association, 1994.
– *The New Day Recalled: Lives of Girls and Women in English Canada, 1919–1939*. Toronto: Copp Clark Pitman, 1988.
Strong-Boag, Veronica, Adele Perry, and Mona Gleason, eds. *Rethinking Canada: The Promise of Women's History*, 4th edition. Toronto: University of Toronto Press, 2002.
Struthers, James. *The Limits of Affluence: Welfare in Ontario, 1920–1970*. Toronto: University of Toronto Press, 1994.
– 'A Profession in Crisis: Charlotte Whitton and Social Work in the 1930's.' In Allan Moscovitch and Jim Albert, eds, *The Benevolent State: The Growth of Welfare in Canada*, 111–25.

– *No Fault of Their Own: Unemployment and the Canadian Welfare State, 1914–1941.* Toronto: University of Toronto Press, 1983.

Sutherland, Neil. 'Introduction: Children and Families Enter History's Main Stream.' *Canadian Historical Review* 78, 3 (September 1997): 379–84.

– *Growing Up: Childhood in English Canada from the Great War to the Age of Television.* Toronto: University of Toronto Press, 1997.

– *Children in English Canadian Society: Framing the Twentieth-Century Consensus.* Toronto: University of Toronto Press, 1976.

Symons, G.L. 'Her View from the Executive Suite: Canadian Women in Management.' In Katerina Lundy and Barbara Warme, eds, *Work in the Canadian Context: Continuity Despite Change,* 337–53.

Thompson, Elizabeth. 'Public and Private in Middle-Eastern Women's History.' *Journal of Women's History* 15, 1 (Spring 2003): 52–68.

Thompson, John, and Allen Seager. *Canada, 1922–1939: Decades of Discord.* Toronto: McClelland and Stewart, 1985.

Thompson, Paul. *The Voice of the Past: Oral History,* 2nd ed. Oxford: Oxford University Press, 1988.

Thomson, Alistair. 'Four Paradigm Transformations in Oral History.' *Oral History Review* 34, 1 (2007): 49–71.

Thornton, Margaret, ed. *Romancing the Tomes: Popular Culture, Law and Feminism.* London: Cavendish, 2002.

Todd, Selina. *Young Women, Work, and Family in England, 1918–1950.* Oxford: Oxford University Press, 2005.

Trofimenkoff, Susan Mann, and Alison Prentice, eds. *The Neglected Majority: Essays in Canadian Women's History.* Toronto: McClelland and Stewart, 1977.

Valverde, Mariana. 'Families, Private Property, and the State: The Dionnes and the Toronto Stork Derby.' *Journal of Canadian Studies* 29, 4 (1994–5): 15–35.

– *The Age of Light, Soap and Water: Moral Reform in English Canada, 1885–1925.* Toronto: McClelland and Stewart, 1991.

– 'The Love of Finery: Fashion and the Fallen Woman in Nineteenth-Century Social Discourse.' *Victorian Studies* 32, 2 (Winter 1989): 169–88.

van Die, Marguerite. *Religion and Public Life in Canada: Historical and Comparative Perspectives.* Toronto: University of Toronto Press, 2001.

Van Kirk, Sylvia. *Many Tender Ties: Women in Fur Trade Society in Western Canada, 1670–1870.* Winnipeg: Watson and Dwyer, 1980.

Vibert, Elizabeth. 'Real Men Hunt Buffalo: Masculinity, Race and Class in British Fur Traders' Narratives.' *Gender and History* 8, 1 (1998): 4–21.

Vicinus, Martha. *Independent Women: Work and Community for Single Women, 1850–1920.* London: Routledge, 1985.

Vipond, Mary. *Listening In: The First Decade of Canadian Broadcasting, 1922–1932.* Montreal and Kingston: McGill University Press, 1992.

Walkowitz, Judith. *City of Dreadful Delight: Narratives of Sexual Danger in Late-Victorian London.* Chicago: University of Chicago Press, 1992.

White, Randall. *Too Good to Be True: Toronto in the 1920s.* Toronto: Dundurn Press, 1993.

Woodcock-Tentler, Lesley. *Wage-Earning Women: Industrial Work and Family Life in the United States, 1900–1930.* Oxford: Oxford University Press, 1979.

Wright, Cynthia. '"Feminine Trifles of Vast Importance": Writing Gender into the History of Consumption.' In Franca Iacovetta and Mariana Valverde, eds, *Gender Conflicts: New Essays in Women's History,* 229–60.

Wright, Richard. *Clara Callan.* Toronto: McClelland and Stewart, 2001.

Young, Peter. *Let's Dance: A Celebration of Ontario's Dance Halls and Summer Pavilions.* Toronto: Natural Heritage Books, 2002.

Yow, Valerie Raleigh. *Recording Oral History: A Guide for the Humanities and Social Sciences.* New York: Altamira Press, 2005.

Zucchi, John E. *Italians in Toronto: Development of a National Identity, 1875–1935.* Montreal and Kingston: McGill-Queen's University Press, 1988.

Index

STUDIES IN GENDER AND HISTORY

General editors: Franca Iacovetta and Karen Dubinsky